IMAGES
of America

ALPINE TOWNSHIP

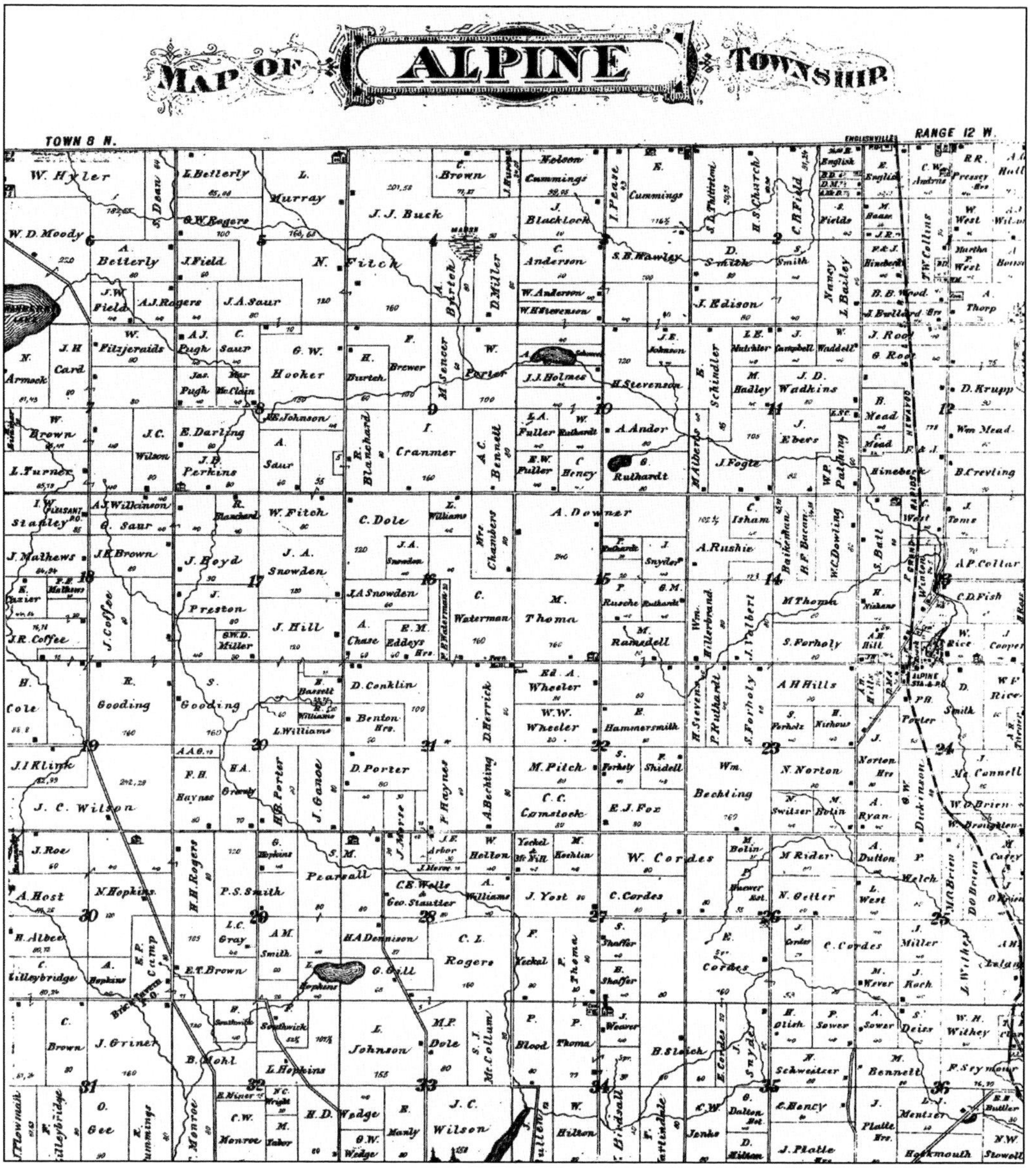

Seen here is an 1876 plat map of Alpine Township.

On the cover: The Frank Ebers family has come out to take a picture to remember this harvest. It was a time when wooden baskets and barrels were used to store apples, maybe 1918. A horse pulls the wagon, and the tray to sort the apples is a simple small wooden box that is on an angle so the apples will flow into the barrels. The apples on the Frank Ebers farm were taken to Englishville to go by train wherever there was a market for them. Frank's wife, Anna Ebers, is standing on the right. Avery and Walter Ebers are two of the young men in the picture. Vernie Ebers is near the horse, on top of a ladder, with Lila Ebers, then Violet Ebers, below her. Maude Birdsey is seated on the far right. Frank Ebers, Bill Birdsey, and Adolph Hawks are in the picture, but it is hard to tell which one is which with their hats and work clothes on. Jack Olson is the man on a ladder. (Courtesy of the Ebers family.)

IMAGES
of America

ALPINE TOWNSHIP

Mary Rasch Alt

ARCADIA
PUBLISHING

ISBN 978-0-7385-5104-3

Published by Arcadia Publishing
Charleston, South Carolina

Printed in the United States of America

Library of Congress Control Number: 2006939094

For all general information, please contact Arcadia Publishing:
Telephone 843-853-2070
Fax 843-853-0044
E-mail sales@arcadiapublishing.com
For customer service and orders:
Toll-Free 1-888-313-2665

Visit us on the Internet at www.arcadiapublishing.com

This book is dedicated to my parents, who taught me the important things in life. Faith and family are first. Two other very important things are to take photographs and to keep records.

CONTENTS

Acknowledgments

A photograph is a great treasure. In an older photograph, you can see just how your son looks like grandpa or how your daughter resembles grandma. You can see what the "home place" looked like years ago. You can marvel at a hand-sewn wedding dress and understand why the bride is standing and her groom is seated for the picture. You can see how advanced farming has become when you imagine working with a pair of horses.

To bring this book together, I visited families in Alpine Township for a few months. I enjoyed both the photographs and the stories people so generously shared. The drawings came from the 1876 *Illustrated Historical Atlas of the Counties of Ottawa & Kent*, done by H. Belden and Company; the 1878 *Memorials of the Grand River Valley*, by Franklin Everett; and the 1881 *History of Kent County, Michigan* by Chas. C. Chapman and Company.

In the creation of this book, I wish to thank Patricia (Rasch) Cederholm, Phyllis (Wahlfield) Dunneback, Barb Erhart, and Elizabeth (Dietrich) Rasch for all they taught me and for all their great help. I would also like to thank Francis Alberts, Marv and Rosie Alt, Norbert and Florence Antor, Kaye Chase, Kathy Coffee, Ron Cordes, Phillip Cranmer, Christine Dennison, Thomas Dilley, Helen (Loveless) Dunneback, Mary (Waldherr) Dunneback, Ginny Ebers, Cindy Heinbeck, Alvin Hill and Janet (Usher) Hill, Judy Ingersoll, Joyce Kilmer, Madelyn (Schindler) Klenk, Merlin Kraft, Shirley (Klenk) McCracken, Marcia (Seekman) Momber, Edna Mae (Cordes) Morse, Charlene Rasch, Josephine Reister, Florence (Rasch) Robach, Frances (Ebers) Rollert, David Schantz, Jim Schindler, Sue Ann (Dunneback) Shoemaker, Jim and Gloria Schweitzer, Fritz and Jan Schweitzer, Vince Schweitzer, Marlene (Vogel) Smith, Beth Vogel, Marlene (Brown) Wahlfield and Fritz Wahlfield, Pat Woolworth, and Frances (Schweitzer) Yost.

I would also like to thank my Arcadia Publishing editor, Anna Wilson, for the encouragement to do this book and for answering all my questions.

INTRODUCTION

It was the Treaty of Washington in 1836 that opened land north of the Grand River to settlers and speculators.

In 1837, Solomon Wright brought his family from Wayne County, New York, to Kent County and settled on a piece of property next to Indian Mill Creek on the road we call Four Mile Road today. The Wright family is thought to have been the first white settlers of Alpine Township. Many were to follow and locate first on streams or near lakes. Soon the heavily forested area north of Walker was surveyed, sectioned, cleared, and busy with very productive farms.

On April 5, 1847, a group organized the 36 square miles of North Walker. It met at a schoolhouse. The name for the township, All Pine, was suggested for the heavy concentration of pine trees in one area of the township. It was shortened after Adelia (Hubbell) Hills suggested Alpine.

At this first meeting, township officials were elected: Edward Wheeler, supervisor; C. D. Shenich, clerk; Casper Cordes, treasurer; and William H. Withey, John Coffee, John Colton, and John Tuxbury, justices. The next meeting was held at Edward Wheeler's home, which was a central location in the township. Soon a small log school was erected on a corner of the Wheeler farm and was used to hold the township's meetings. In about 1860, a wood frame town hall was built on the northeast corner of section 21, the location of the present Alpine Township Historical Museum.

This area of Michigan was nearly all forest before the pioneers came. The township was only a seasonal residence for Native American tribes in Michigan. On the northwest edge of the township is Cranberry Lake, named for the fruit Native Americans harvested there.

In 1839, John Coffee and Richmond Gooding came to Alpine Township and settled five miles west of the Wright family. They named their post office after the township they left in Ohio—Pleasant.

It was not long before sections of Alpine Township were being claimed, cleared, and farmed by families by the name of Hills, Brown, Snyder, Hildebrant, Waterman, Dole, Card, Ruthardt, Rogers, Hilton, Denison, Herrick, Tuxbury, Lillibridge, Pearsall, Snowden, Cassidy, Davenport, Thome, Buck, Miller, Umlor, Boyd, Childs, Withey, Ballard, Fox, Scheidel, Cordes, Chase, Wheeler, and Platte. All can be found on the 1855 plat map and census records. Some of these same families have remained, enjoying the rich fruits these founding families hewed out of the forest.

One of Michigan's great explorers, John Ball, also purchased land in Alpine Township. He could see the richness of the lumber and goodness of the land when he surveyed it.

Family and faith gave these early settlers the strength to work from dawn to dusk building a life in this new wilderness of Michigan. As more families came to homestead in the township, churches and schools were organized and then buildings were built.

Logging was a major industry at the township's beginning. At one time, seven sawmills were located on Indian Mill Creek. There are several small lakes in the township. It is interesting to see what is said about the streams in the township in the 1881 *History of Kent County, Michigan*, as the amount of water running through these streams has changed:

> The source of Mill Creek is Cranberry Lake, which is situated on the line between Kent and Ottawa Counties. From there to Pickerel Lake, on Sec. 10, Mill Creek is but a small rivulet. From Pickerel Lake to its mouth, it is fed by several small streams, one of which comes from Downer Lake on the southeast quarter of Sec. 10. The main stream passes about one and one-half miles north of the center of the township, thence southeasterly until it unites with the Grand River in the southwest corner of Plainfield. For a distance of five or six miles from its mouth, the water power is sufficiently good for manufacturing purposes.

Even though Alpine Township was named for its pine trees, oak, beech, and maple made up two-thirds of the township's wooded area. After the "logging-out" period, this good land was tilled for excellent yields of corn, wheat, and oats. Peach Ridge and Fruit Ridge Avenues were named for the orchards that were found to flourish on what is now known as the Ridge.

Along with the families came schools. Those early schools were not only for the children's learning but also were a great avenue for social gatherings. Imagine the loneliness of a family who came from an area that was more heavily populated to this wilderness with no neighbors within five miles, no schools, and no churches.

According to the 1881 *History of Kent County, Michigan*, Antoine Cuvier's son was the first child born to the early settlers in the township in 1838. The Cuvier family house was located one mile east of Erastus Clark's house.

The first death was that of a Mr. Nicolls, who died in 1839 on his land in section 31.

The first marriage was that of Electa Hilton to Allen Meeker in the autumn of 1844. The ceremony was performed by Rev. Elder Jones.

In this 160th year of Alpine Township, most farms have the state designation of Centennial Farm. This means the farm has been owned by the same family and their direct descendants for at least 100 years.

The worse natural disaster in Alpine Township was the Palm Sunday tornado that swept through the middle of the township on April 11, 1965. It took down many homes, barns, and businesses and did damage to Trinity Congregational Church on Four Mile Road and Holy Trinity Catholic Church on Alpine Church Road.

On May 31, 1998, this area experienced "straight line winds." They were just short of a tornado. The severe winds damaged many barns and ruined many orchards.

In this book, the schools are in order according to their district numbers. I tried to find a photograph to represent every early settler's family in the township. I am sorry if I missed anyone. It is my wish that you enjoy these photographs enough to take good care of your own and to label them.

One

LUMBERING

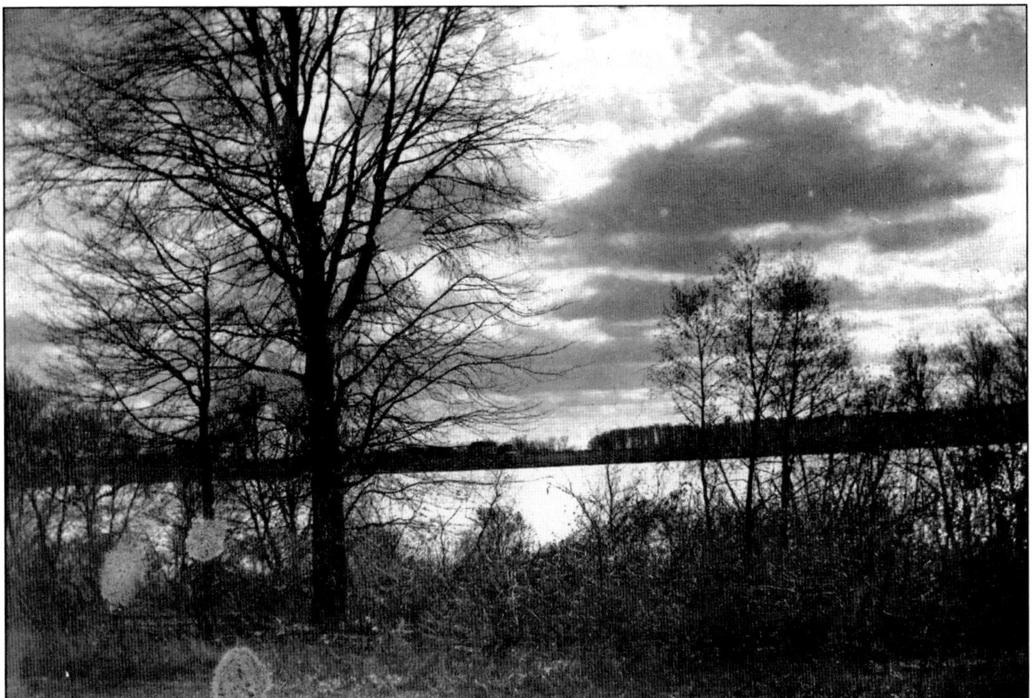

In this early photograph of Cranberry Lake, only trees can be seen, no homes. On the plat map of 1876, the W. D. Moody farm was on the north side of the lake. The N. Armock and J. H. Card farms were on the south side of the lake.

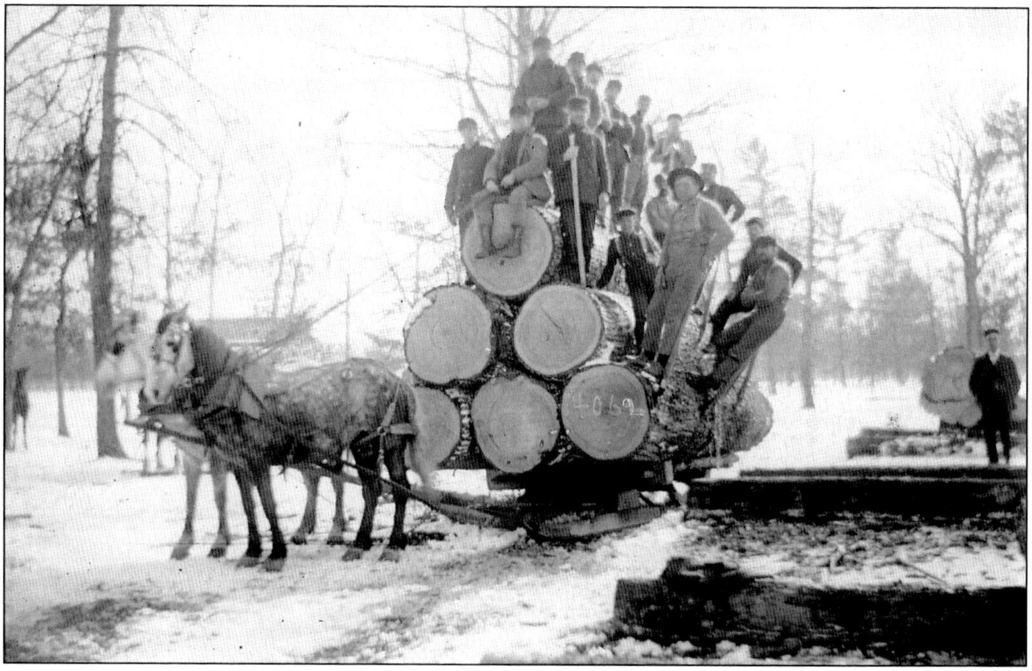

Every settler who came to establish a farm in the earliest days of Alpine Township had to clear the forest. It was heavy work to cut and haul the lumber. When a photographer stopped this sleigh from the Courtade property, all workers jumped on board after making this pyramid of wood.

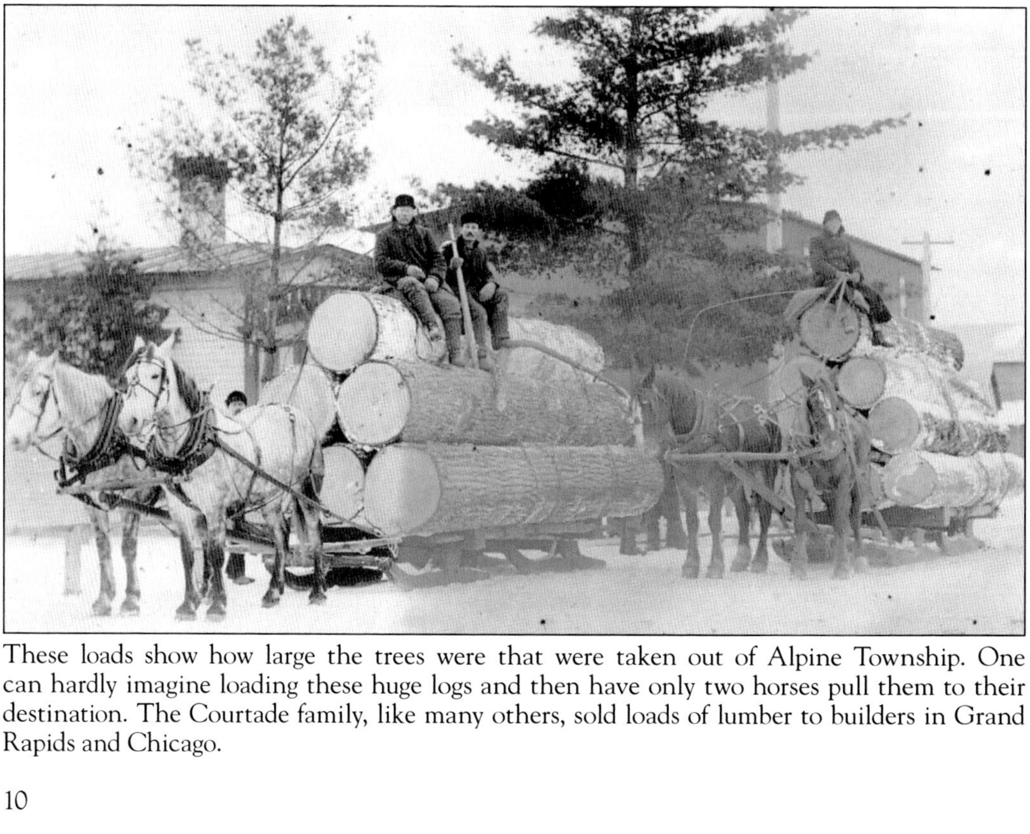

These loads show how large the trees were that were taken out of Alpine Township. One can hardly imagine loading these huge logs and then have only two horses pull them to their destination. The Courtade family, like many others, sold loads of lumber to builders in Grand Rapids and Chicago.

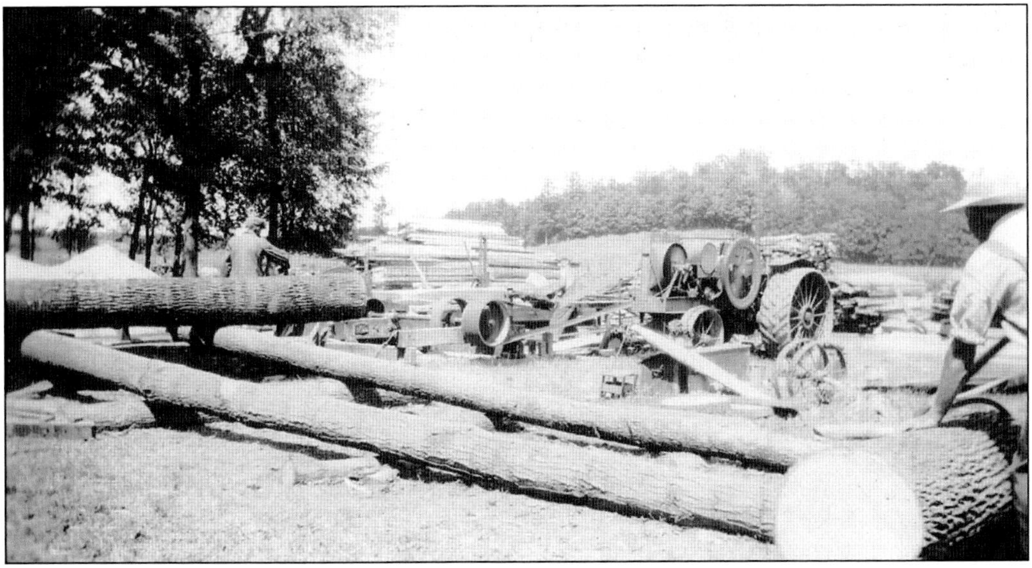

It is said that Michigan lumber built Chicago twice. Chicago was rebuilt after the great fire of 1871. On the Cranmer farm, they are debarking the logs with this equipment.

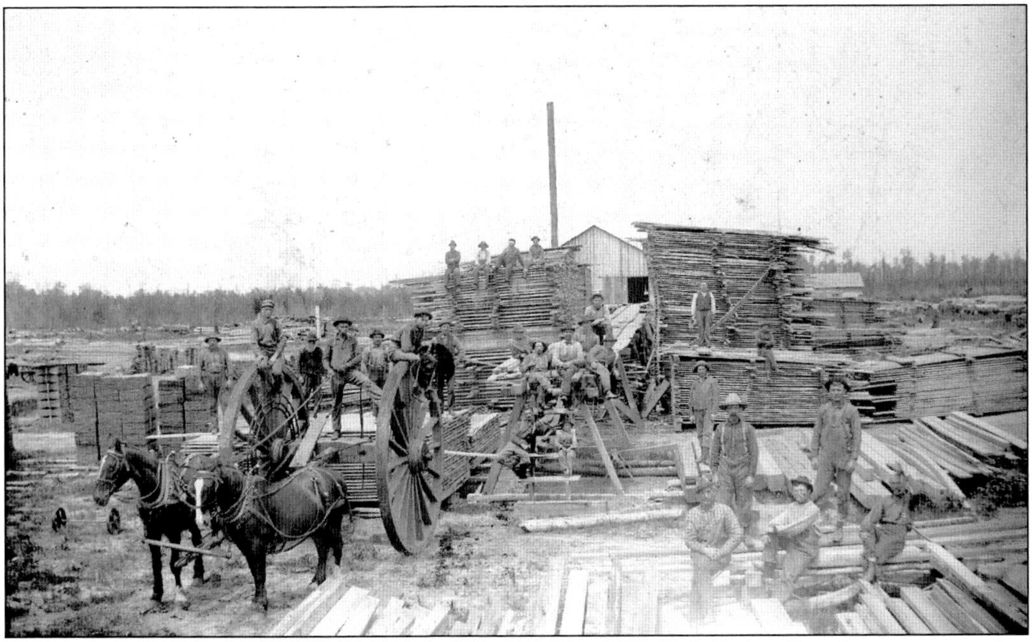

Richard English had one of the lumber mills in Alpine Township. He employed many men at his mill in 1888. Strong horses were needed to work with the men. Big wheels on the wagon must have helped move a heavy load.

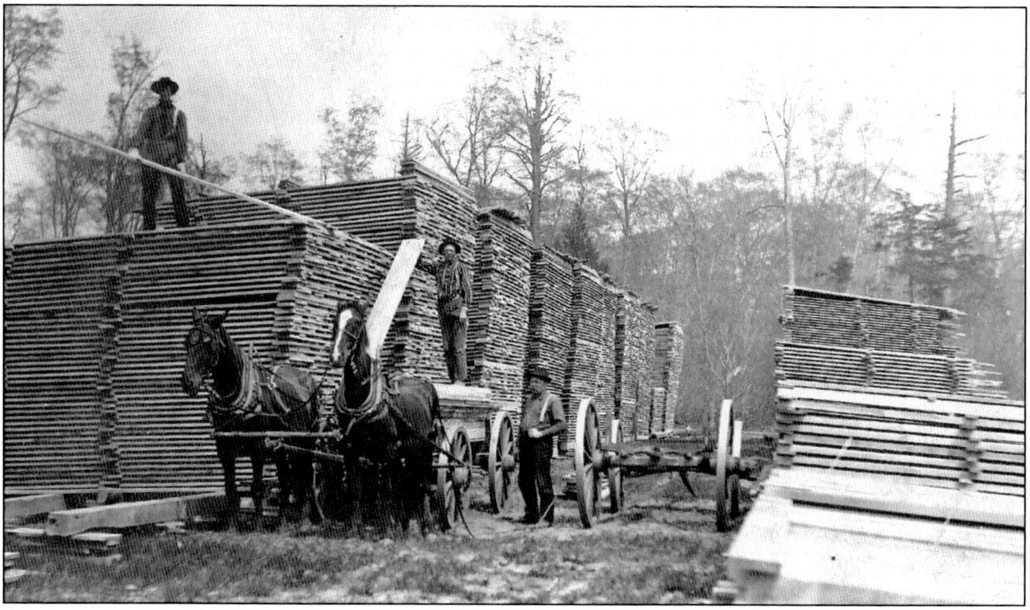

The village of Englishville was formed as Richard English gave his workers wood and property to build their homes. After trees were cut, debarked, and split, the wood was stacked to age. Note how, in this 1888 photograph, the wood is placed so that air can circulate to dry the wood.

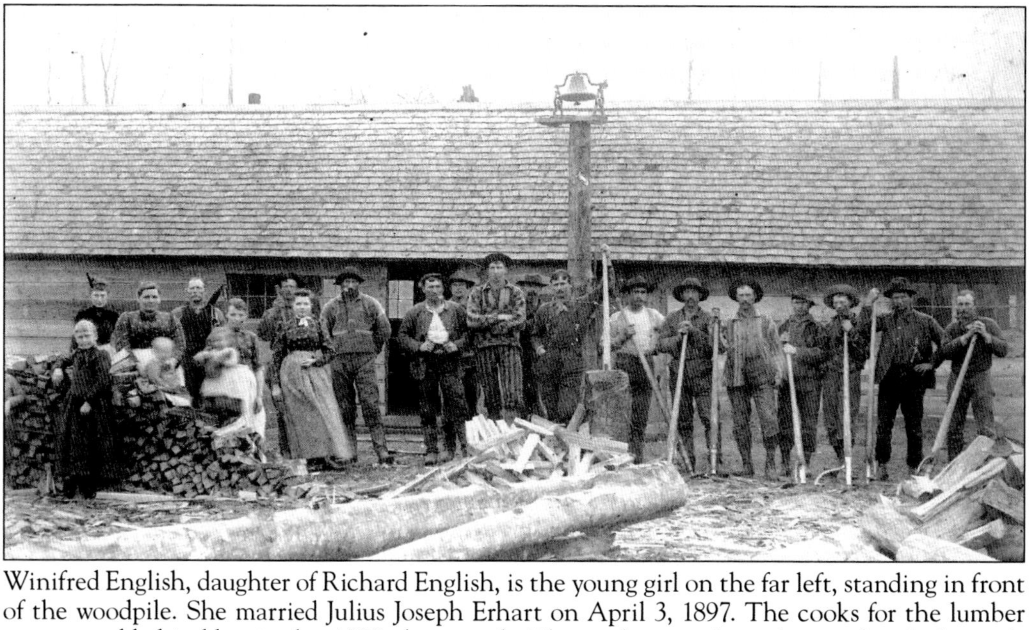

Winifred English, daughter of Richard English, is the young girl on the far left, standing in front of the woodpile. She married Julius Joseph Erhart on April 3, 1897. The cooks for the lumber camp stand behind her in this 1889 photograph. The workers on the right stand with the tools of their trade.

Two

EARLY SETTLERS

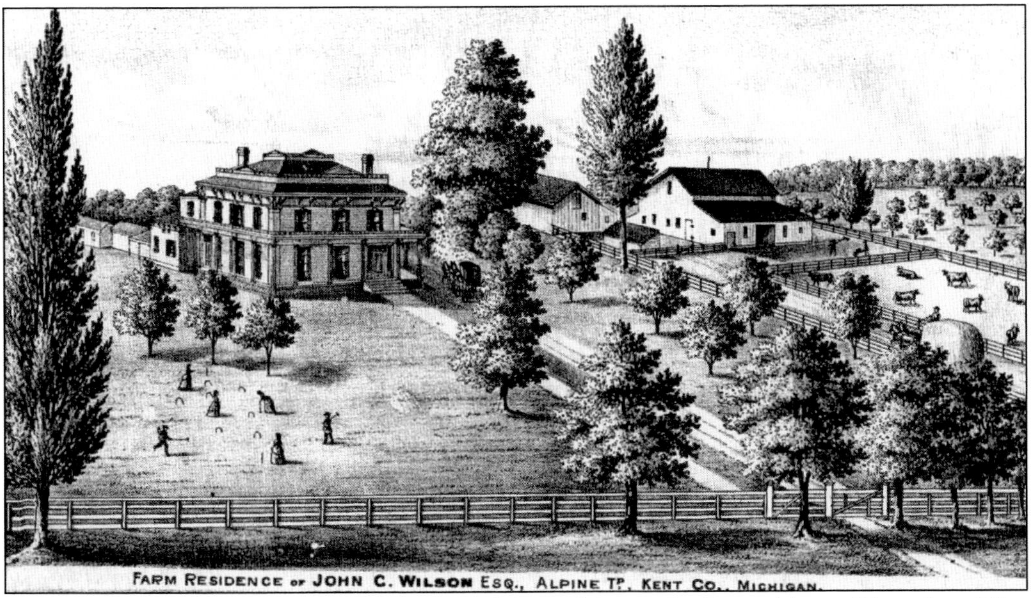

Solomon Wright's home was the first wood-framed house built in Alpine Township. This house became the Wright/Wilson home in 1873 when Helen, the daughter of Solomon and Mary Wright, married Albert Wilson. This farm is now Gracewil Country Club Golf Course, located at Four Mile Road and Walker Avenue. Solomon was at the organizational meeting of neighboring Wright Township. He was the oldest person in attendance and agreed to let them use his name for the township.

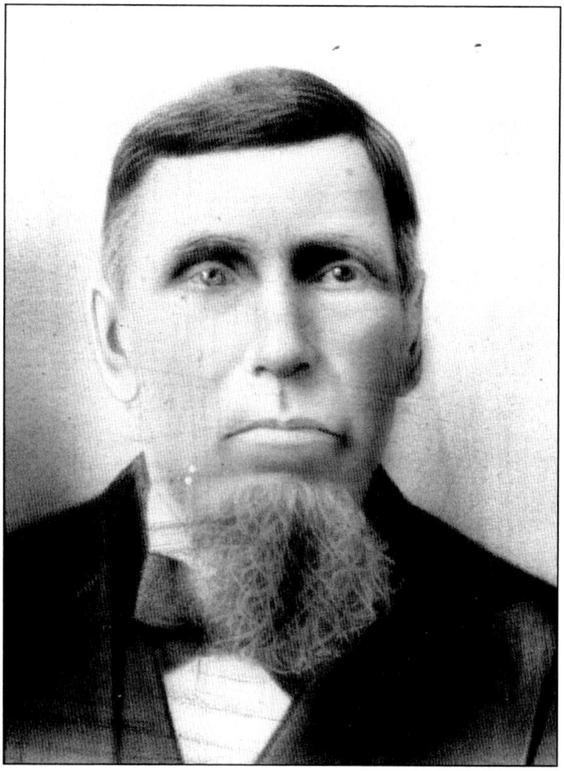

Adam Antor came to America, arriving in New York on July 26, 1850, on the ship *Marathon* at the age of 28. He had come from Obermoellrich, Bavaria, Germany. In 1854, Antor married Dorothy Day Albert in Ohio. He moved his family to Alpine Township around 1864.

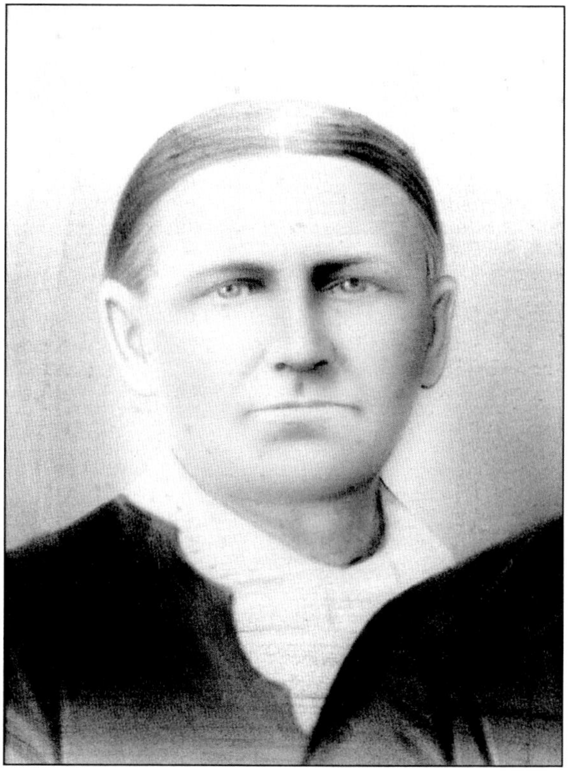

Dorothy Day (Albert) Antor gave her husband five children: William, Albert, Mary, Margaret, and John. William married Josephine Rothenthaler; Albert married Elizabeth Rusche, then he married Rosa Krupp; Mary married Joseph Fleet; Margaret married George Miller; and John married Helena Heinbeck.

Elisha T. Brown married Laura Brodish. They bought 80 acres of land on section 29 in Alpine Township. When they purchased the land there was not even a footpath through the woods. Their first house on the property was 20 feet wide by 26 feet long. It would be added on to and lived in for 28 years. They had five children: Julia, Francis, George, Martha, and J. Warren.

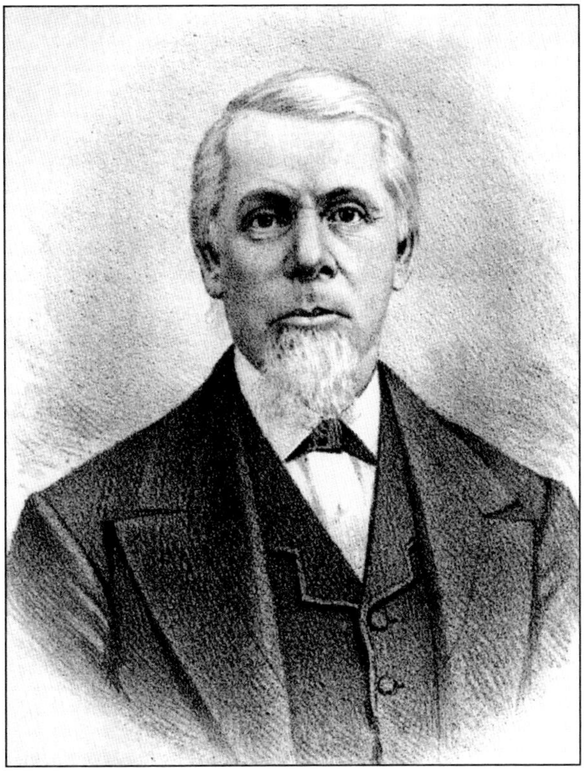

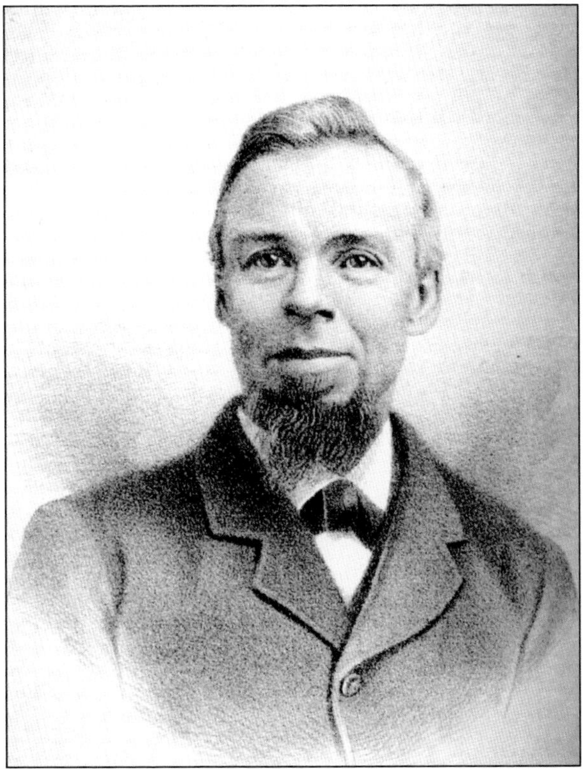

Kent Jarvis Brown was a tailor in his early years, then he purchased 80 acres on section 18 in Alpine Township. In 1857, he married Betsy Clark. They had four children: Helen, Clara, Perley, and Kent H. Brown. Helen married Edward Darling, and Clara married Willis Darling. Their home is on page 30 of this book.

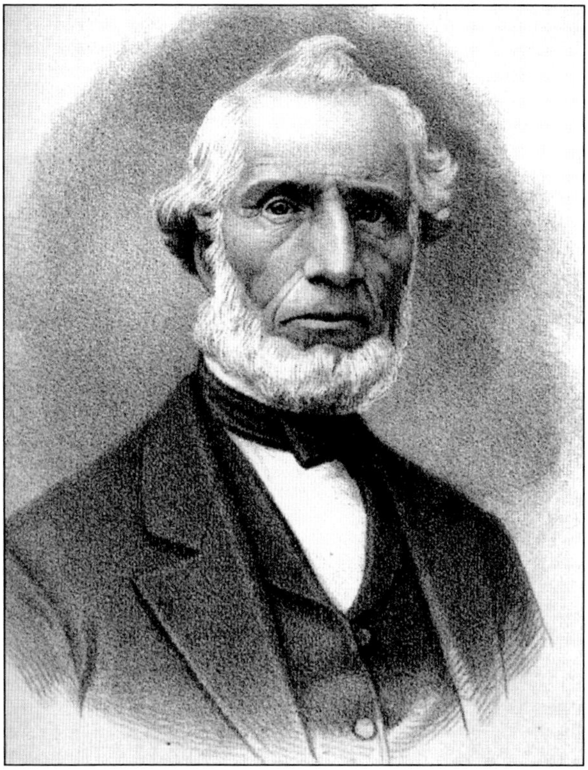

Erastus Clark was born in 1803 in Ontario, Canada, to Moses Clark and Patty (Bill) Clark. He married Hannah Phillips. Their first three children were born in Canada: William, Elizabeth and Cyrus. They moved to Alpine Township in 1838 and purchased a farm on Peach Ridge Avenue and Four Mile Road. Their next two children were born there: Charles and Hannah Maria. Cyrus married Helen Anderson, Charles married Lavange Grey, and Hannah Maria married Marcus Taber.

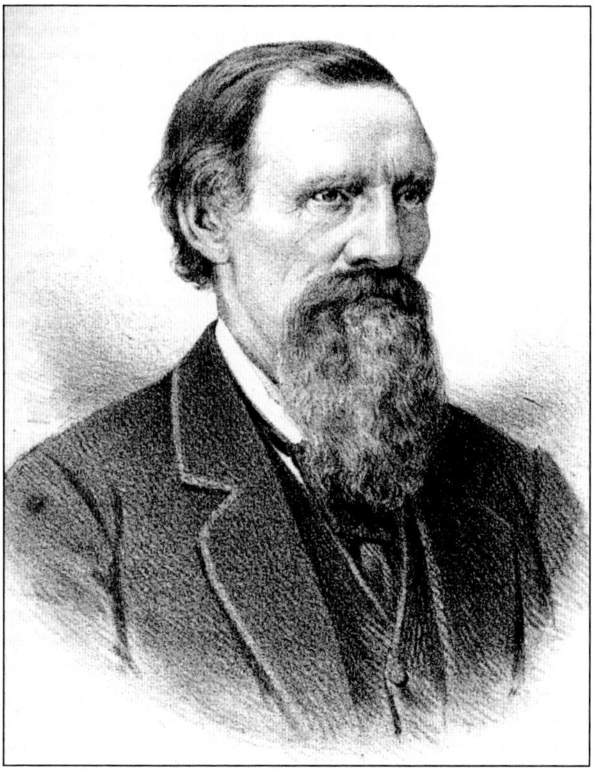

William Cordes, son of Anthony and Elizabeth Cordes, came to America in 1836. He went to California in 1850 and made $2,000 within a year of mining. In 1856, William married Catharine Hoffman. Their farm is in section 26. They had seven children: Josephine, Adelaide, Francisca, Albert, Elizabeth, Emma, and Richard, who died young. Josephine married George Fehsenfeld, Adelaide married Henry Steinbrecher, Francisca married A. Hammerschmidt, Albert married Angie Bullis, Elizabeth married Matthew Sadler, and Emma married John VanEwen.

Phil and Hannah Cummings had four children: Edwin, Norman, Nelson, and Phebe. Norman married Mary Stevenson, Nelson married Adelaide Stevenson, and Phebe married Ruben Wheeler. Edwin Cummings (pictured) came to Alpine Township with his father, Phil Cummings. Edwin owned a farm on Ten Mile Road and Sparta Avenue. He married Hannah Fenton and was a preacher. They had five daughters: Frances, Helen, Florence, Effie, and Grace. Frances married Thomas Montgomery, Helen married Sylvester Field, Florence married Charles Ballard, and Effie married Hugh Montgomery. Grace Cummings never married. Edwin sold his farm to Frank Ebers.

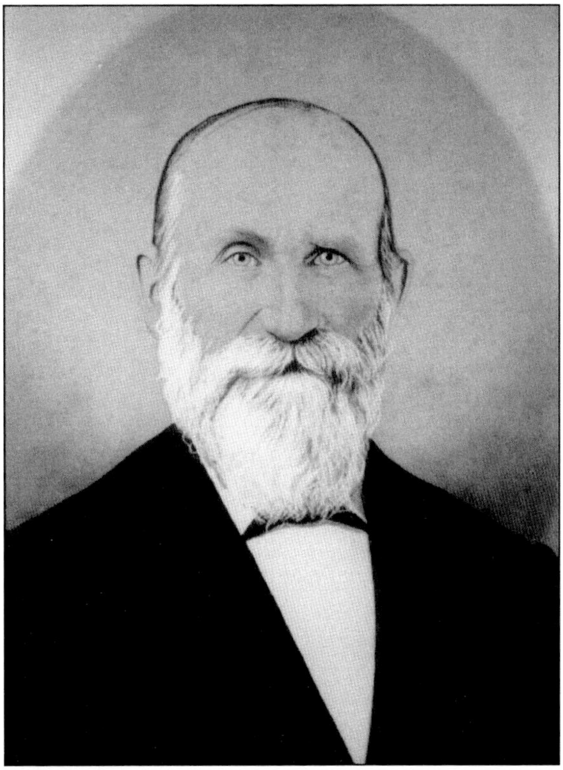

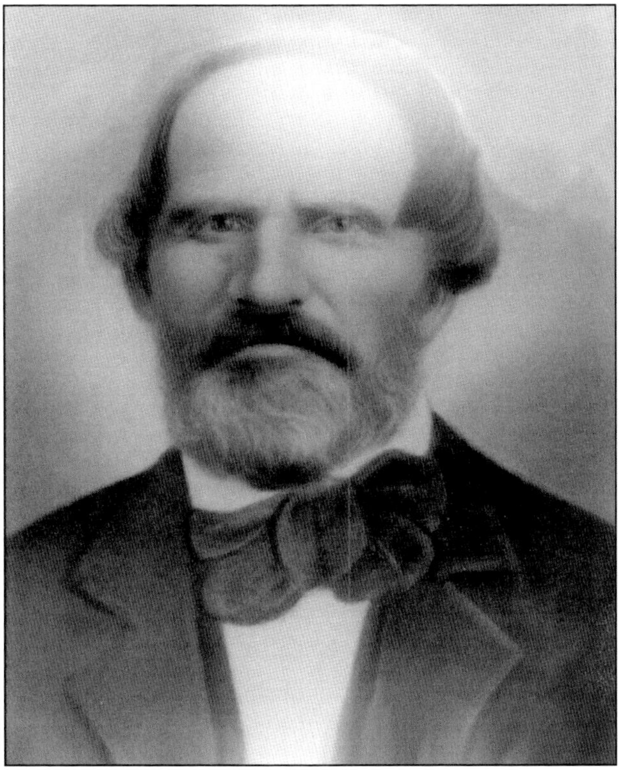

Henry Ebers came to America before he sent for his family. When he learned that a lawyer had taken his wife's money, Ebers bought what he thought was a lesser, cheaper farm. As it turned out, he had a good farm on hilly ground.

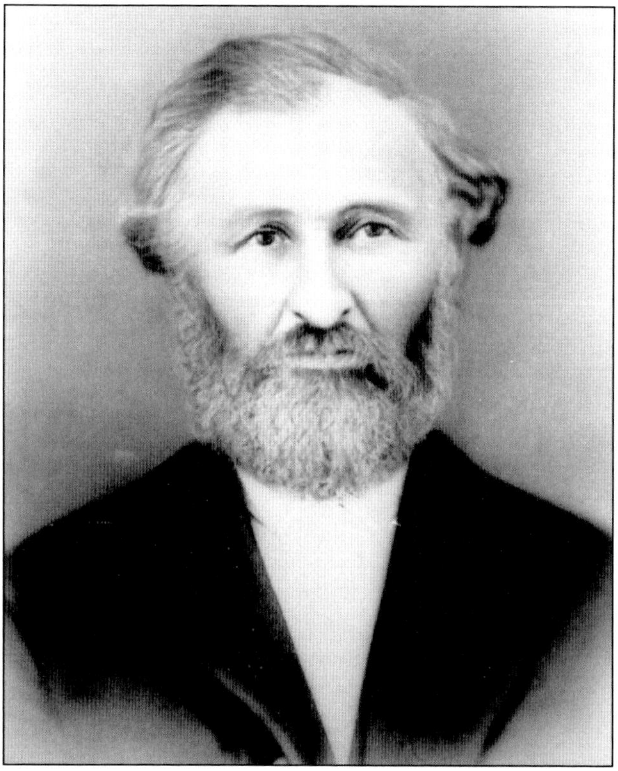

Joseph English started a sawmill on Ten Mile Road, east of what is now Alpine Avenue. His son Richard English built the mill into a very successful business. It is said that they gave their workers land and lumber to build their homes. The village of Englishville was then created. Simpson was their family name in England. When they came to America, everyone called him English, so that became the family name.

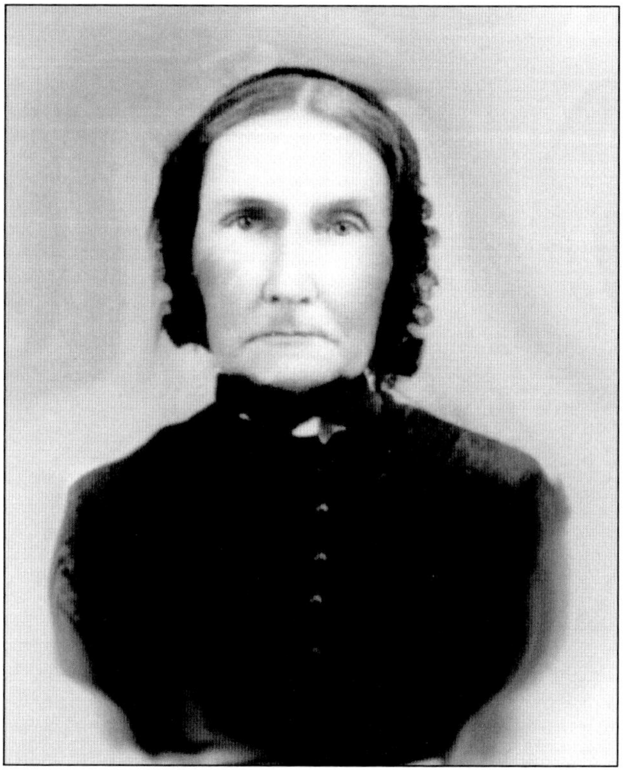

Diana English was the wife of Joseph English. They had two children, Abraham and Dinah Simpson, who were born in England and did not come to America. The children born to Diana and Joseph in America were William, Joseph, Richard, and Edward. William married Nancy Orser, Joseph married Catherine Mapes, Richard married Carrie French, and Edward married Jennie Stuart.

Norton Fitch came to Alpine Township when he was 15 years old, in 1848. He married Sophia Murray in 1855. They had 280 acres in section 4. Fitch served his country during the Civil War with the 1st Regiment U.S. Sharpshooters in Company C for three years. He was engaged in the Siege of Yorktown and a battle near Manassas in 1862. He received an honorable discharge on October 18, 1862, as he lost his left arm in battle.

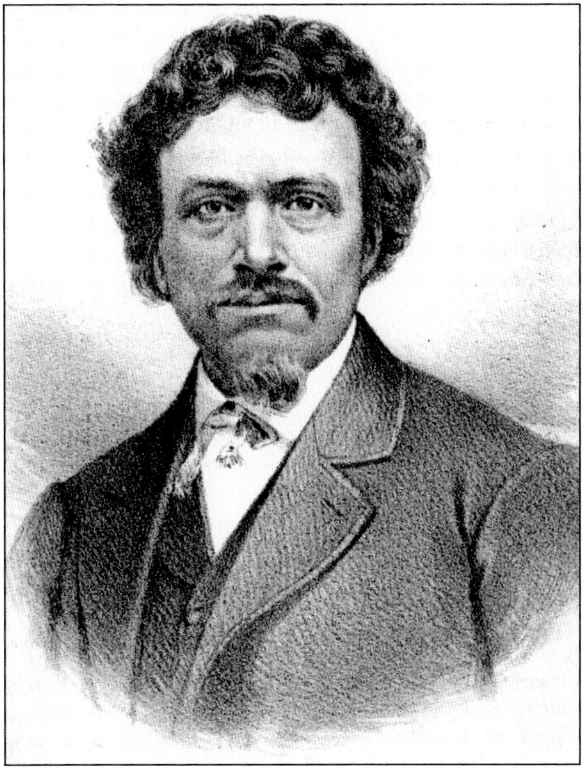

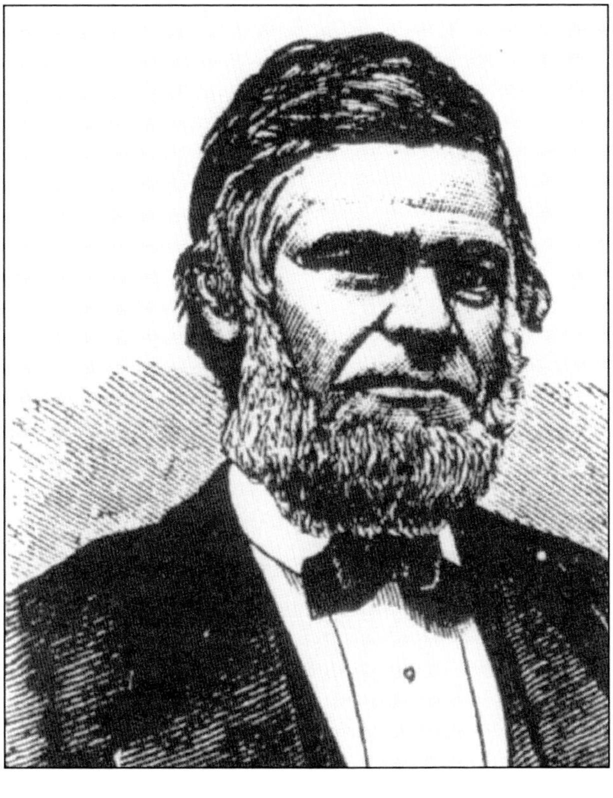

Sherman M. Pearsall was born in New York in 1817. He moved to Michigan in 1827 and married Catherine Bailey in 1841. Pearsall bought a farm in Alpine Township in 1843 and is best known for hosting a barn raising without allowing any liquor. When the day was over, the people who helped him raise his barn gave three cheers, one for Pearsall, one for his barn, and the third for his baked pigs.

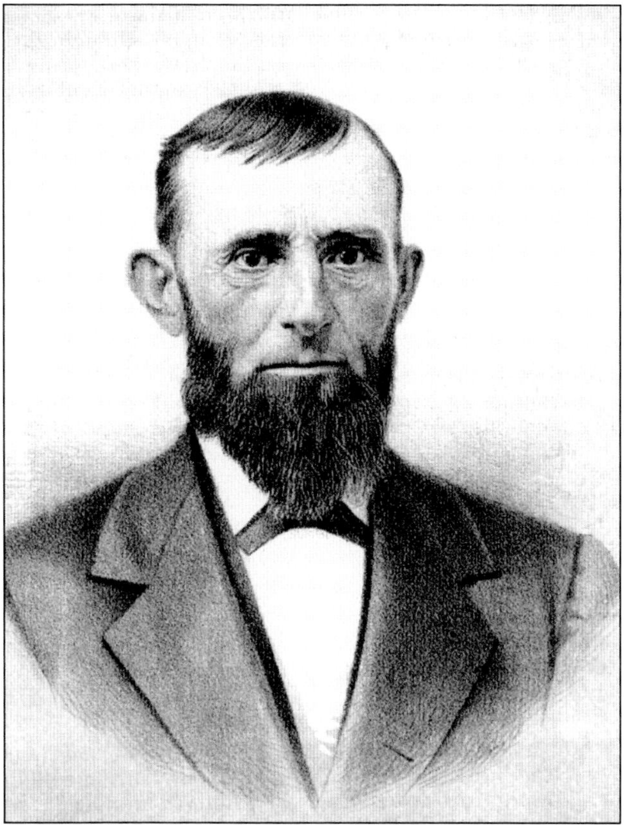

Marcus Taber married Erastus and Hannah Clark's daughter Hannah Maria Clark in the 1860s. Their children were L. D. and Hansen Taber. Hansen married Clementine Manly. Hansen and Clementine were the parents of Horace Taber.

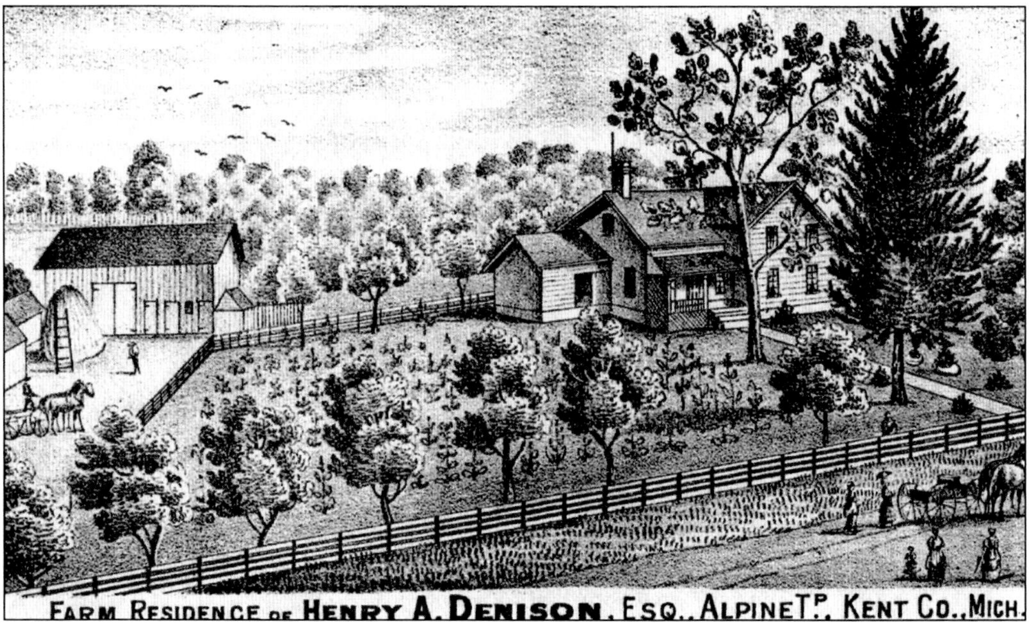

Henry and Agnes Denison from New York owned this farm of 80 acres in section 28. Their post office was Indian Creek. On the 1850 federal census, Henry's farm value was $1,000. Their children were Elizabeth, Emeline, and Lydin.

William Birdsall secured a farm that was on Four Mile Road and Baumhoff Avenue in 1846. As he cleared this wilderness site, William might have crossed paths with a bear or even a pack of wolves. William and Salina, his wife, had 14 children: Alonzo, John, infant twins who died, Salina, Marta, Oliver, Albert, William, an infant who died, Charlotte, Ira, another infant who died, Martin, and Jena Birdsall.

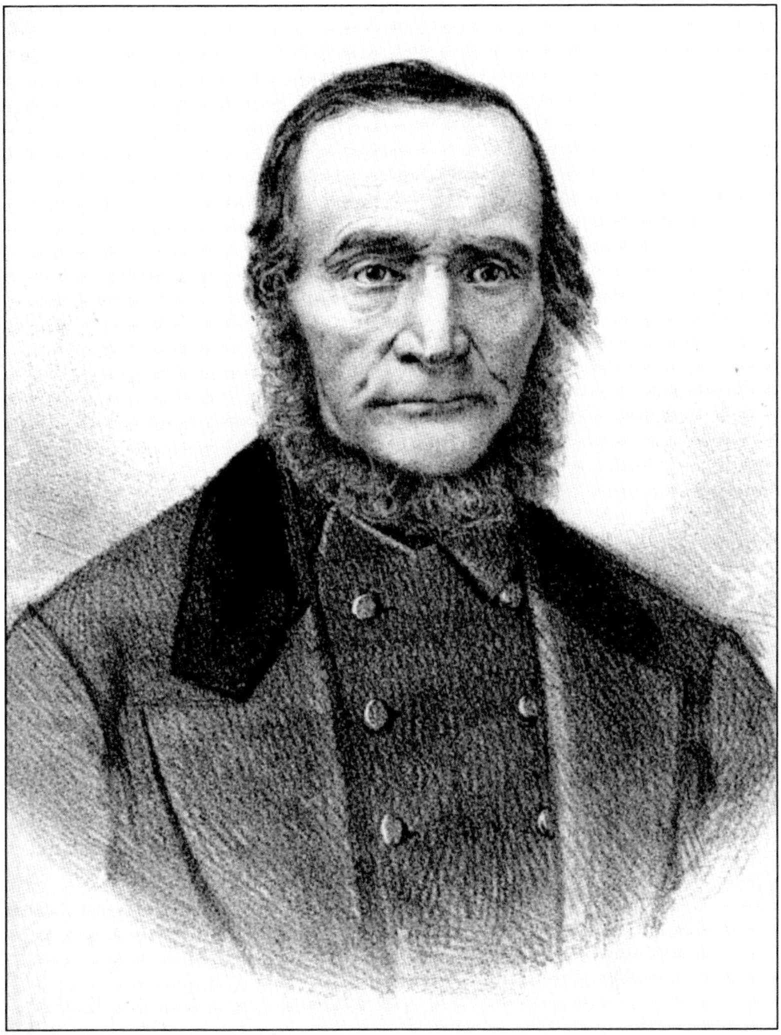

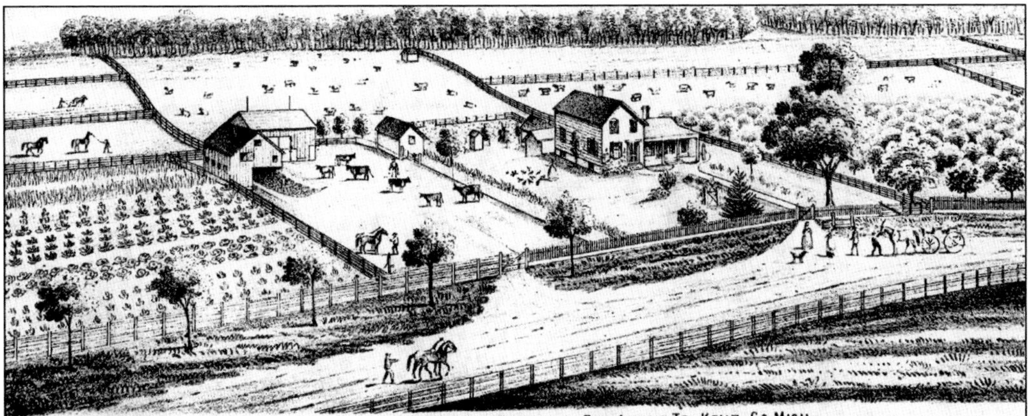

Seen here is William Birdsall's farm. At one time, he had cleared 300 acres of forested land and owned 2,000 acres in the state of Michigan.

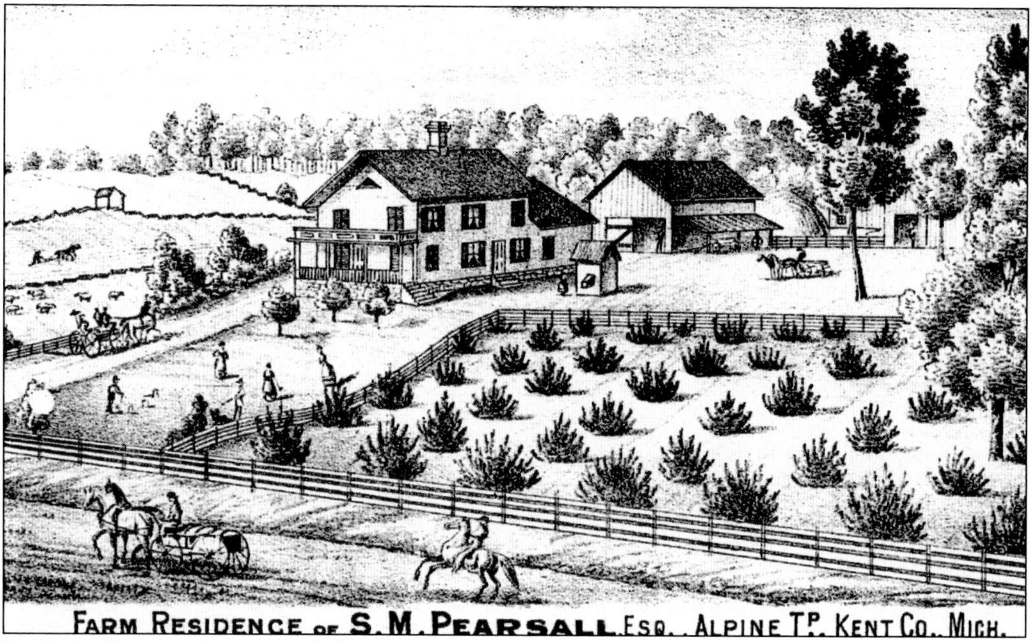

In 1843, Sherman M. Pearsall found property in Alpine Township on the southwest corner of Peach Ridge Avenue and Six Mile Road.

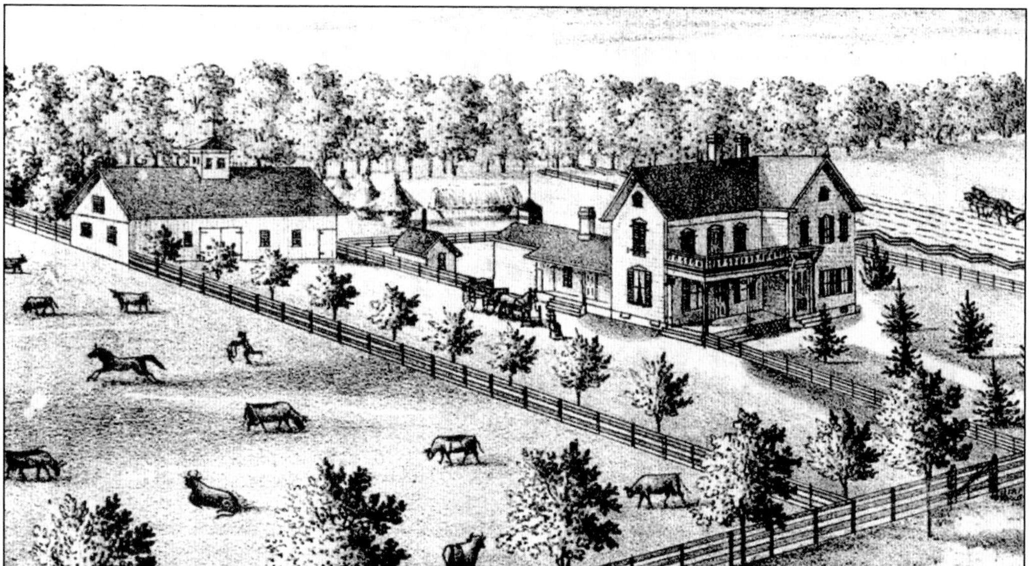

A Civil War veteran, Capt. Hanson H. Rogers had been with his unit at Gettysburg and the Battles of the Wilderness, Winchester, and Cedar Creek. In 1865, Hanson married Martha Hiler. They had three children: John, Albert, and Hattie. Hanson was an Alpine Township clerk for six years.

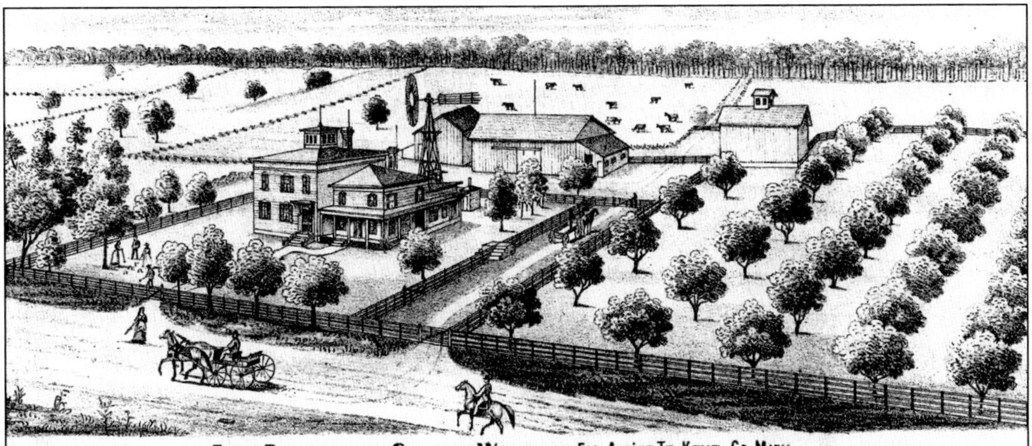

FARM RESIDENCE OF CHARLES WATERMAN ESQ. ALPINE TP. KENT CO. MICH.

Charles Waterman acquired this farm on Seven Mile Road from the state. As one can see, he could survey his farm from his cupola on top of his house. They had a well powered by the windmill next to the house. Waterman sold this farm to Marcus Alt and Josephine (Hoffman) Alt in 1893.

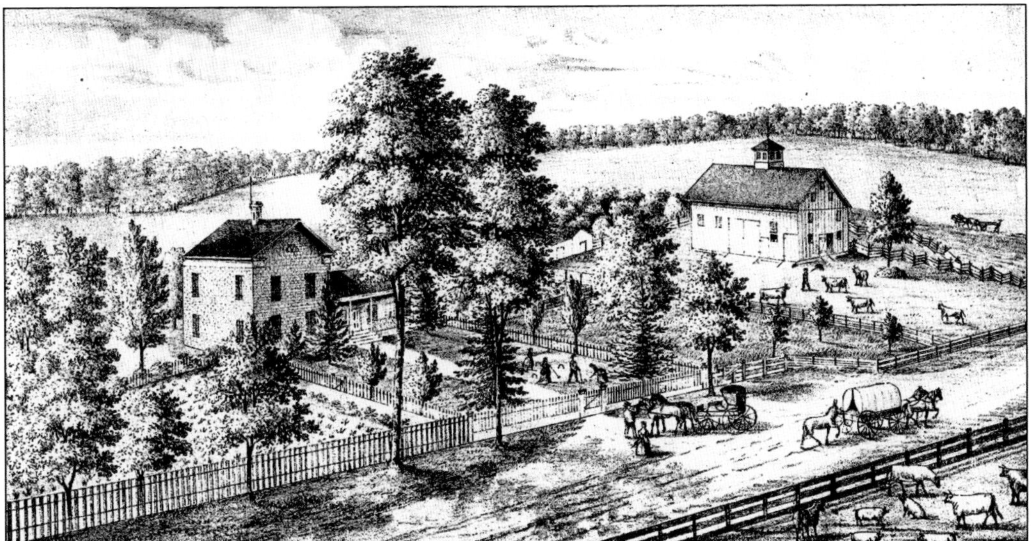

FARM RESIDENCE OF JOHN C. WILSON, ESQ., ALPINÉ TP. KENT CO., MICH.

The John C. Wilson farm was at the corner of Six Mile Road and Stage Avenue. He married Sarah Palmer. Stage Avenue is pictured here. The unique barn still stands with the house.

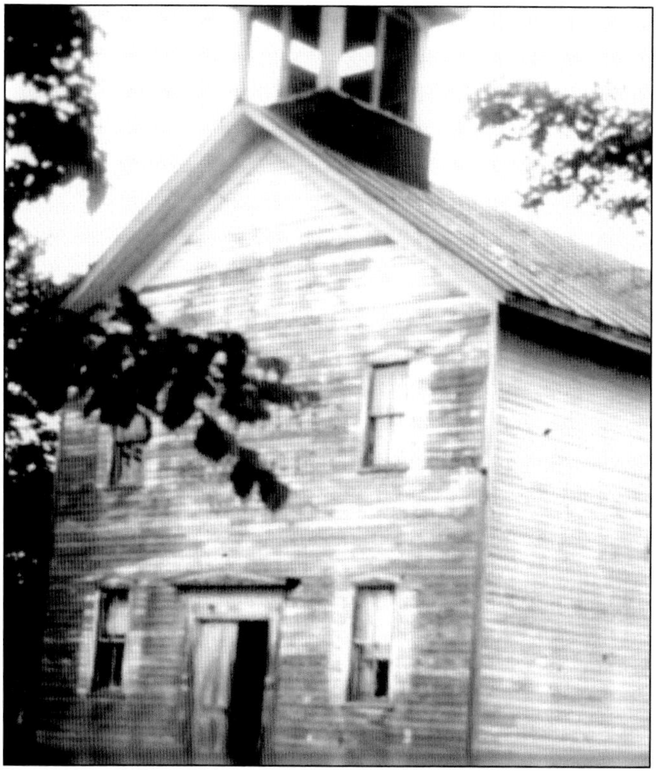

The farmers in this township established the Alpine Grange on March 17, 1874. The Grange was a rural organization "to promote the interests of the agricultural community." This two-story hall was built on Seven Mile Road and Peach Ridge Avenue in 1877 on land donated by Abel Chase.

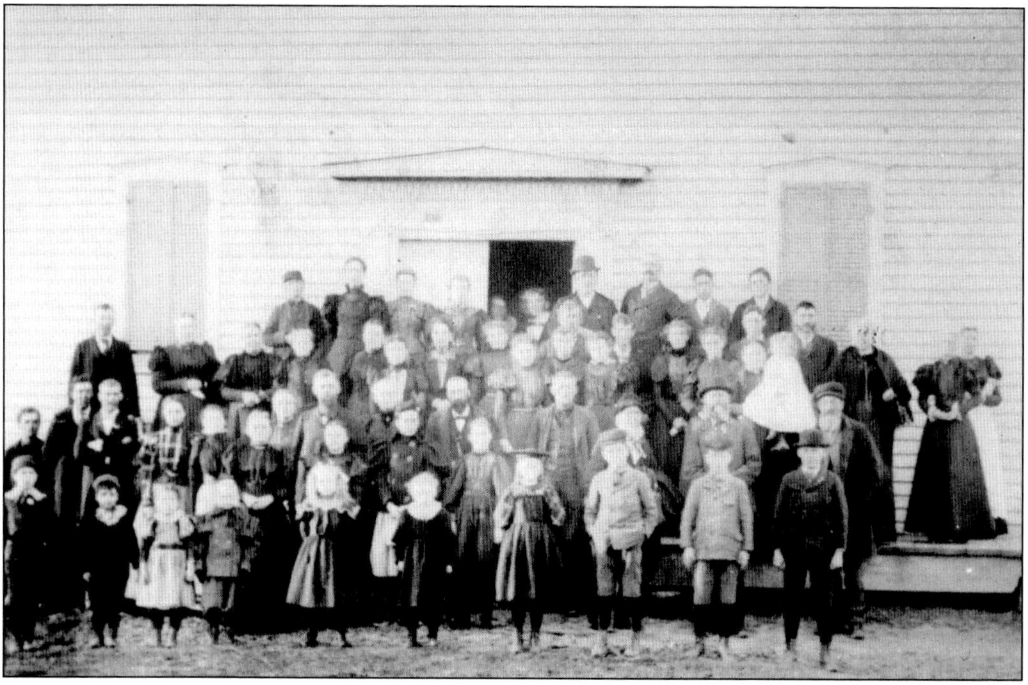

In 1899, the Alpine Grange is shown here celebrating its 25th anniversary. The Grange was a center for social activities. The Alpine Grange was active for 114 years. In 1974, this building was torn down.

Three

HOMES AND BARNS

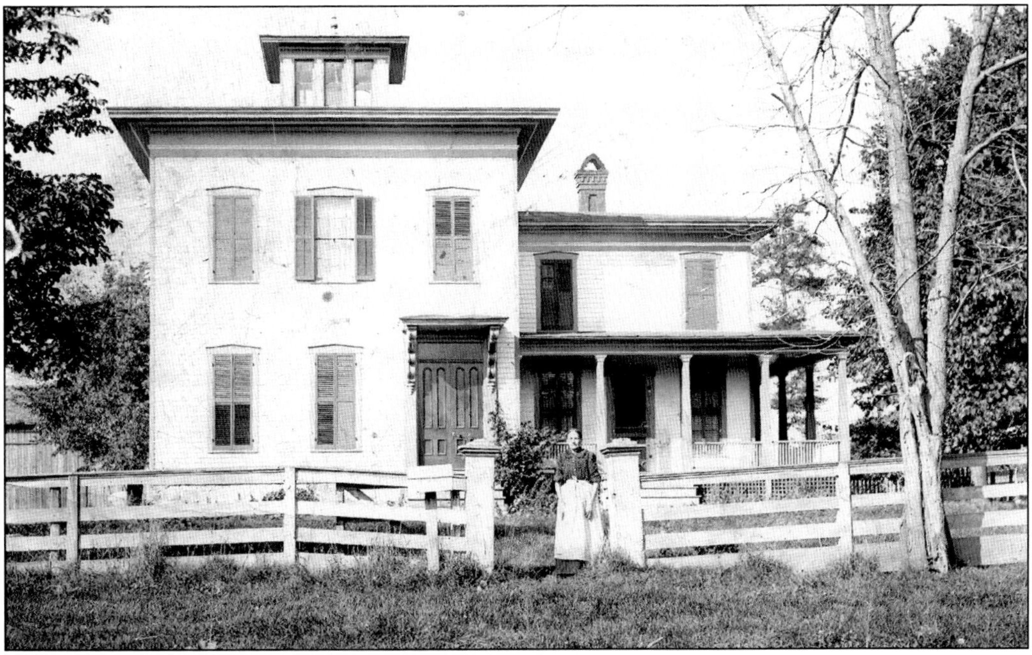

Josephine (Hoffman) Alt, wife of Marcus Alt, stands at the gate in front of their home on Seven Mile Road, west of Walker Avenue. She had been born in neighboring Wright Township. While visiting in Alsace, Germany, she met and married Marcus Alt. They had 10 children, 7 of whom survived to adulthood. After three daughters had married, Marcus and Josephine came to America with their children Joseph, Anthony, Melanie, and Albert. They bought the Charles Waterman farm in 1893. After Joseph's wife died, he moved back to Germany. Joseph married Mary Spinner, Anthony married Matilda Dietrich, Melanie married John Rothenthaler, and Albert married Anna Brechting. John Rothenthaler came from Württemberg, Germany, in 1898. He is the brother of Josephine (Rothenthaler) Antor. John worked for the Alt family before he married Melanie Alt.

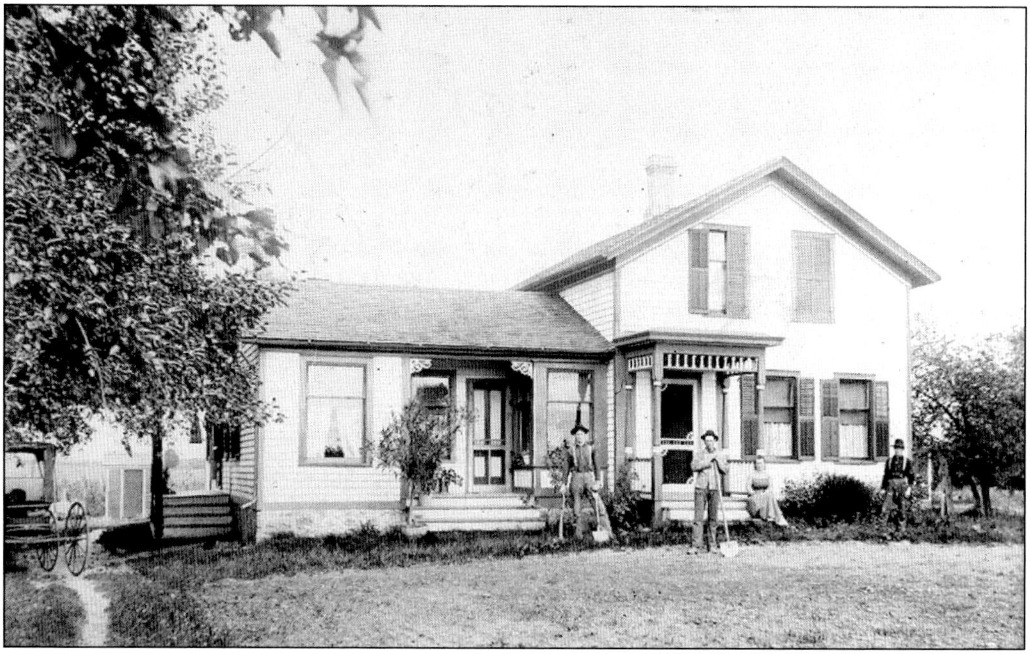

This is the Ernest and George Alberts family home on Seven Mile Road, west of Baumhoff Avenue. It is no longer there, as it burned to the ground in 1948.

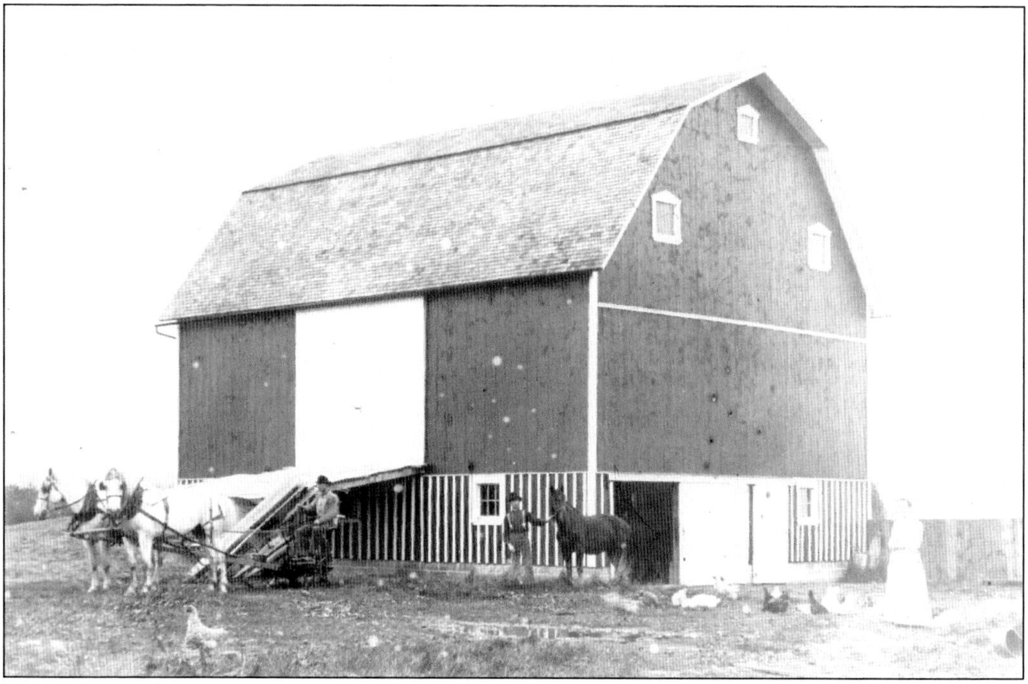

At the Ernest Alberts barn, someone has the team of horses hitched for work. Mom has the chickens out in the yard too. This was a time for general farming. Most people had a little of everything: a few cows for milking, pigs for ham, chicken for eggs, a garden for vegetables, an orchard for fruit, and horses to help with the work.

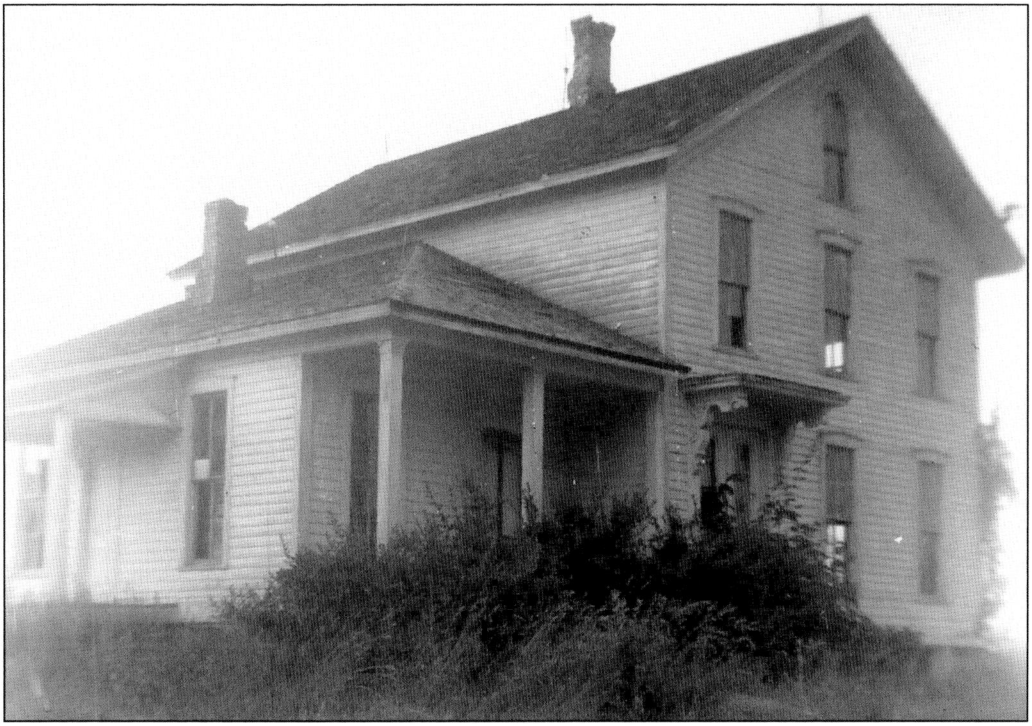

Anthony Alt and Matilda (Dietrich) Alt bought the Isaac W. Stanley farm on Stage Avenue and Eight Mile Road when he came to America in 1894. This was considered the village of Pleasant, named after the township John Coffee and Richmond Gooding had come from in Ohio. Stanley was the postmaster of Pleasant. His office was in this two-story house. The staircase in this home was very beautiful and opened to the upstairs bedrooms.

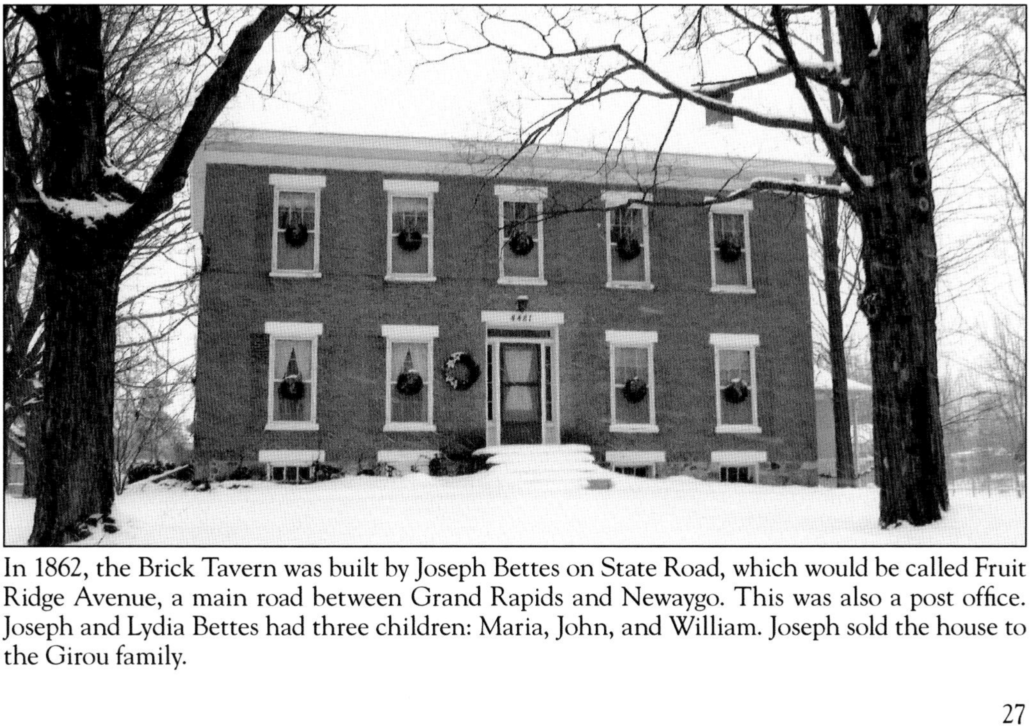

In 1862, the Brick Tavern was built by Joseph Bettes on State Road, which would be called Fruit Ridge Avenue, a main road between Grand Rapids and Newaygo. This was also a post office. Joseph and Lydia Bettes had three children: Maria, John, and William. Joseph sold the house to the Girou family.

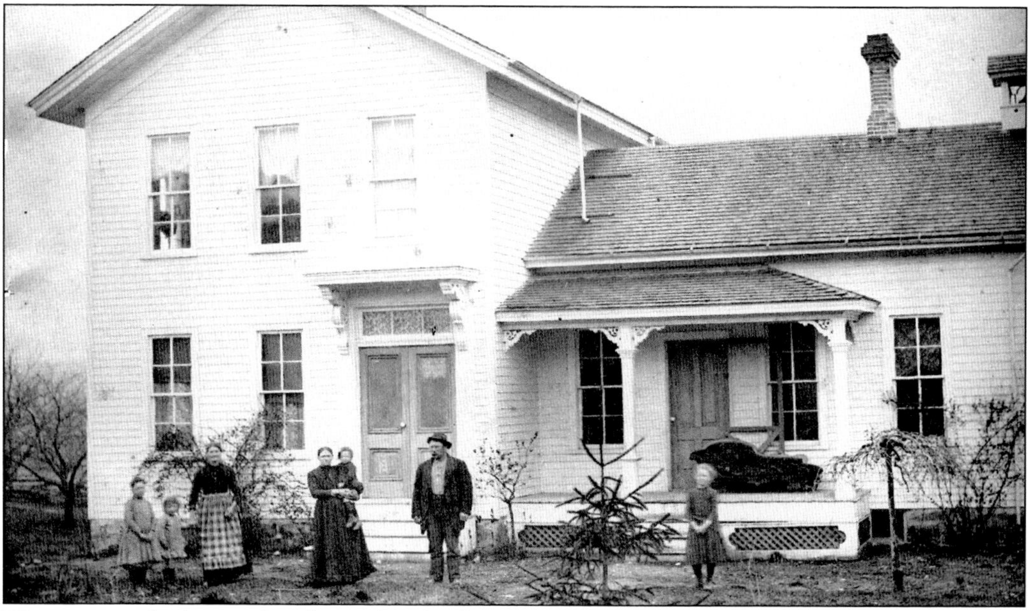

This is an early August Brechting family photograph in front of their home on Six Mile Road. August left his parents in Dorlar, Westphalia, Germany, to join his brother William in America. Two more brothers came, Franz and Julius Brechting. It is said that they helped lay original foundations in the copper mines of the Upper Peninsula of Michigan. When one broke his leg, they came south to the Grand Rapids area. Franz and Julius ran a wagon maker and repair shop in Grand Rapids.

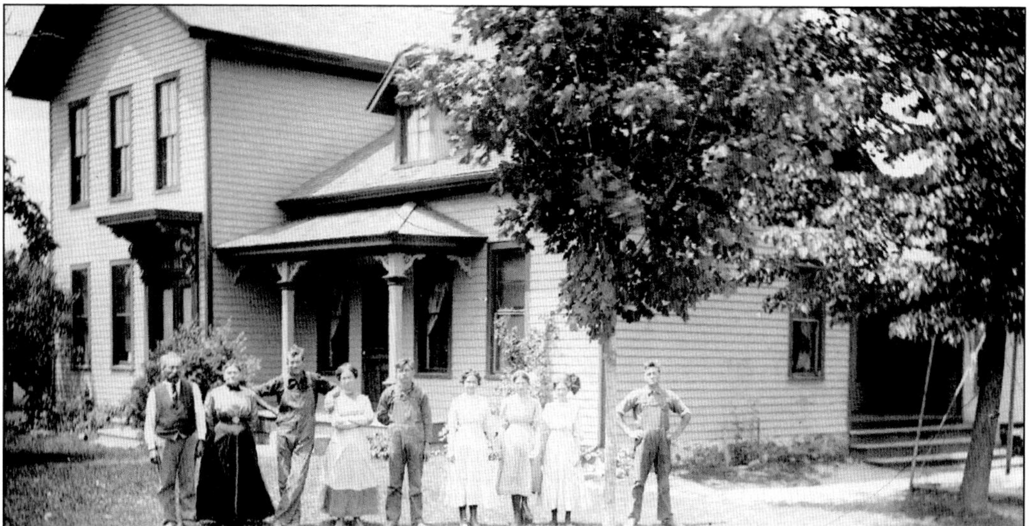

August Brechting stands on the left with his wife, Margareth Gertrude (Schoettler) Brechting and their children, from left to right, Anthony, Mary Florentina, August, Louise, Bernadine, Matilda, and Julius, about 1909. Anthony married Julia Bergman, Mary Florentina entered the convent as Sister Fidelis, August married Nina Antor, Louise married Joseph Nickolas Schweitzer, Bernadine married Richard Thome, Julius married Theresa Antor, and Matilda never married. Anna Brechting had already married Albert Alt in 1903, and Emma had married Frederick Schindler in 1905.

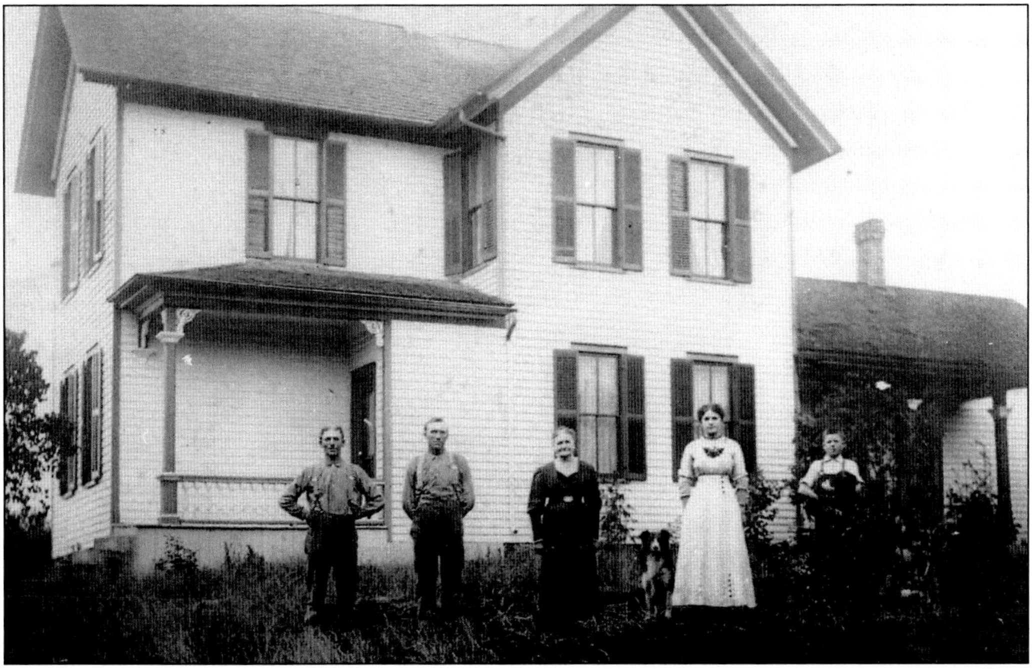

Looking for work, William Brechting was the first of four brothers to come to America from Dorlar, Westphalia, Germany. Here William Brechting's family stands at their home on Six Mile Road after his passing in 1909. From left to right are Fred, Joseph, Florentine (Schoettler), Mary, and Frank. Fred married Elizabeth Zweers, Joseph married Elizabeth Homan, Mary married Fred Schweitzer, and Frank Brechting married Mary Henze. Daughter Frances is not in the photograph, as she had married Pearly Ebers in 1908.

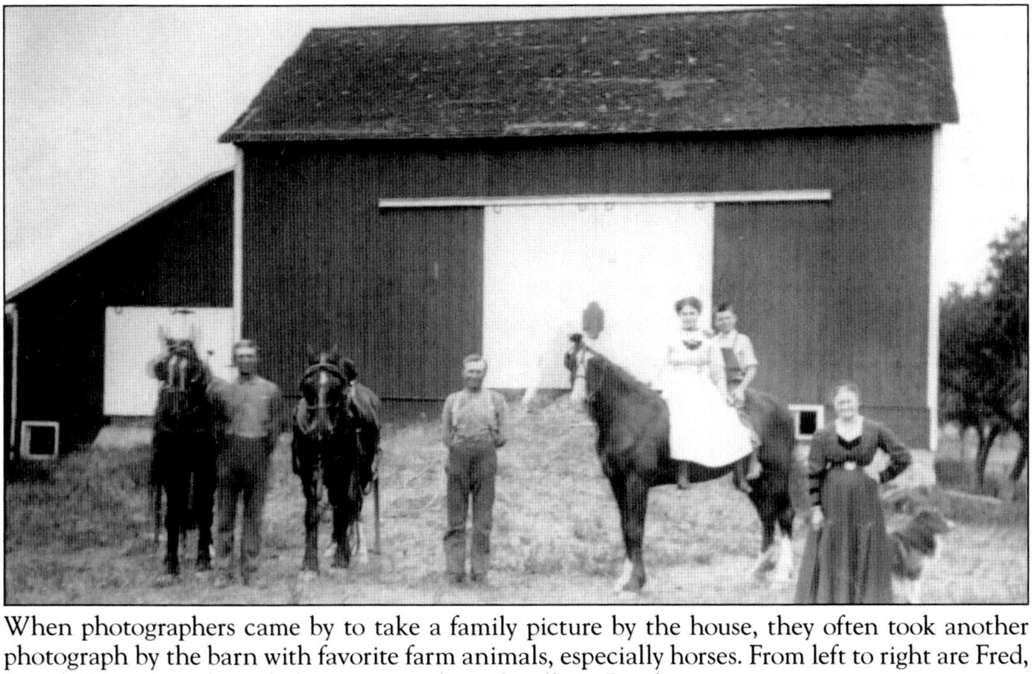

When photographers came by to take a family picture by the house, they often took another photograph by the barn with favorite farm animals, especially horses. From left to right are Fred, Joseph, Mary, Frank, and Florentine, widow of William Brechting.

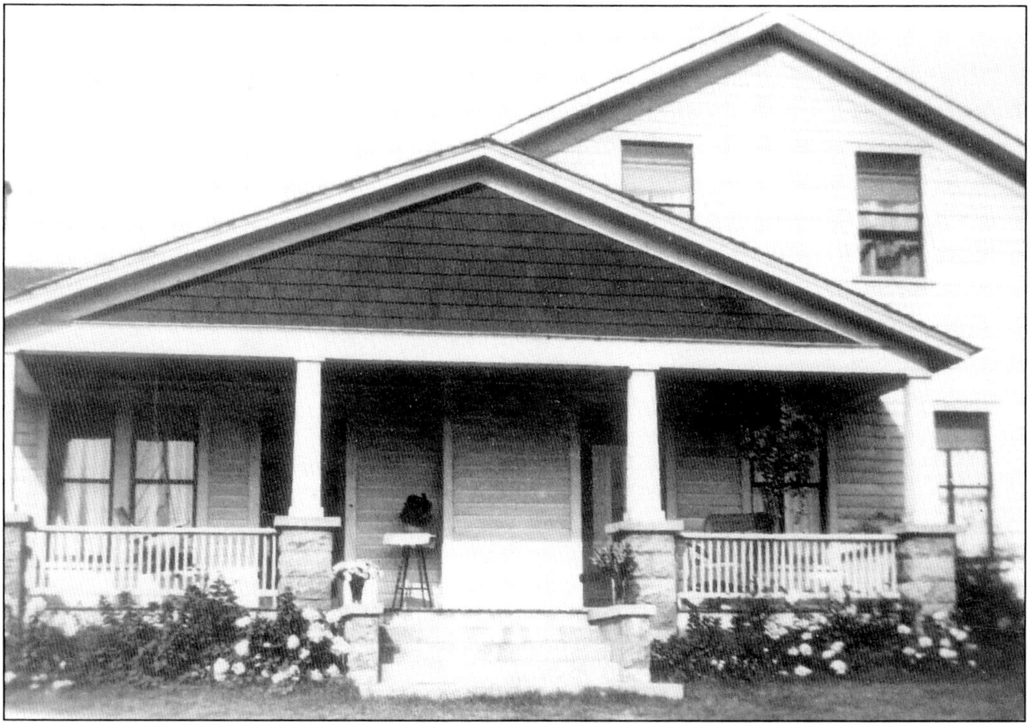

Charles Bremer's home and farm were on the northwest corner of Alpine Avenue and Six Mile Road. The Alpine Township offices and library are now located on this site. Bremer married Christine Ruthardt in October 1887. Their children were Mabel, William, Helen, Arthur, Alma, and Walter. Mabel married William Fuller.

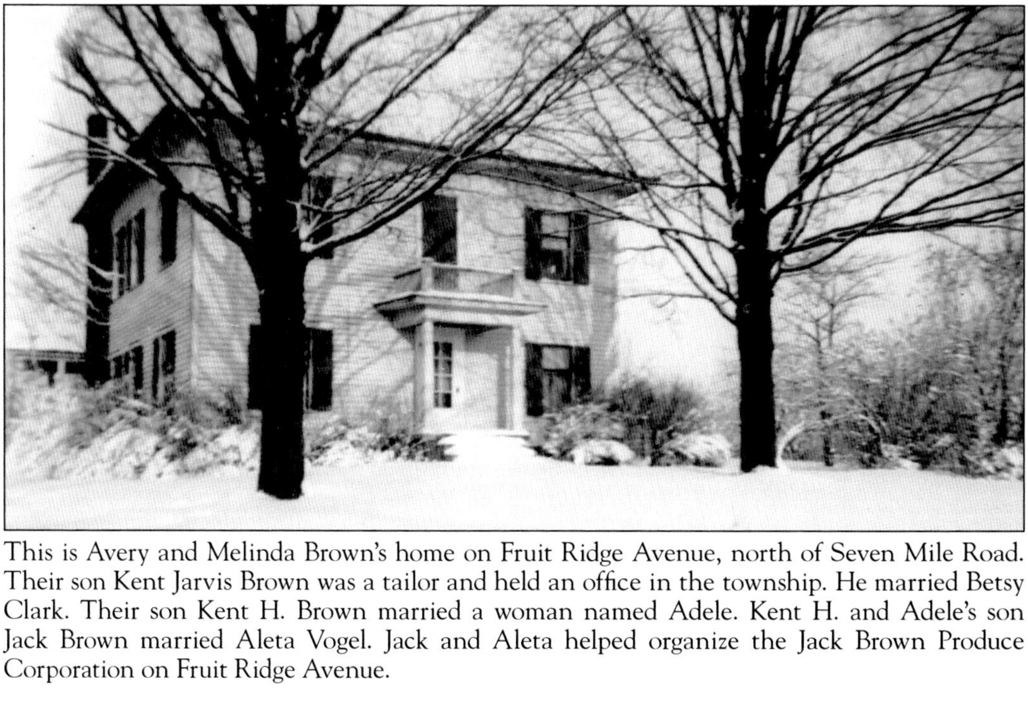

This is Avery and Melinda Brown's home on Fruit Ridge Avenue, north of Seven Mile Road. Their son Kent Jarvis Brown was a tailor and held an office in the township. He married Betsy Clark. Their son Kent H. Brown married a woman named Adele. Kent H. and Adele's son Jack Brown married Aleta Vogel. Jack and Aleta helped organize the Jack Brown Produce Corporation on Fruit Ridge Avenue.

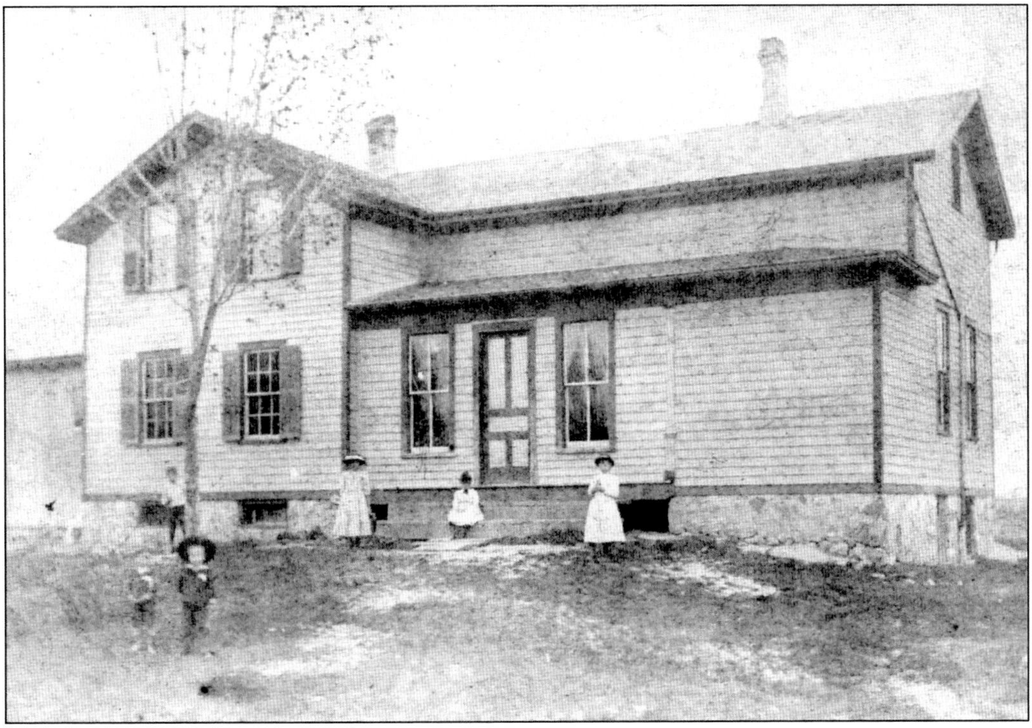

This is the Abel Chase home on Peach Ridge Avenue and Seven Mile Road in section 16.

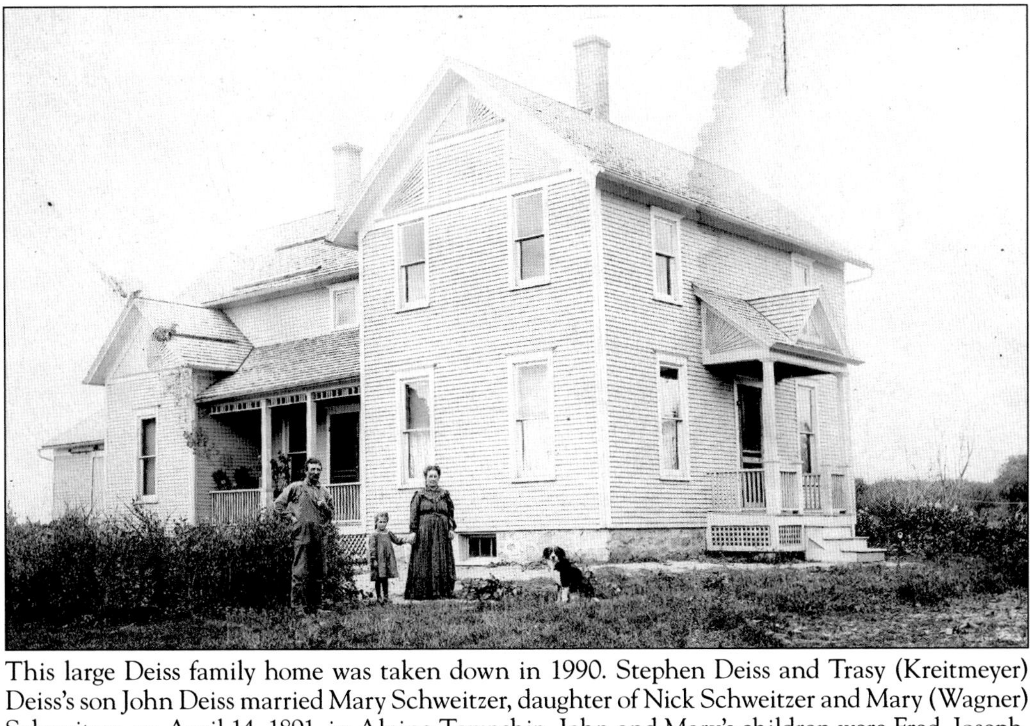

This large Deiss family home was taken down in 1990. Stephen Deiss and Trasy (Kreitmeyer) Deiss's son John Deiss married Mary Schweitzer, daughter of Nick Schweitzer and Mary (Wagner) Schweitzer, on April 14, 1891, in Alpine Township. John and Mary's children were Fred, Joseph, and Anna Deiss. Fred married Rose Frances Erhardt.

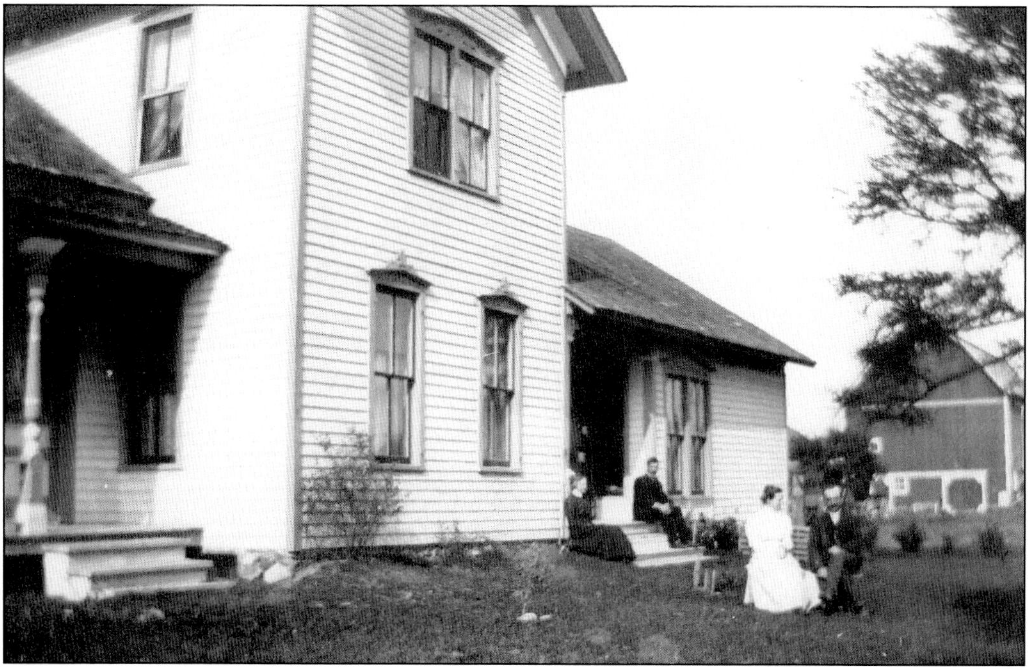

On a lovely summer day, two daughters of Philip and Lisetta Ruthardt are enjoying the afternoon with their husbands. Charles and Rosina Dietz visit with Charles and Christine Bremer in the front yard. Charles and Rosina Dietz never had any children.

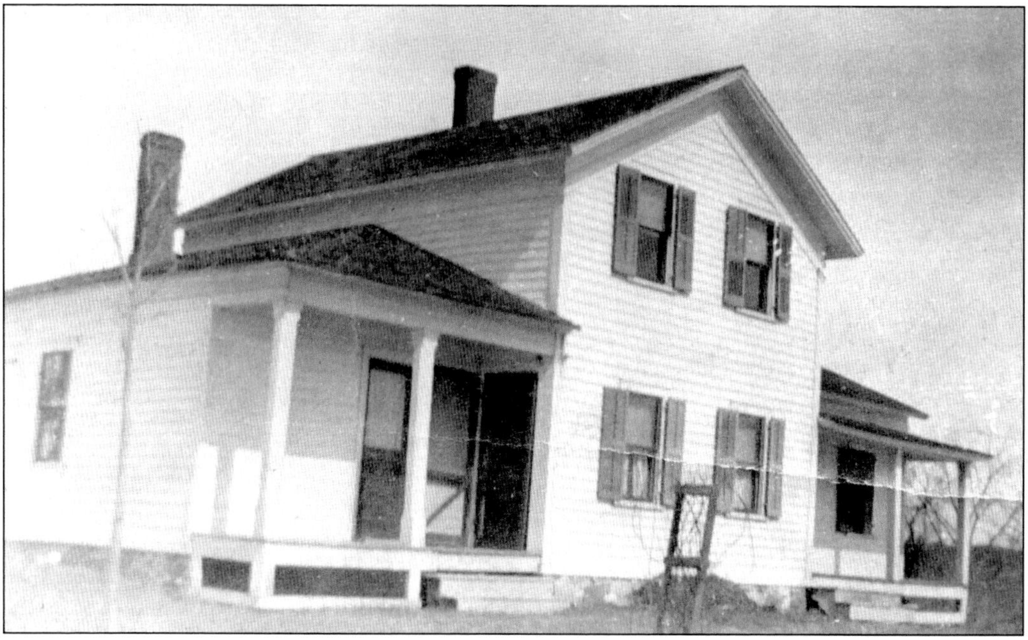

This Dunneback home on the corner of Six Mile Road and Peach Ridge Avenue was purchased by Elizabeth (Schulte) Dunneback and Joseph Dunneback with the inheritance she received from her first husband, another Joseph Dunneback. It was the birthplace of Edwin, Leo, Anthony, Harry, and Clara (Vierheilig) Dunneback. Anna (Dunneback) Hendershot and Theodore Dunneback were also raised here.

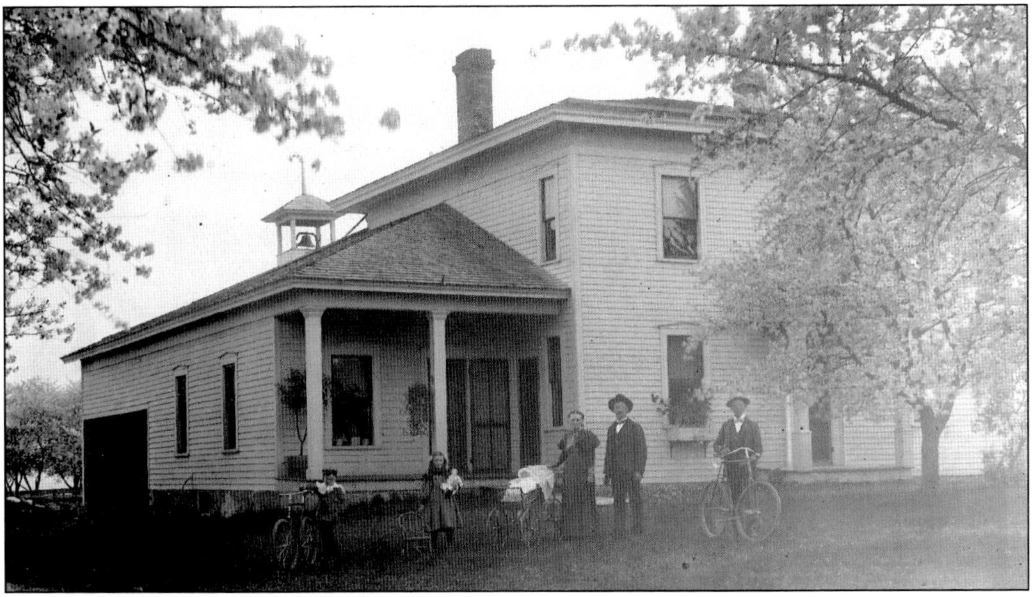

It is springtime. Anna and Frank Ebers are standing in front of their home on the south side of Ten Mile Road. They had purchased the farm in 1890 from the Edwin Cummings family. Son Avery has his bicycle, daughter Vernie has her doll, and son Walter Ebers is in the baby buggy. The man on the right is unidentified.

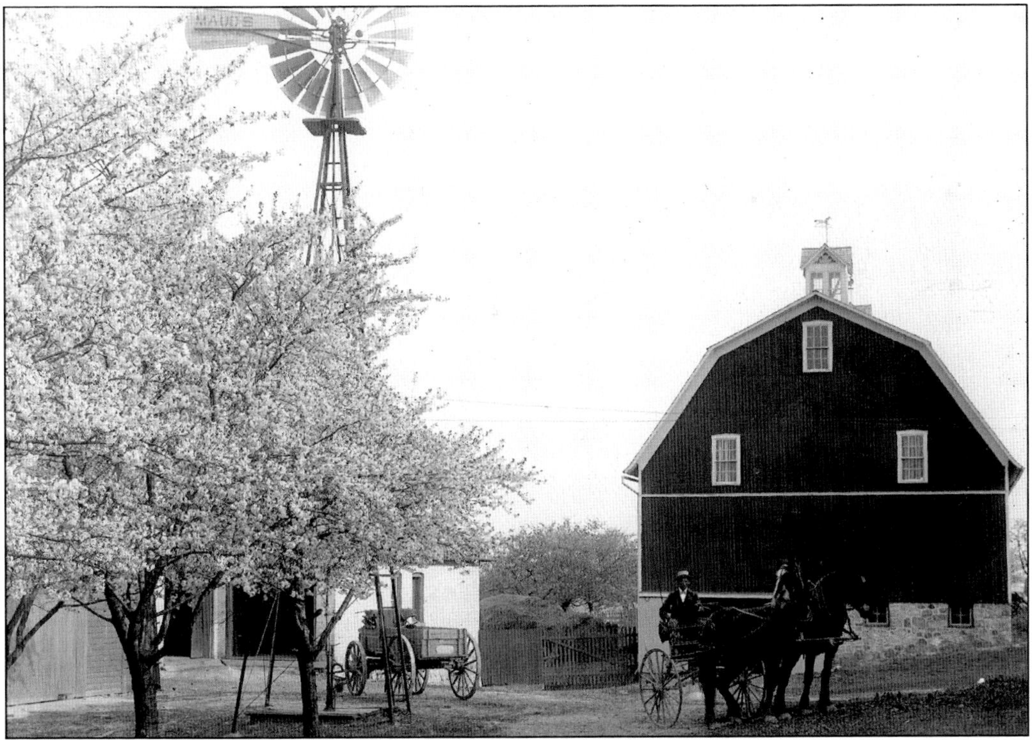

The trees are in bloom. It is the most beautiful and fragrant time of the year in the area known as the Ridge. Frank Ebers brought his team of horses out with the buggy for this photograph. The farm wagon sits behind them. Frank's son Walter Ebers took this barn down in the 1950s.

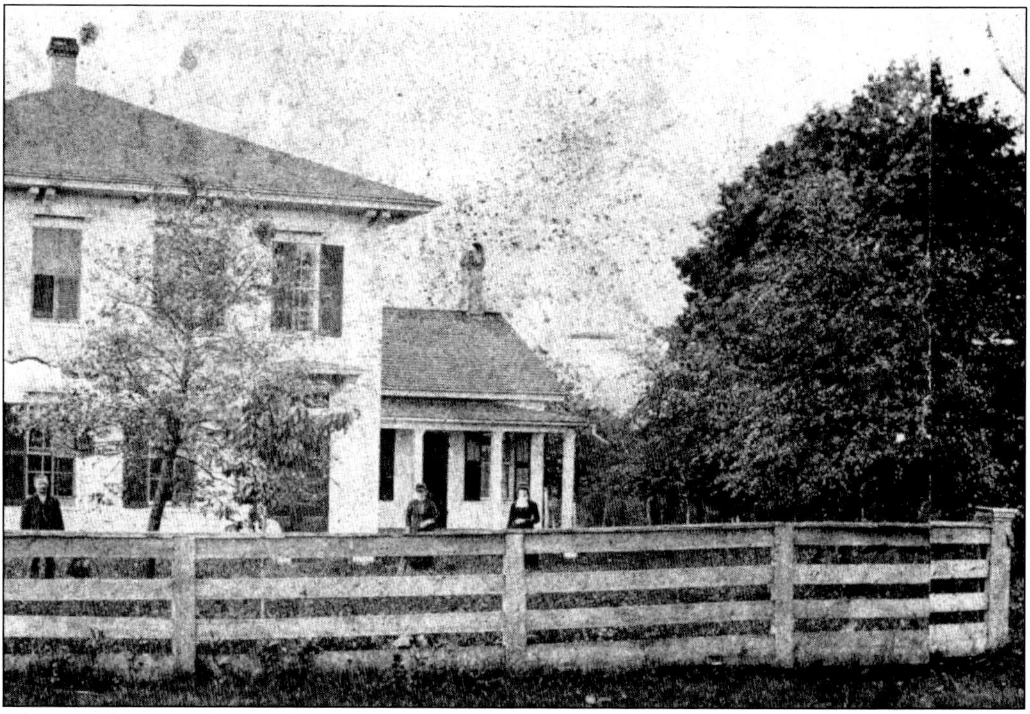

John H. Ebers stands, on the left, with his son little Pearly Ebers, who is peeking through the fence. John was the son of Henry and Christine Ebers. His wife, Mary (Rusche) Ebers, is one of the ladies on the right.

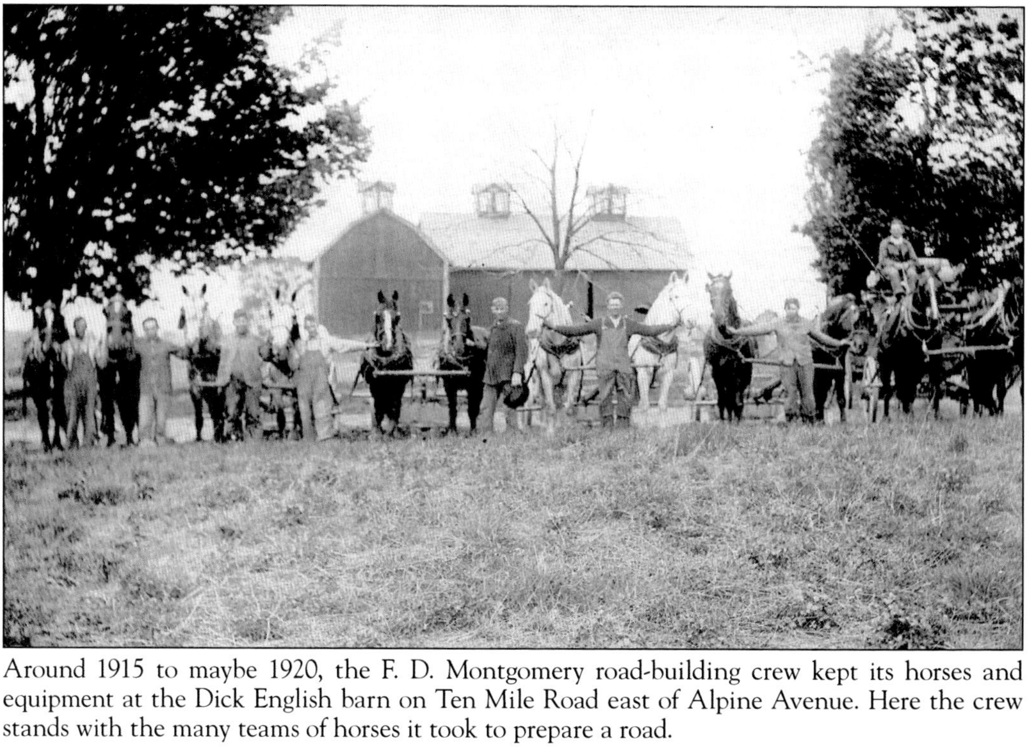

Around 1915 to maybe 1920, the F. D. Montgomery road-building crew kept its horses and equipment at the Dick English barn on Ten Mile Road east of Alpine Avenue. Here the crew stands with the many teams of horses it took to prepare a road.

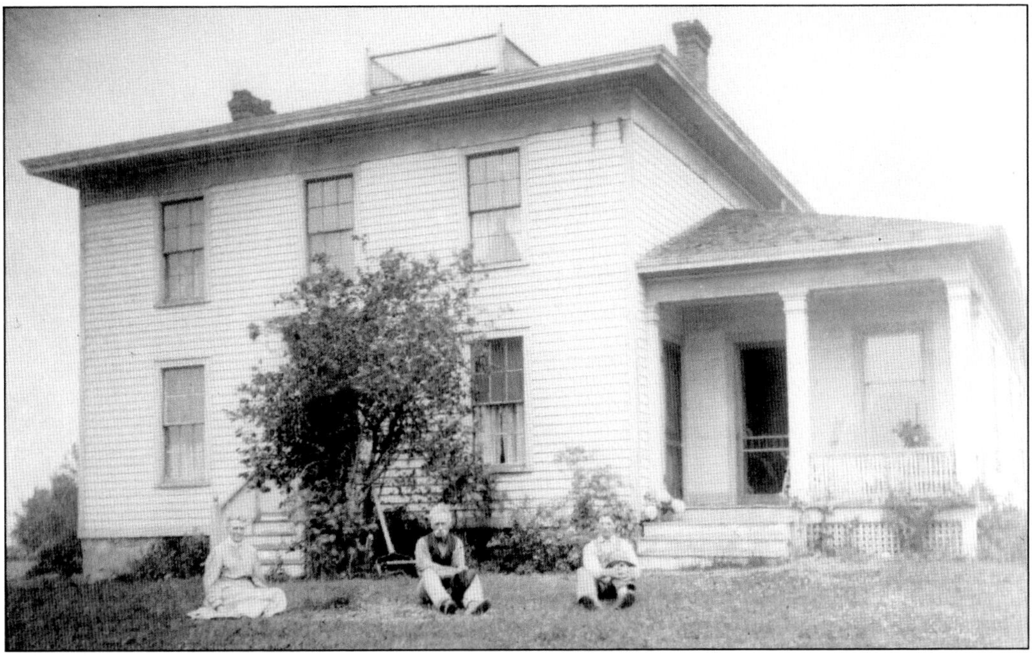

This is the Fuller family house on Peach Ridge Avenue. Layfette and Lucy Fuller had a daughter, Ida (Fuller) Alberts, who was a teacher at the Wheeler School in Alpine Township. Ida married Ernest Alberts.

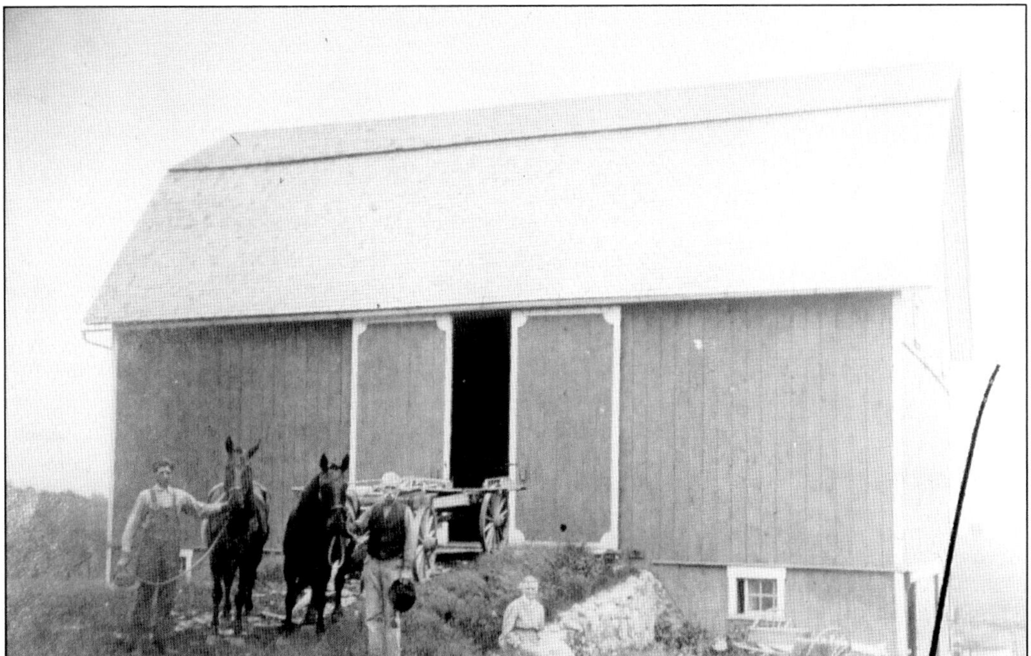

Layfette Fuller stands on the right with his horse by the barn as his wife, Lucy, sits on the barn bridge hill. The son, Freddie, was listed as eight months old on the 1880 federal census.

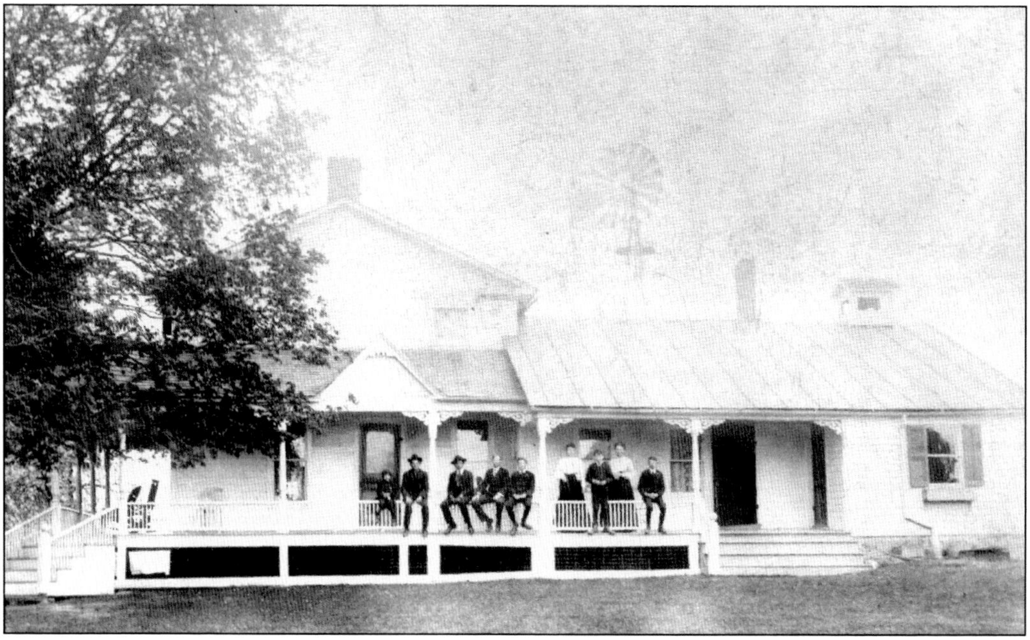

The first John Coffee and his good friend Richmond Gooding came from Ohio to Alpine Township in 1839. They purchased land and returned home to marry and bring their brides, Marinda Jane Gooding and Macy Lyon, respectively, to live on the road that would become Fruit Ridge Avenue. This home of Richmond Gooding became John Ransom Coffee and Sarah (Keas) Coffee's home. They stand on the porch with their children, Will (who served in the Civil War), Stephen, Watson, and Bertha (Wolf) Coffee. This house burned down in 1933.

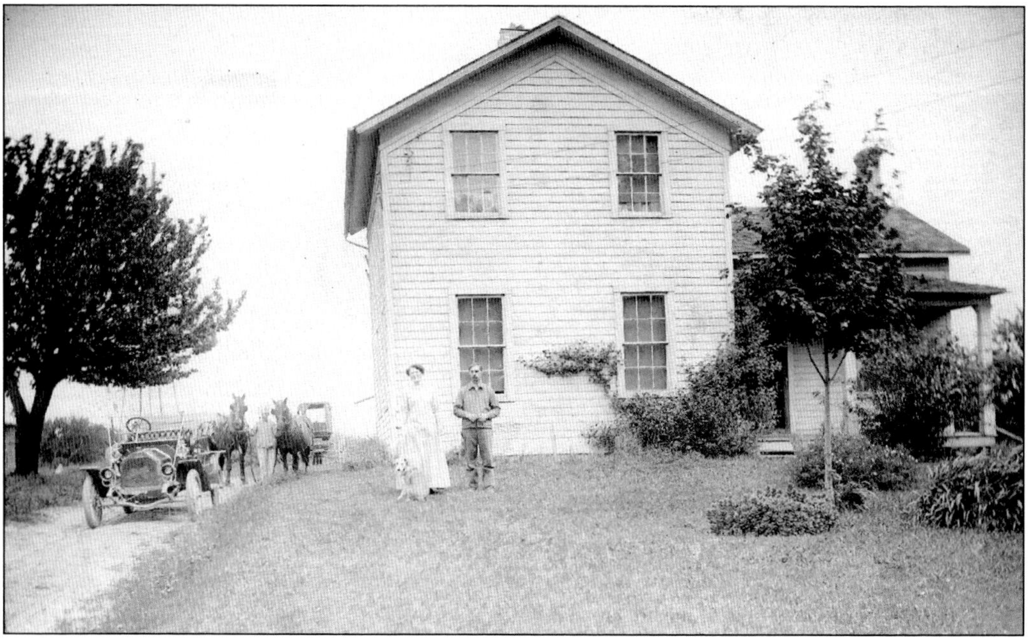

Watson and Bertha Coffee ran a farm on Six Mile Road and Hendershot Avenue. Watson was the son of John R. and John's first wife, Mary (Johnson) Coffee. Watson and Bertha did not have any children. Lester and Mary Dunneback bought this farm and raised their family here.

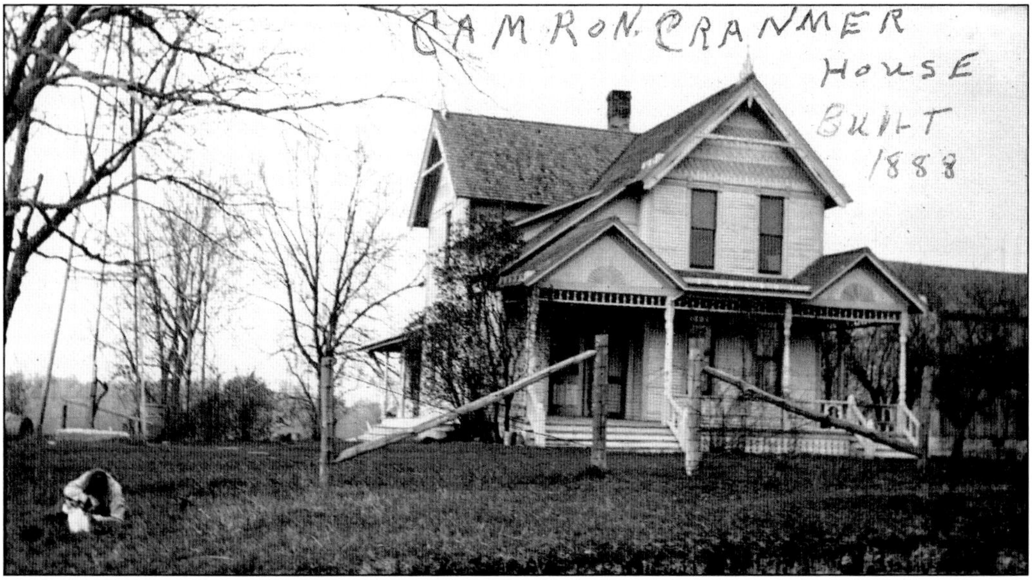

This large farmhouse belonged to the Cranmer family on Eight Mile Road, east of Peach Ridge Avenue. In the foreground are a boy and his dog. He could be Ken Cranmer, who was raised in this house. It was built in 1888 and has been torn down.

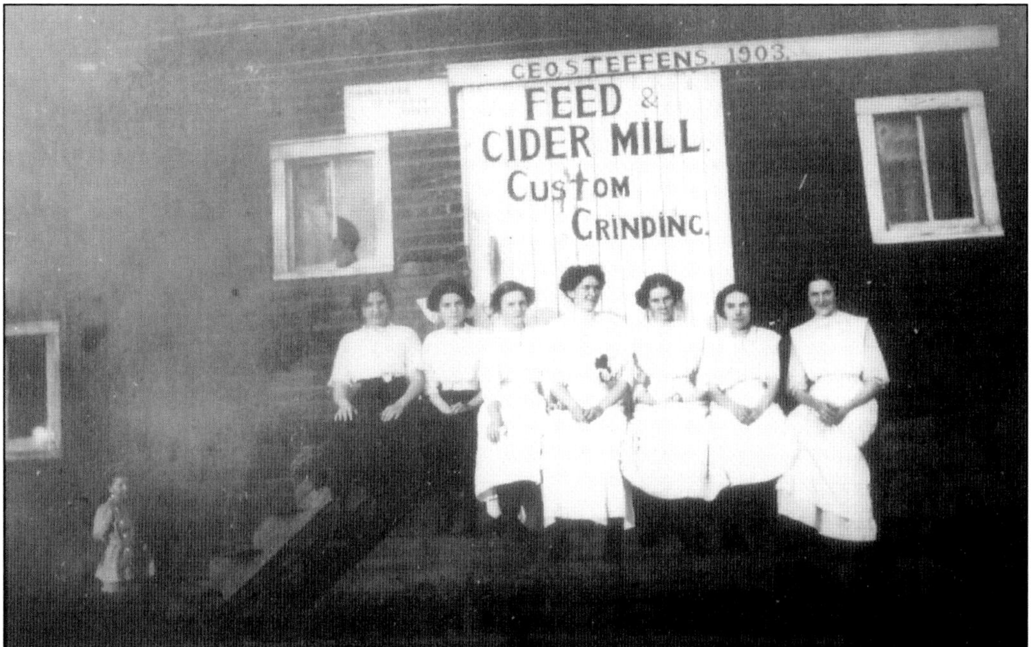

George Steffens build this feed and cider mill in 1903 in section 23. Waterpower from the creek on the property was used to run the mill.

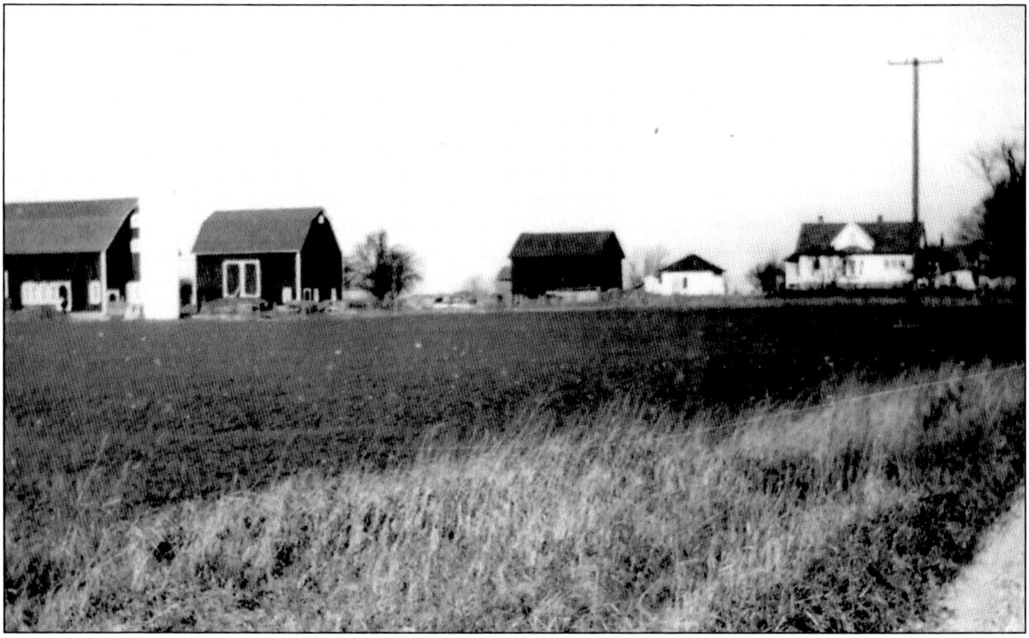

Urban and Catherine Heinbeck came from Ohio and bought this farm in 1845. They paid $1.09 in property tax on 40 acres for that year.

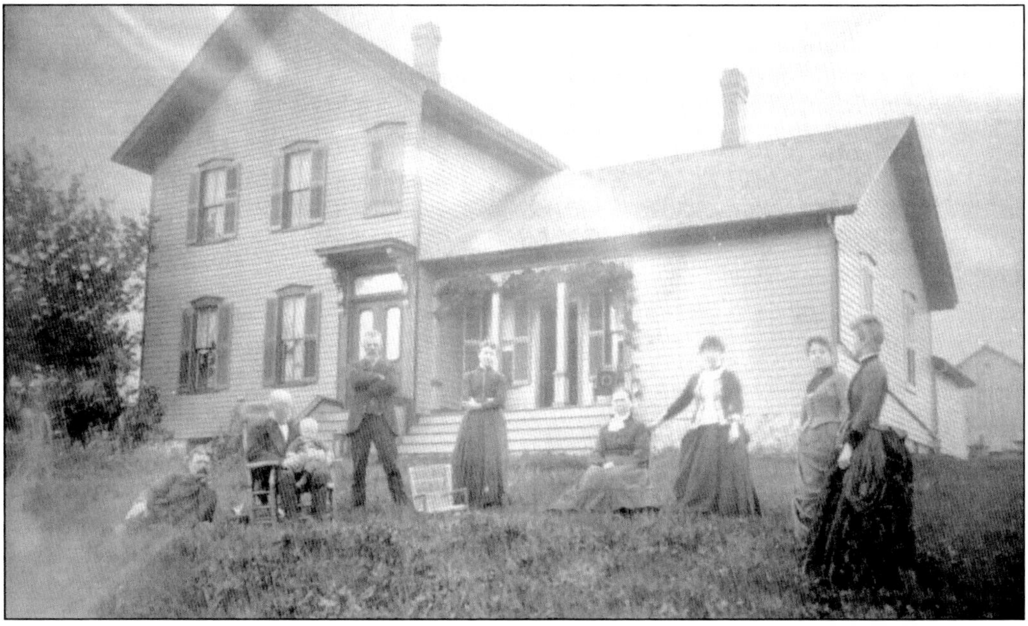

The Casper Henze home stood high on a hill on Alpine Avenue, north of Four Mile Road. In this picture are, from left to right, William, John Casper holding Frank, Casper, Mary (Hahn), Tanta (German for *aunt*) Mary, Therese, Anna, and M. Louise Henze. Currently Henze Street runs west from Alpine Avenue in the middle of a commercial district where their farm and this house had been.

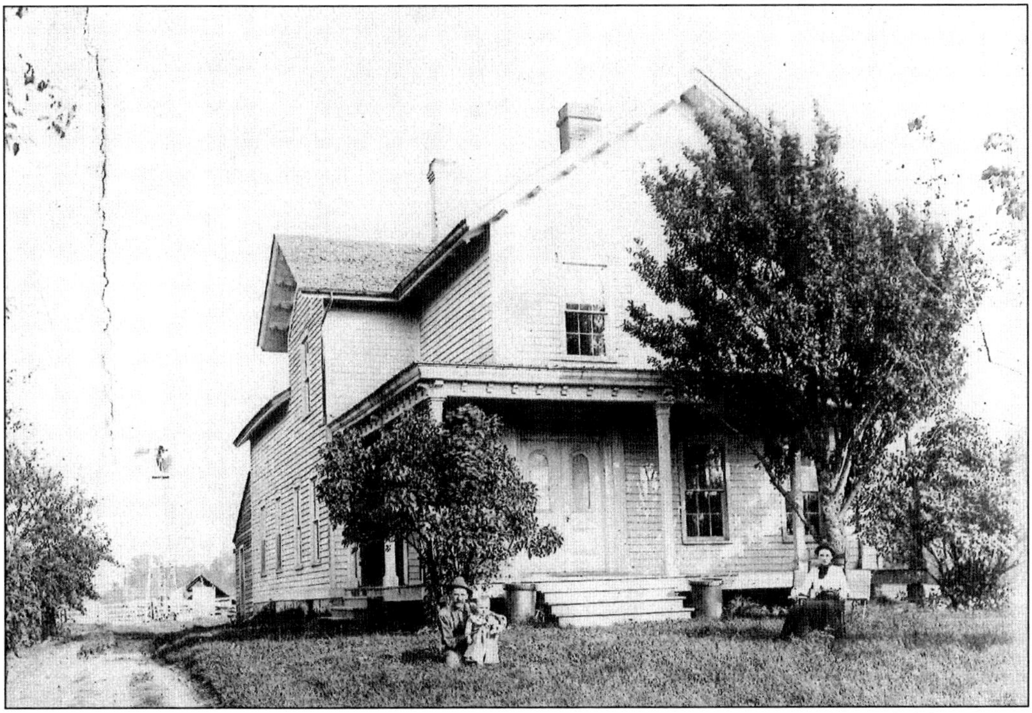

J. F. and Gladys Hillebrand are at their home on Peach Ridge Avenue. Their children were William and Richard Hillebrand.

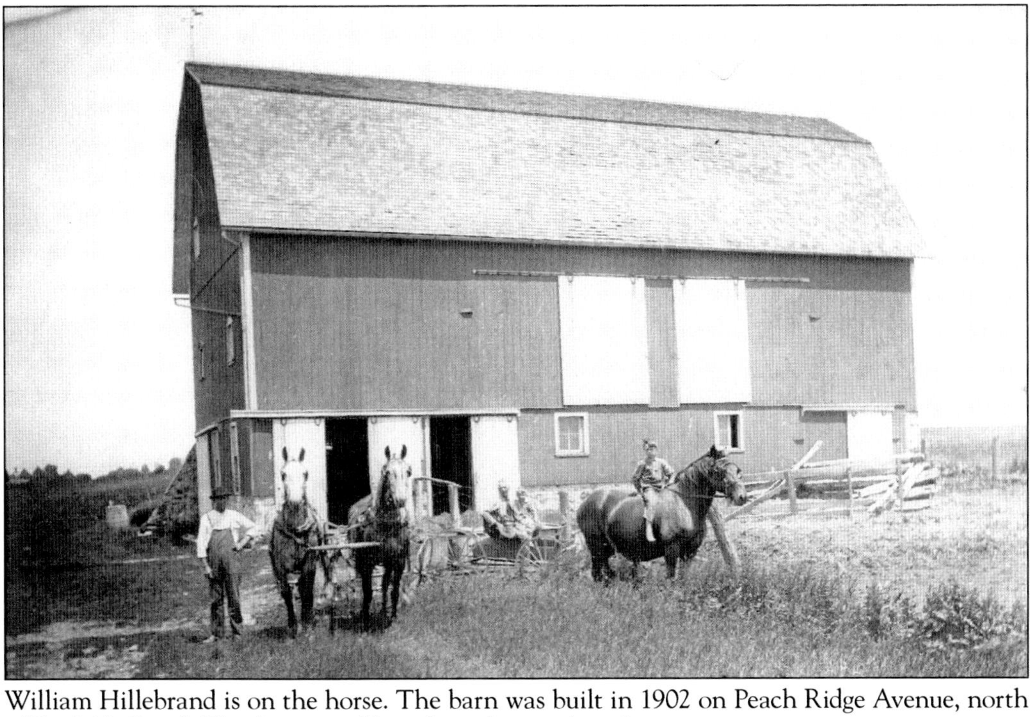

William Hillebrand is on the horse. The barn was built in 1902 on Peach Ridge Avenue, north of Six Mile Road. This house and barn have been taken down.

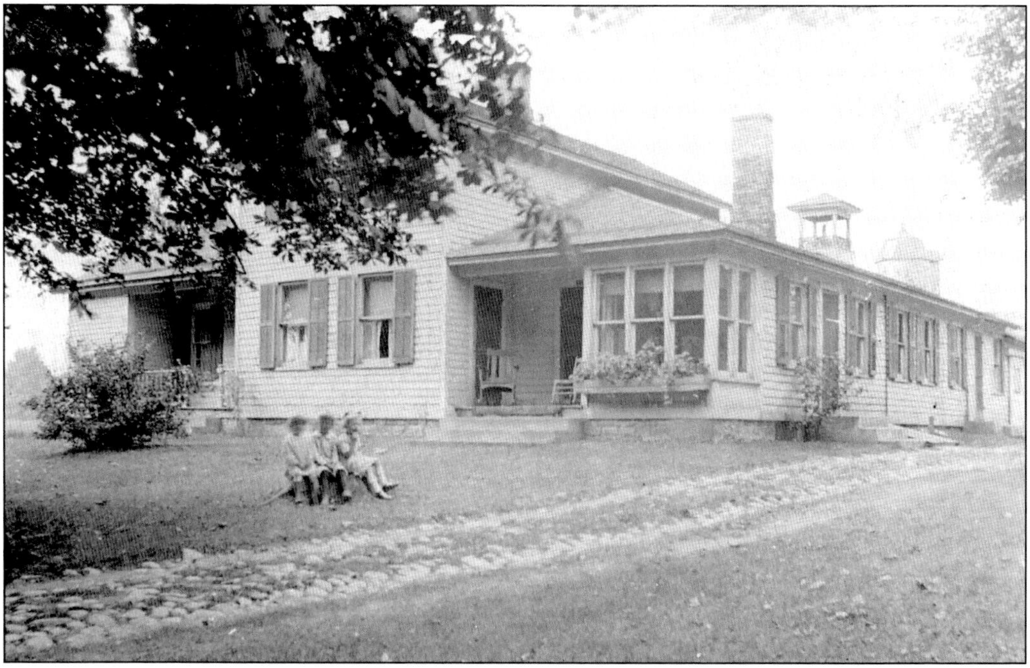

This is the home of Aaron Hubbell Hills, son of Turner Hills and Adelia (Hubbell) Hills, who moved to the area in 1837. Aaron married Ann Colton in 1852. They purchased the southwest corner of Seven Mile Road and Alpine Avenue. When George Ward bought this home, he remodeled it. A few years later, it was torn down to make room for four lanes on Alpine Avenue.

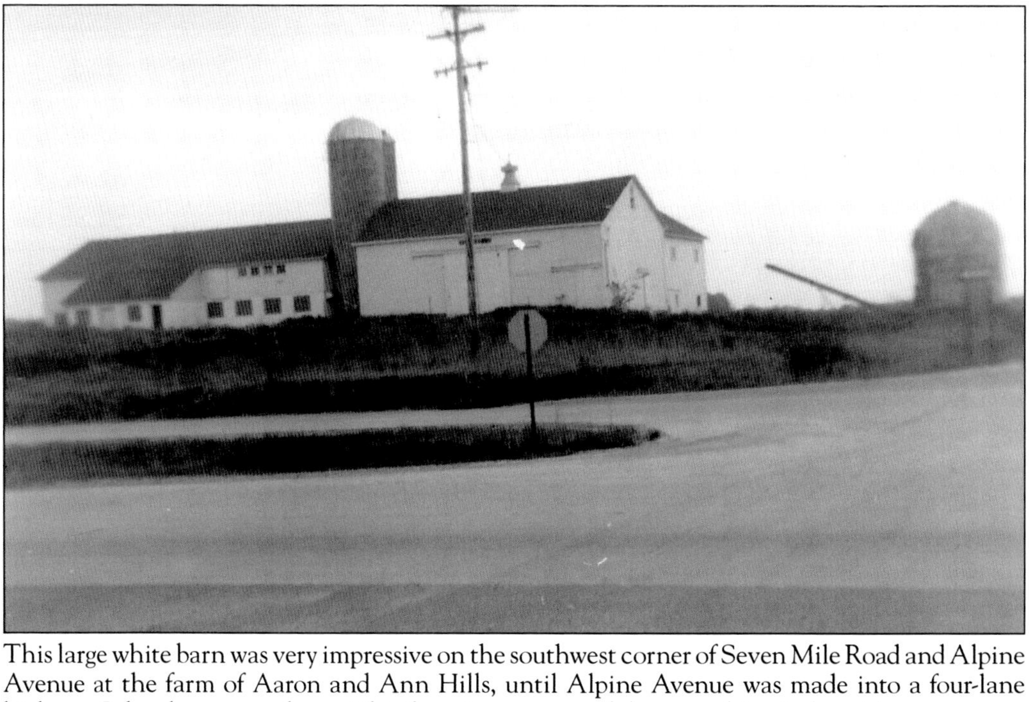

This large white barn was very impressive on the southwest corner of Seven Mile Road and Alpine Avenue at the farm of Aaron and Ann Hills, until Alpine Avenue was made into a four-lane highway. It has been torn down. This farm is now part of the township's industrial area.

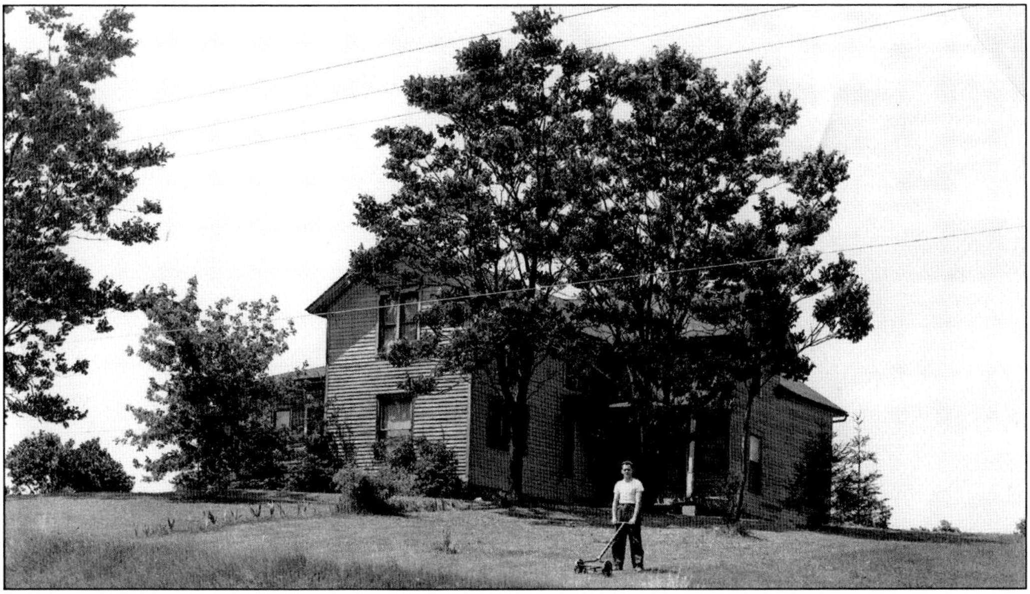

The Ingersoll home on Alpine Avenue, south of Alpine Church Road, was taken down by the Alpine Township Fire Department within the past 10 years as a practice burn. Casper Cordes had owned this property. Then the Fred Cordes family owned it before Martin Ingersoll and Marie (Platte) Ingersoll.

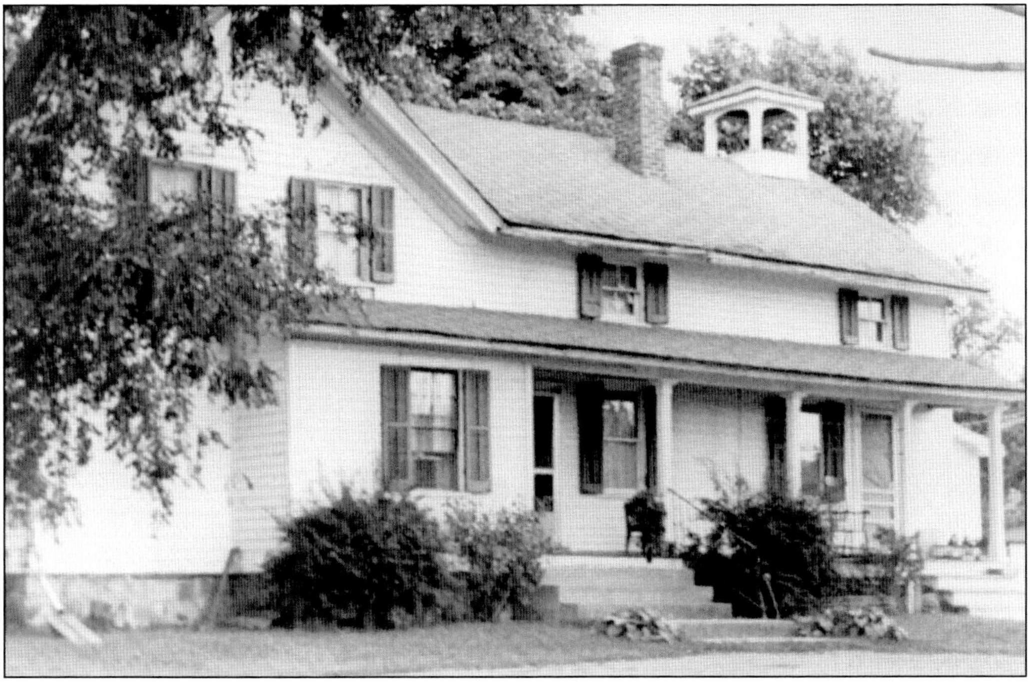

This is the Klenk home on Gibbs Avenue, designated a Natural Beauty Road. John F. Klenk was the first owner of this farm. His son Fred H. Klenk and his wife Julia (Vogel) Klenk raised, sheared, and marketed sheep when they took over the farm. Fred had been in the Battle of Bull Run during the Civil War. Harold Klenk and his wife, Madelyn (Schindler) Klenk, worked the farm and raised their family in this house.

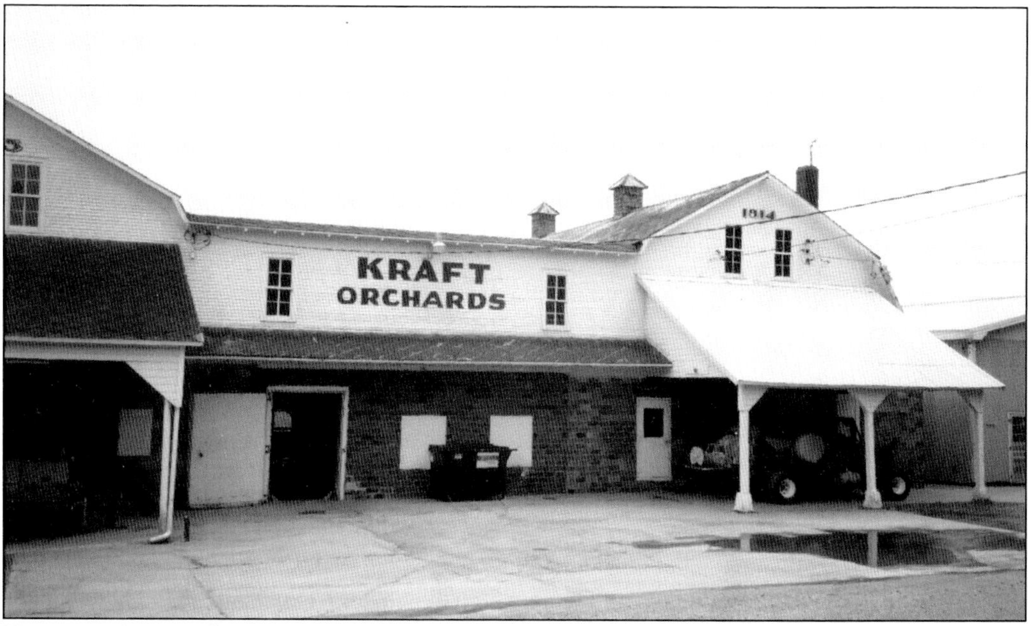

Henry Kraft wanted to get more for his apples at the market. To do this, he had to hold on to his apple crop longer in a cold storage. A salesman suggested that he build a storage area with two walls for insulation. Opening the large doors at night and closing them during the day cooled Kraft's fruit when there was no electricity to do the job. The right side of this apple storage was built in 1914. The left portion was built in 1933. In 1940, the middle portion was built to join both storages.

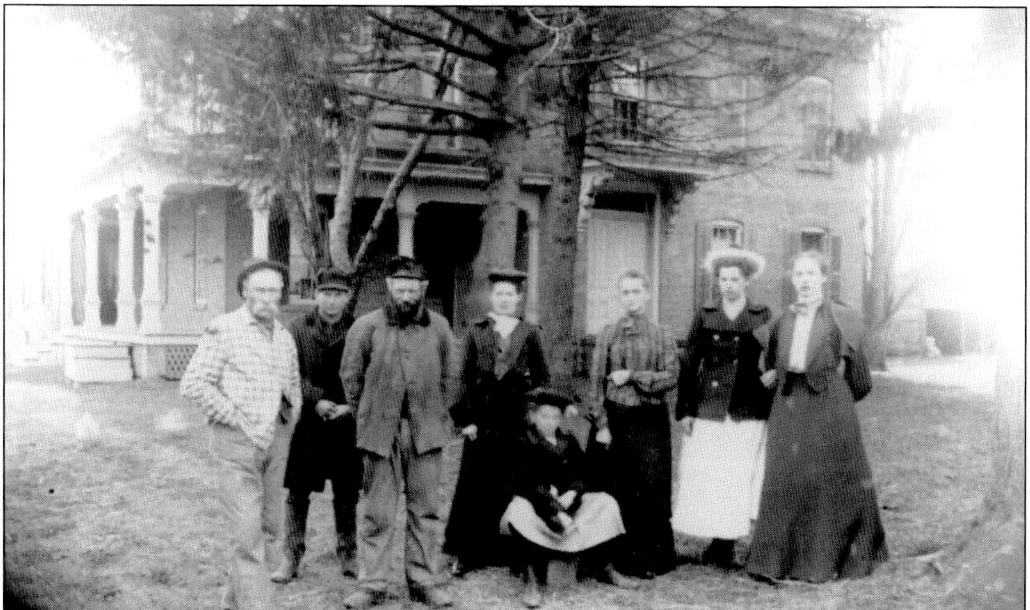

The Johnson family stands by their home on Peach Ridge Avenue. From left to right are Edward Douglas, William Schindler, Luther Johnson, Clara (Johnson) Hankinson, Margaret Johnson, Ann Johnson, Jessie Johnson, and Ruth Johnson.

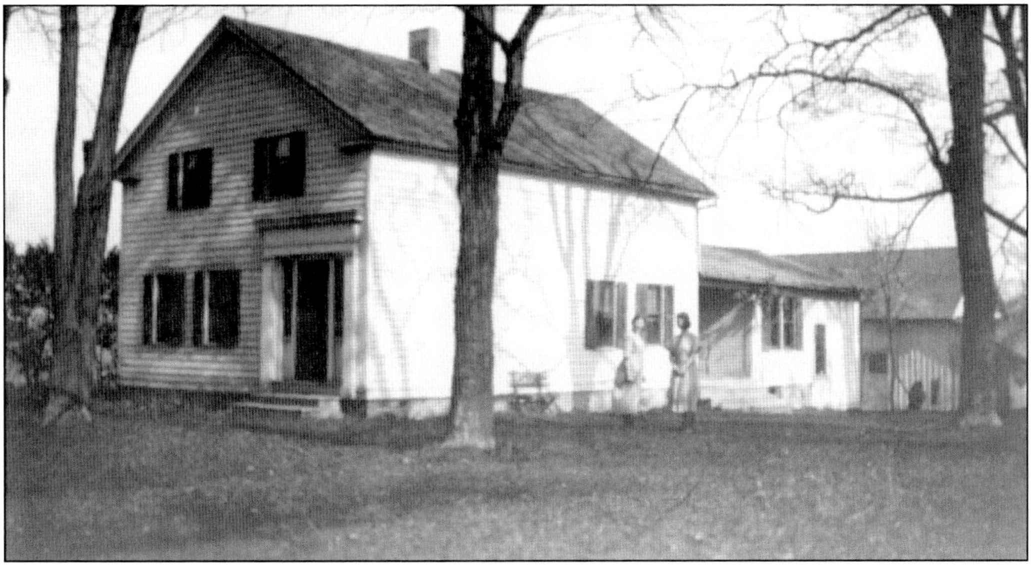

The McConnell house on Seven Mile Road and Alpine Avenue was Aaron Hubbell Hills's property in section 13. This house has been taken down.

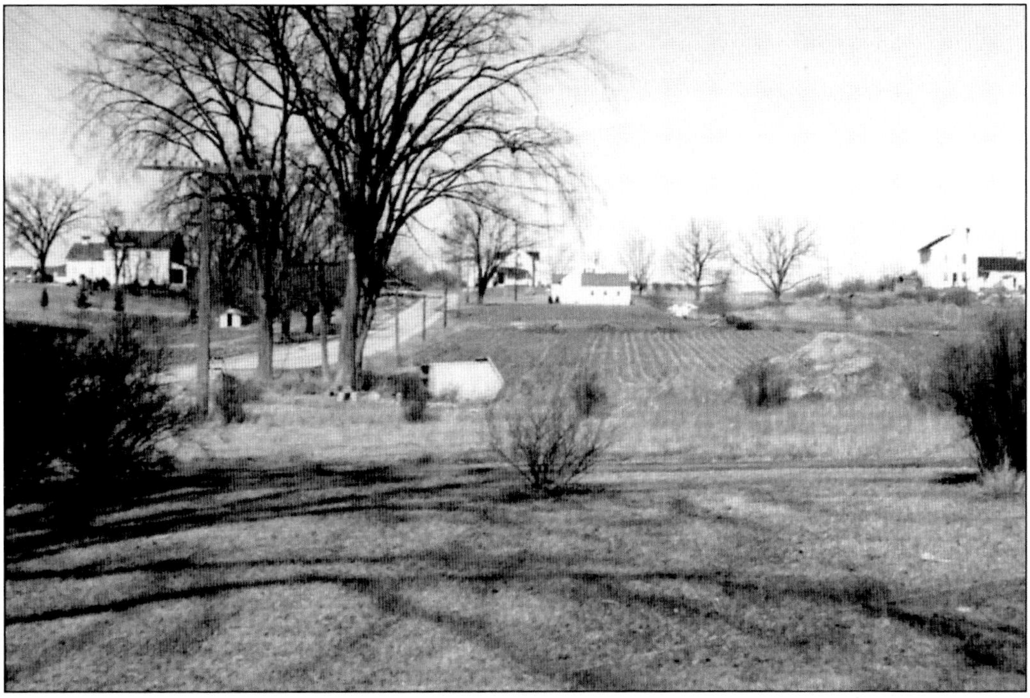

Looking north on Peach Ridge Avenue to Six Mile Road, the Dunneback home can be seen on the left, both Morse homes in the middle, and on the right a house that served as a stagecoach inn. Every bedroom had an outside entrance. In the foreground is an outhouse tipped over from a Halloween prank.

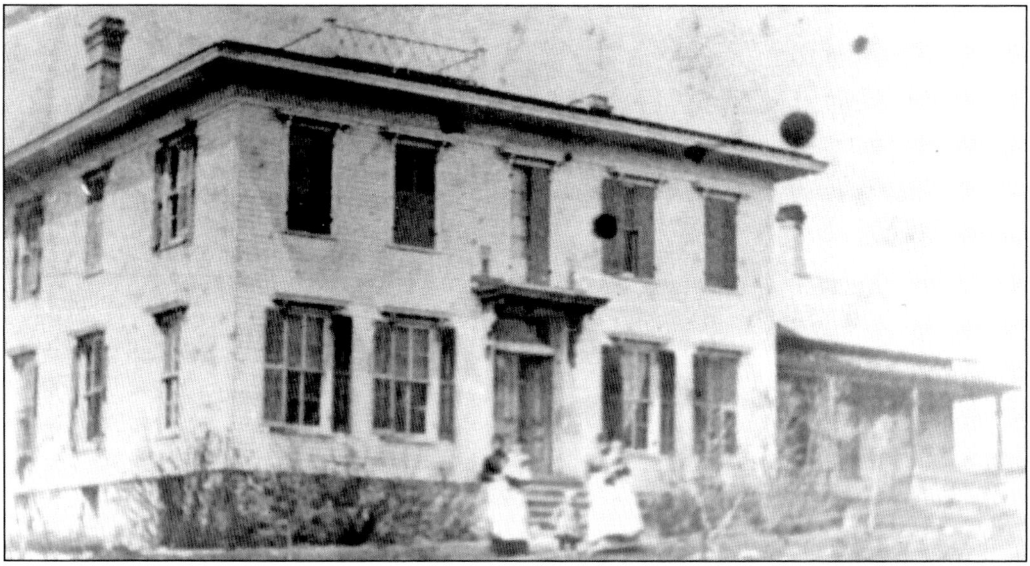

This large home of Joseph Platte and Catherine (Albert) Platte stood on Alpine Avenue, north of Four Mile Road. Edward Platte, born in 1885, is the child standing. One of the women is Catherine, Edward's mother. The other is unidentified. The younger children are Theodore, born in 1886, and Iva, born in 1888. This house was taken down as Alpine Avenue became a commercial center northwest of the city of Grand Rapids.

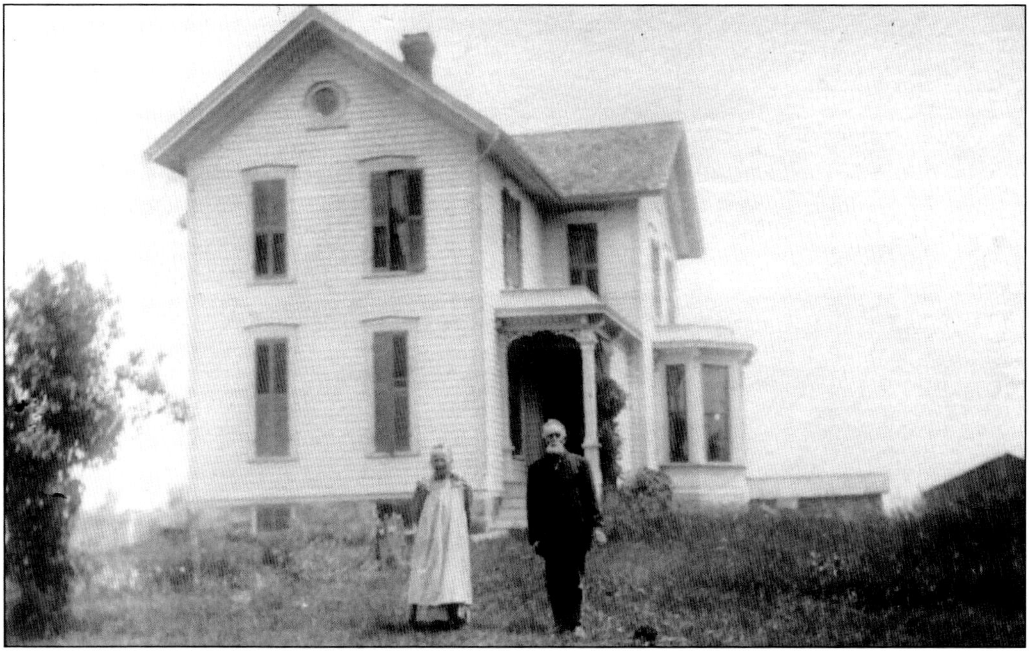

At the age of 16, Adolph Rasch came to America with his family and settled in Centerline. When Adolph's only sister, Frances (Rasch) Jackoboice, and their three brothers, Robert, Alois, and Julius Rasch, located in Grand Rapids, he moved to western Michigan. Unlike the others, who found business success in Grand Rapids, Adolph settled on a farm in Wright Township. When he retired with his wife, Anna Mary (Kaltz) Rasch, they moved to this home in Alpine Township, on Stage Avenue, north of Eight Mile Road. The farm had been owned by L. Turner.

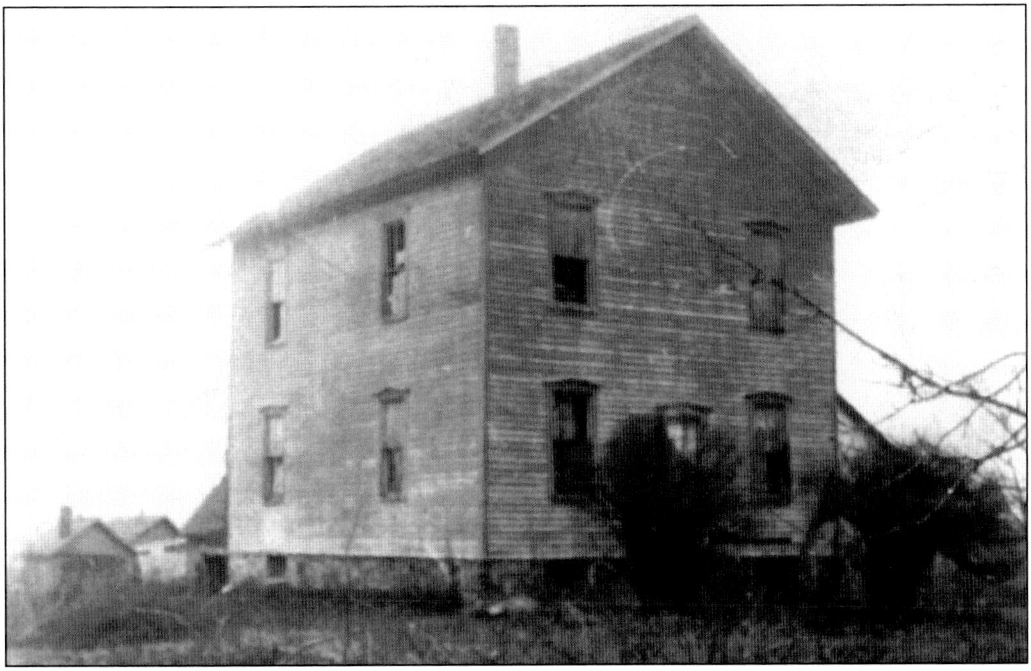

Robert G. Rasch never showed this house to his fiancée, Elizabeth "Bess" Dietrich, before they were married. He felt she would not marry him if she saw the basic condition of it. "I married the man, not the house," said Dietrich. Their first four sons were born and raised in this house before they moved to Robert's father's (Will Rasch's) home in order to care for him.

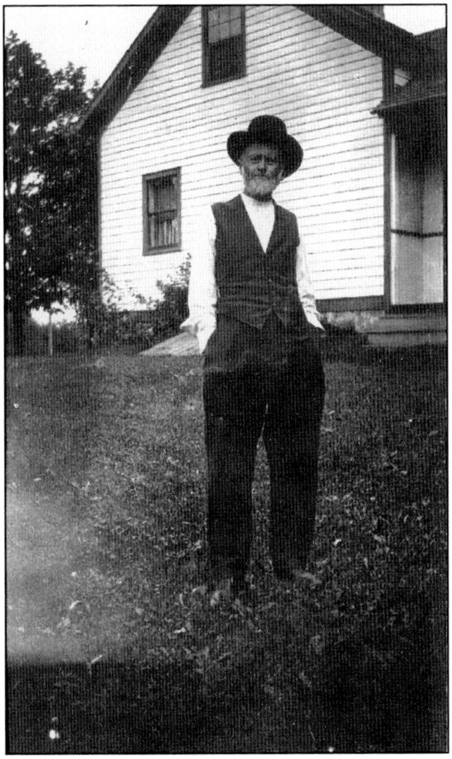

Philip Ruthardt came to America in 1846. Here he is at his home on Seven Mile Road in Alpine Township, where he had settled in 1850. Ruthardt had traveled west looking for gold and got as far as Pikes Peak, Colorado, when he turned back, as that was the end of the train line at that time. He married Lisetta Baumhoff, whom he had met working his way home in Oakfield, Missouri. They had five daughters, pictured on page 78 of this book.

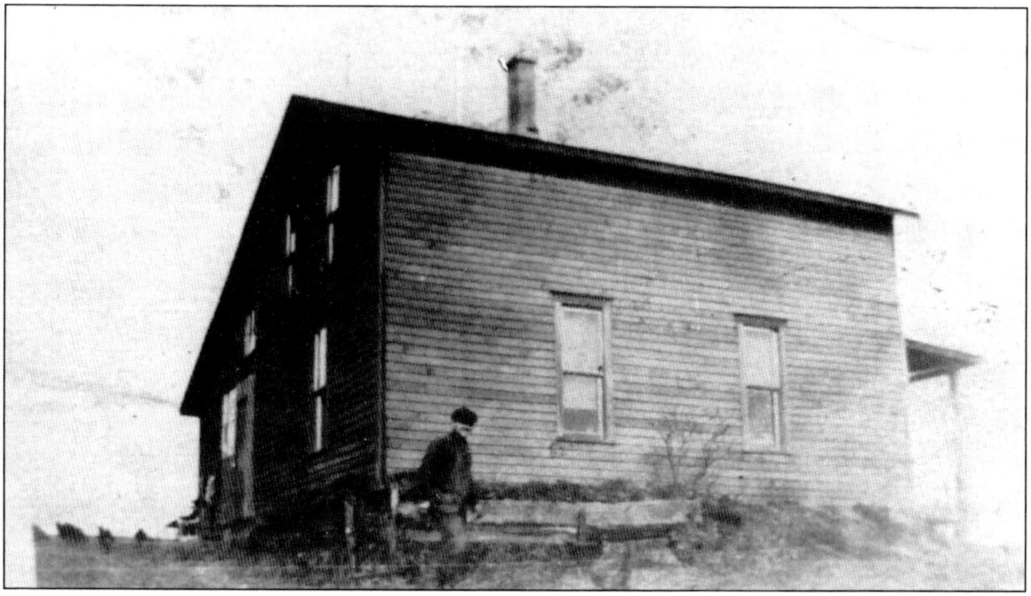

Ferdinand Scheidel came to Michigan in 1851 with Sebastian and George Vierheilig. They walked from Peru, Ohio, to purchase land that the government was offering for $1 per acre. Ferdinand chose instead to buy 40 acres from a Mr. Platte on Bristol Avenue for $74. This is the house he had with his wife, Catherine Vierheilig, whom he married in 1852.

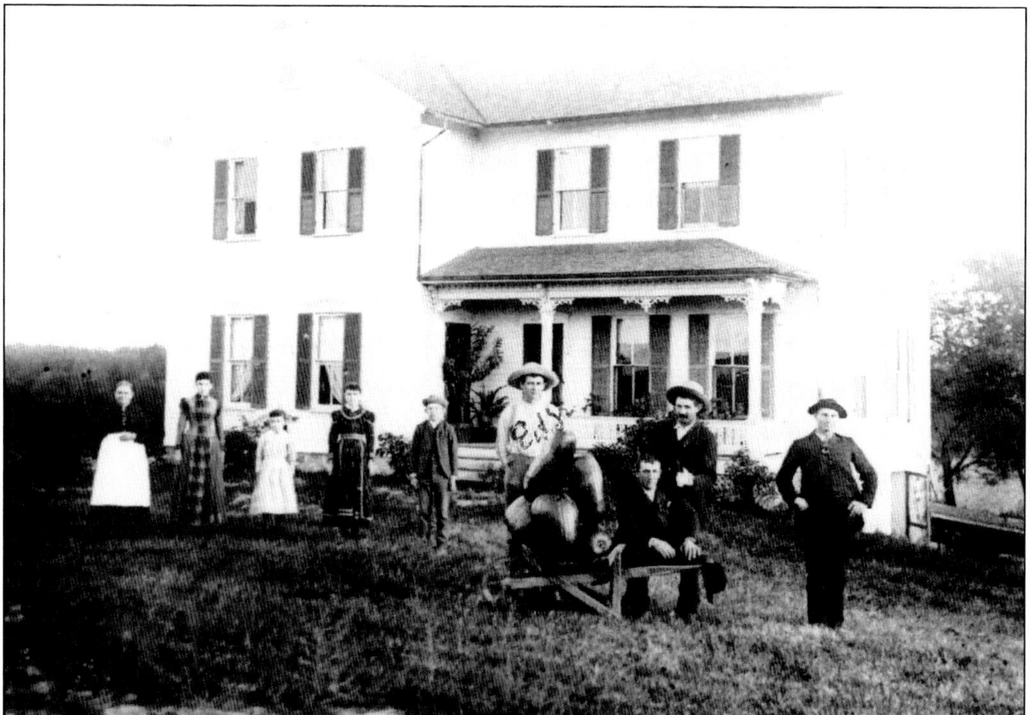

This is the Ed Schindler Sr. homestead, built in 1877 on Nine Mile Road. Standing from left to right are Ed's wife, Emma; Clara; Louise; unidentified; Fred, Ed Schindler Jr., and two unidentified men. The homestead would be sold to Nicholas Schweitzer.

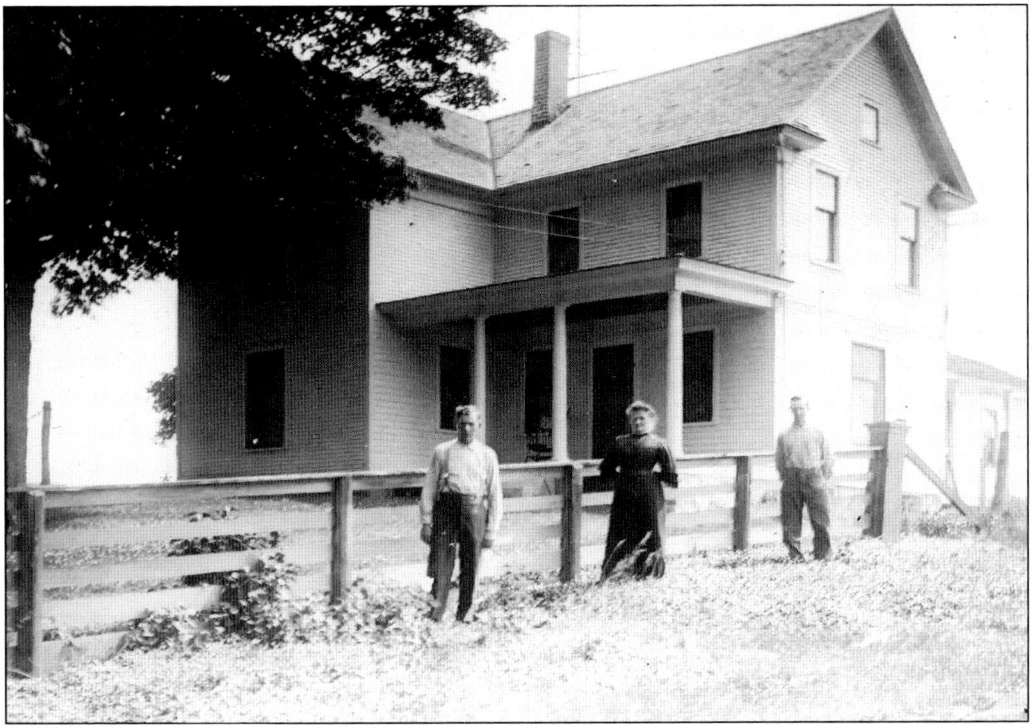

Marie and Bill Schindler, on the right, stand with an unidentified man at their home on Peach Ridge Avenue about 1912. This house burned in 1933. The next house was built in the same place.

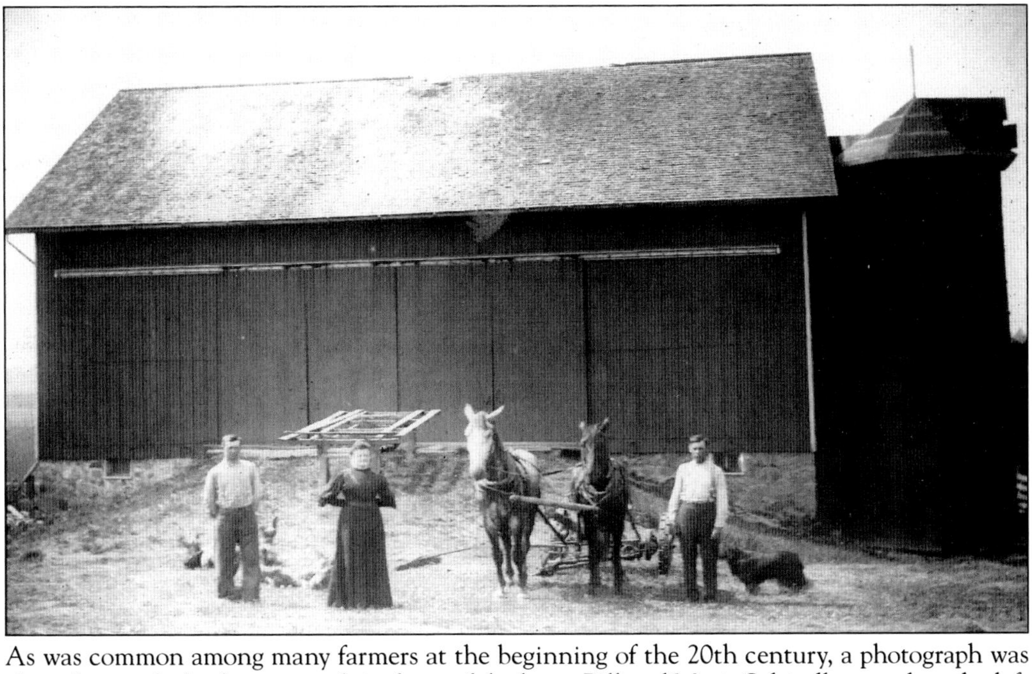

As was common among many farmers at the beginning of the 20th century, a photograph was also taken with the farm animals in front of the barn. Bill and Marie Schindler stand on the left with their hired man and a faithful dog.

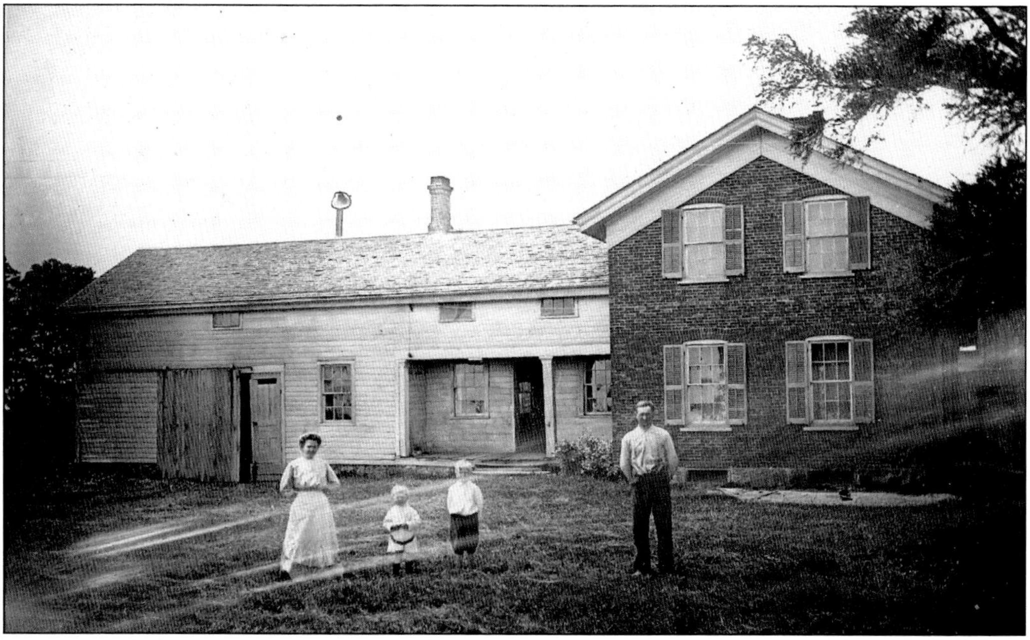

Noel Hopkins built this house in 1863. His sons had to finish it when Noel was killed by runaway horses. The Schindler family bought it. Here Anna, Frank, and Ed Schindler Sr. stand with Anna's brother-in-law Bill Schindler. When renovating this house, three dried apple cores, a bone-handled fork, and a canteen were found wrapped in an 1863 newspaper behind the plaster and lath. This house has been torn down.

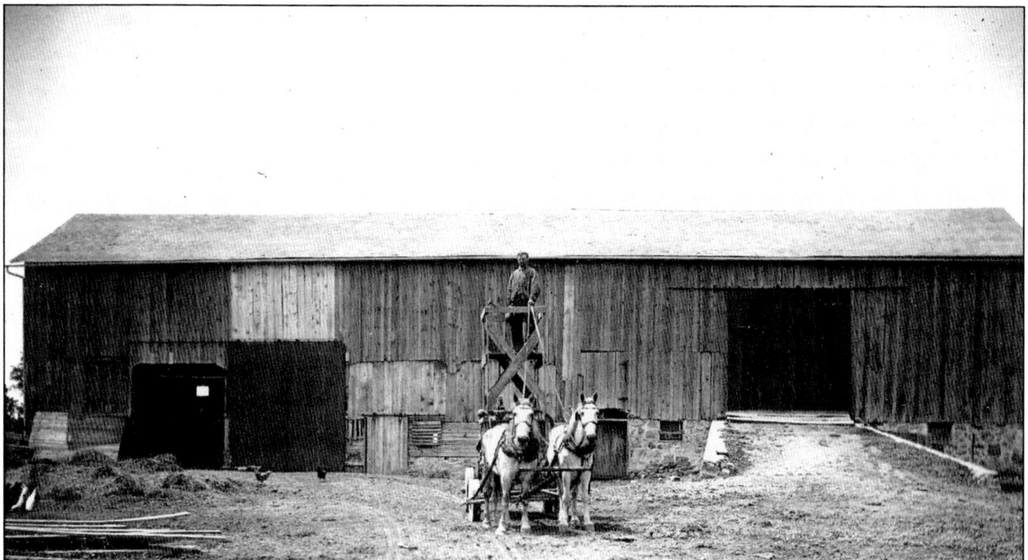

This barn was on Hendershot Avenue, purchased in 1890 by Ferdinand Schindler. It is two barns built together. One barn on the east side of Hendershot Avenue was brought to the west side of the road to make one large barn. The piece of equipment being pulled by the two horses is a spray rig for fruit trees. The object is to spray trees from above. This barn was burned down one Halloween night by vandals.

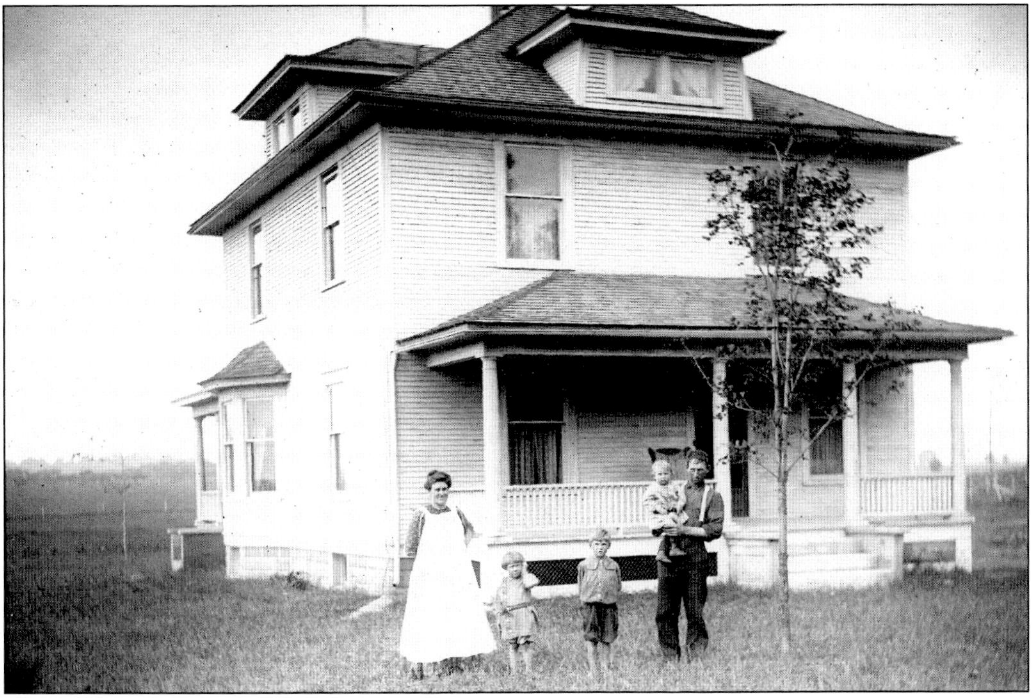

Frederick Schindler and Emma (Brechting) Schindler raised their family on this farm at the corner of Baumhoff Avenue and Six Mile Road. Here Emma is pregnant for her son George, who was born on September 22, 1912. Bob, who would drown in Lake Michigan in 1929, stands next to his mother. Fritz is next, and Frederick is holding Adolph "Stub" Schindler. Three more children would join the family: Madelyn, Rita, and Edgar.

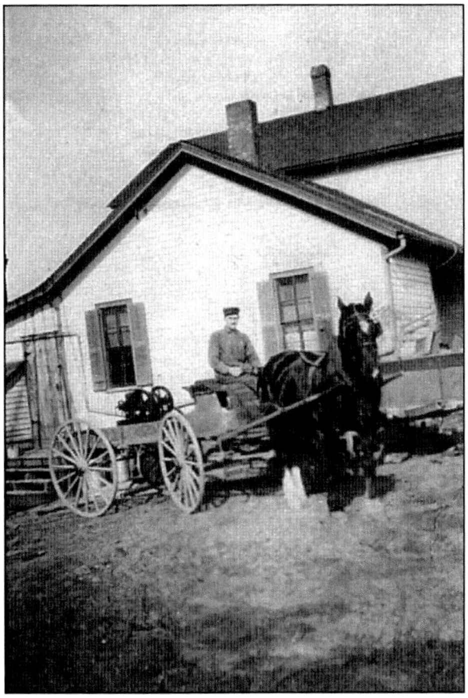

Fred Schweitzer has a piece of equipment in his wagon, pulled by his horse. This was his home on Alpine Avenue, north of Four Mile Road. Where this house stood is now a very busy part of Alpine Avenue's commercial business district in section 35.

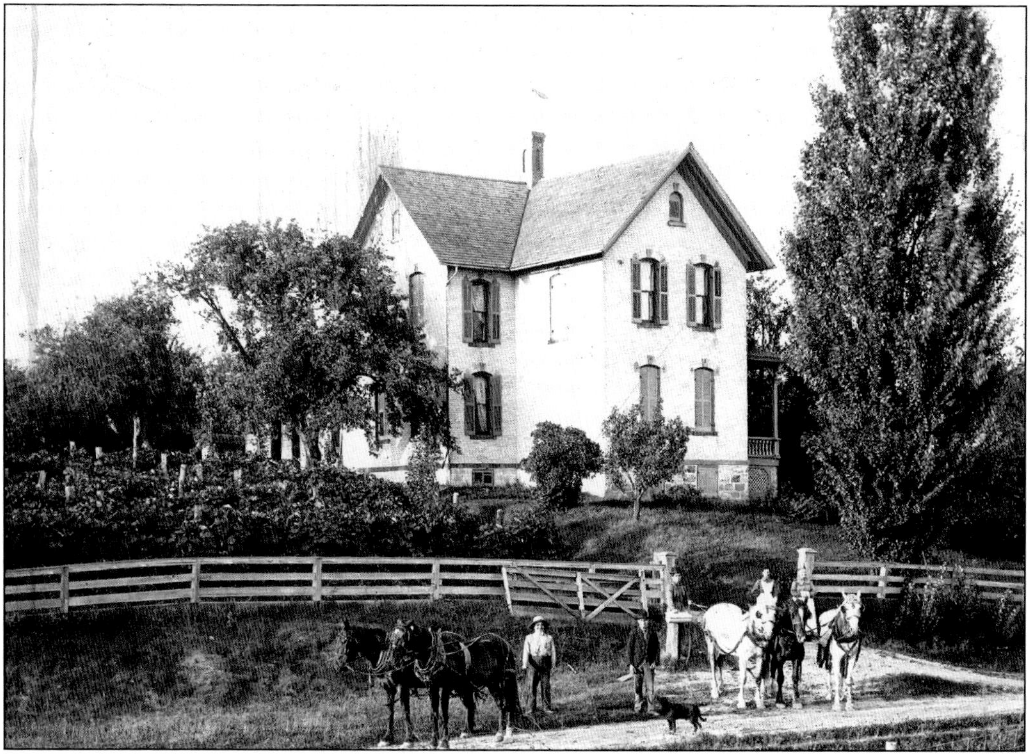

John Vogel married Mary Miller in 1858. They had six children: Jacob, Christine, Fred, Julia, Carl, and Philip. In this photograph, the Vogels are standing in front of their large farmhouse with their teams of horses. Grapes are grown inside the fence that keeps large animals out.

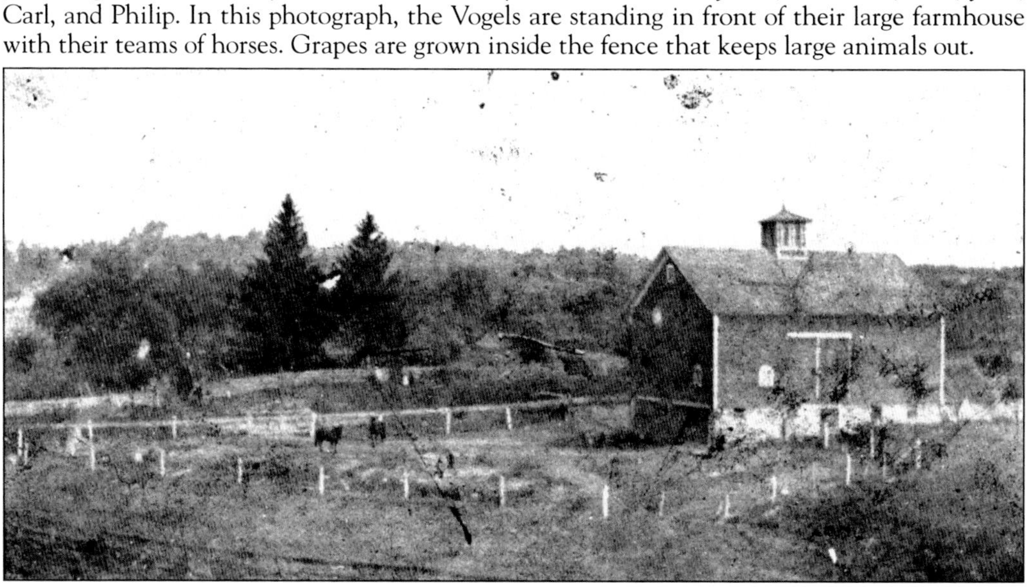

Gottfried Gorke or Yorke had been a lawyer in Prussia when he decided to take his family to America. He purchased a good piece of property in Alpine Township because a creek ran through his 80-acre farm. In 1889, Gottfried and his wife, Louisa, struck an agreement with the township over the use of the creek, which is named after the family. In 1904, the farm went to their son, Gottfried Gork or York Jr., who died of an infection from a pitchfork injury. Gottfried had married Emma Johnson Maves.

Four

PEOPLE AND GATHERING

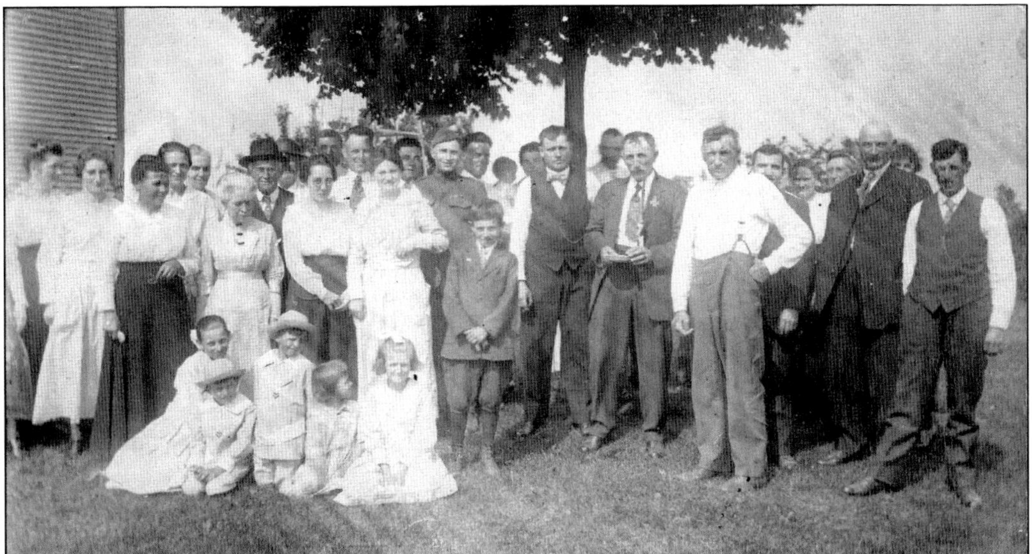

This is William and Josephine Antor's 25th wedding anniversary party. Standing from left to right are Lena Antor, Nina Antor, Josephine Antor, Melanie (Alt) Rothenthaler, Emma Alberts, Luella and Cameron Cranmer, unidentified, Hattie Miller, unidentified, Frank and Minnie (Schweitzer) Antor, unidentified, Pete Rothenthler in Frank's military uniform, Carl Scheidel, Nettie Scheidel with a baby, Albert Alt, unidentified, John Antor, William Antor, two unidentified people, Maggie Miller, John Alberts, unidentified, and John Rothenthaler. The Rothenthaler children in front are, from left to right, Josephine, Joseph, Edward, Tillie (looking back), and Mary Rothenthaler. The young man standing is not identified.

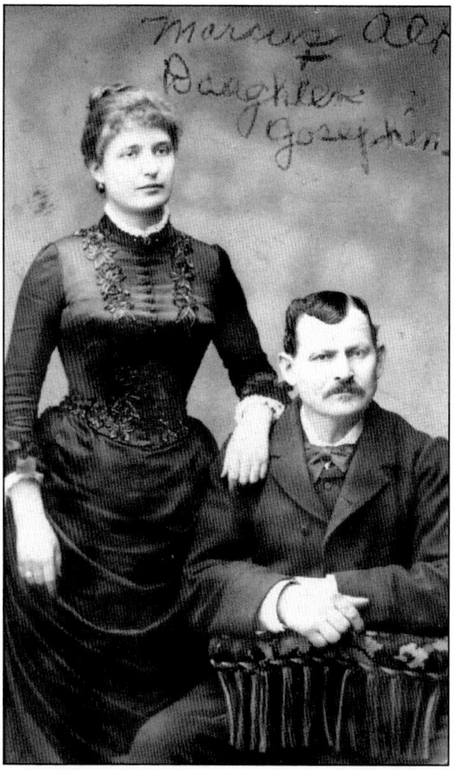

Marcus Alt made his home in Alpine Township in 1892 on the Charles Waterman farm. He went back to Alsace, Germany, which is now a part of France, to visit his three daughters who stayed home because they were married when Marcus and Josephine (Hoffman) Alt decided to come to America. Here Marcus is with his daughter Josephine.

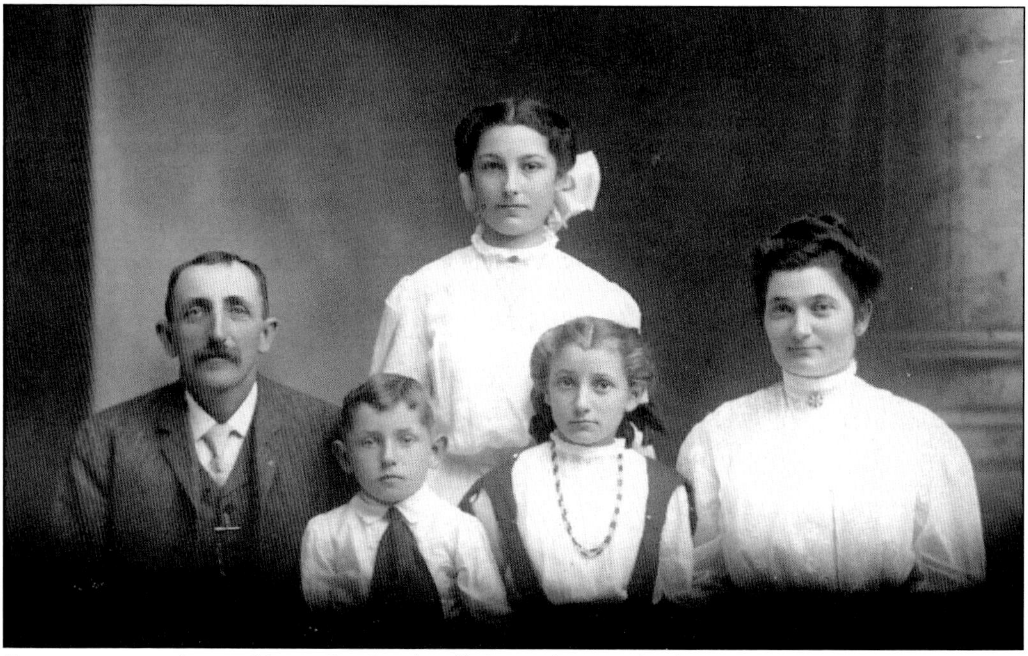

Sometimes people would get the family all dressed up and take a trip into town for a family photograph. Here John Antor and his family did just that. His son Urban married Elizabeth Dietrich. Nina (second from right) married August Brechting Jr. Standing is Irene, who married Bert Thome. Seated on the far right is John's wife, Lena (Heinbeck) Antor.

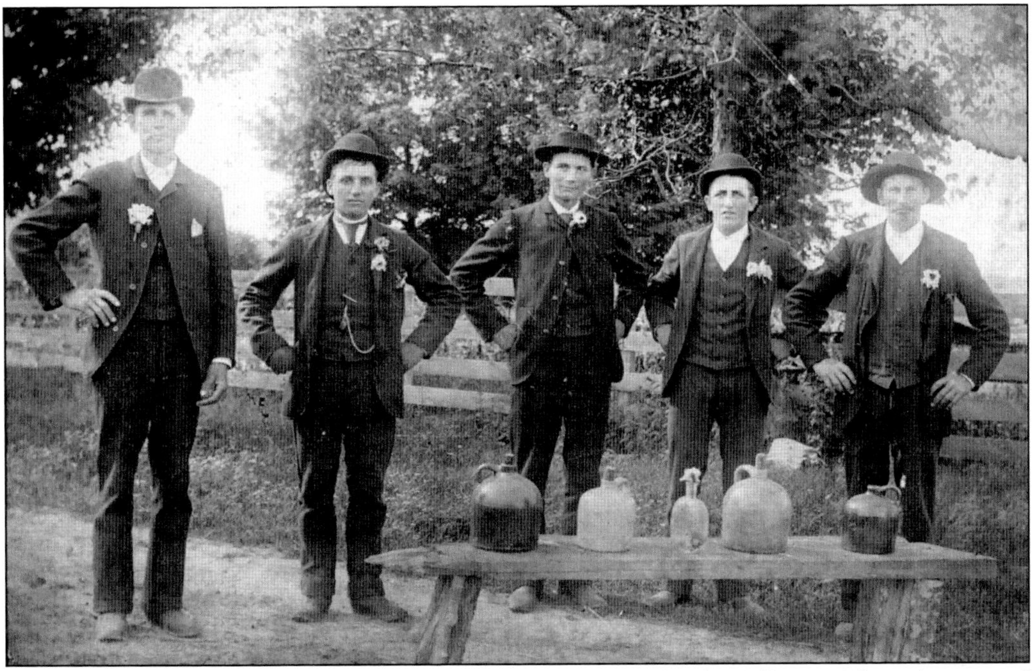

The year is 1890. From left to right are Bill Antor, Jake Vogel, John Alberts, Albert Antor, and Fred Alberts. Note the style of suits they are wearing. The suit includes a vest, and when the jacket was closed, it was fashionable only to close the top button. If this is a wedding, the groom is not listed.

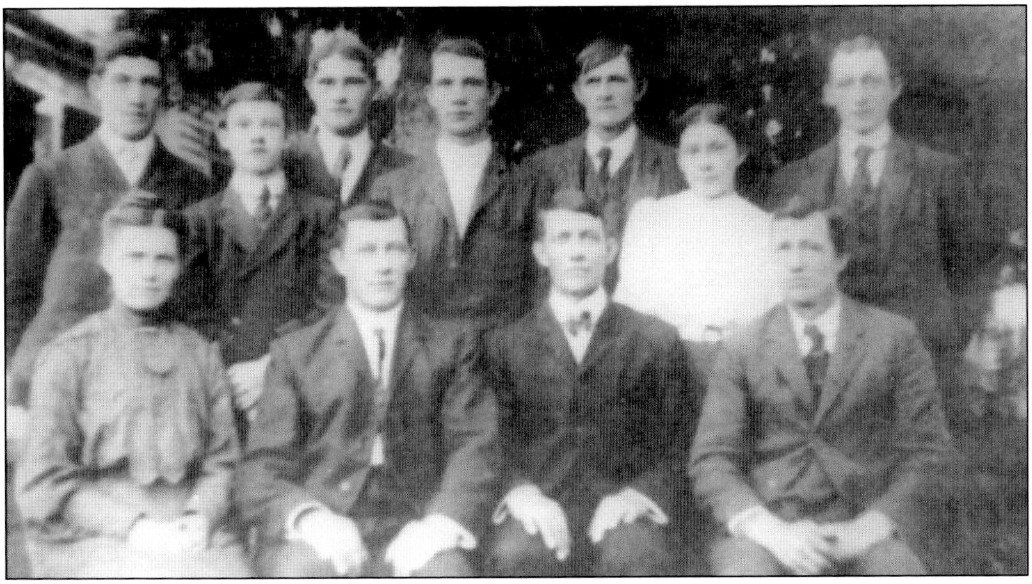

Nicholas and Catherine (Kluting) Armock raised these children on the shores of Cranberry Lake. Pictured are, from left to right, (first row) Veronica, Enoch, John, and Anthony; (second row) Ben, William, Frank, Paul, Albert, Rose, and Daniel Armock. Veronica married Charles Courtade, Enoch married Mary Shoemaker, John married Elizabeth Finkler, Ben married Rhoda Moore, William married Princess Fuller, Frank married Dora Stockton, Paul married Jennie Scholton, Albert married Nellie Leinaar, and Daniel married Ida Witt.

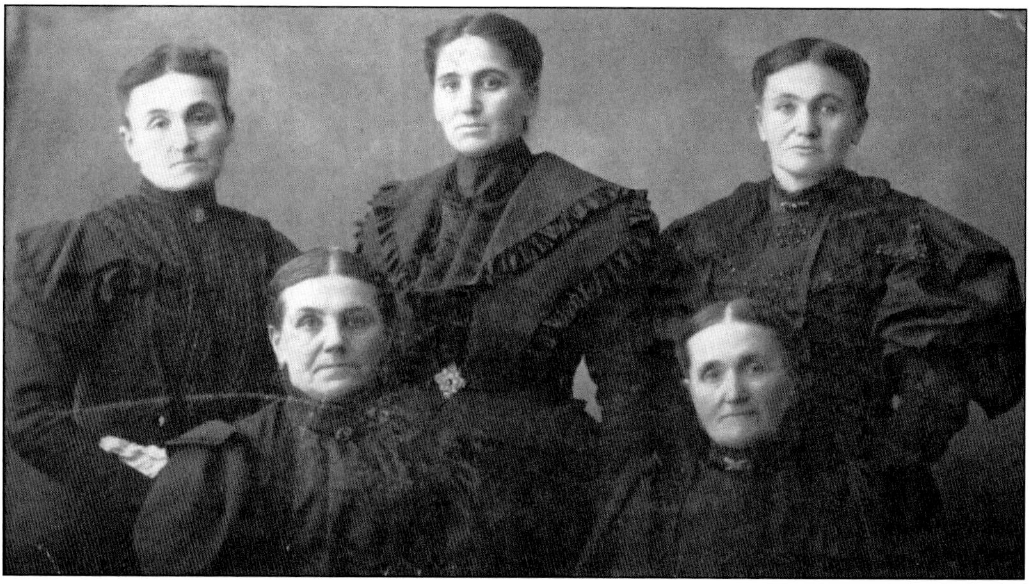

Anna and Todakus Schoettler came to America with their five daughters. Three of these daughters married three Brechting brothers, who came to Michigan from Dorlar, Germany. From left to right are (first row) Theresa and Florentine; (second row) Gertrude, Elizabeth, and Frances. Gertrude married August Brechting, a farmer in Alpine Township.; Elizabeth married Joseph Hessman, a cabinetmaker in Grand Rapids; Frances married Anthony Dunneback, who ran a grocery store in Grand Rapids; Theresa married Frank Brechting, who was a wagon maker in Grand Rapids; and Florentine married William Brechting, a farmer in Alpine Township. Anna and Todakus spent their last days in the home of William and Florentine Brechting, in section 23.

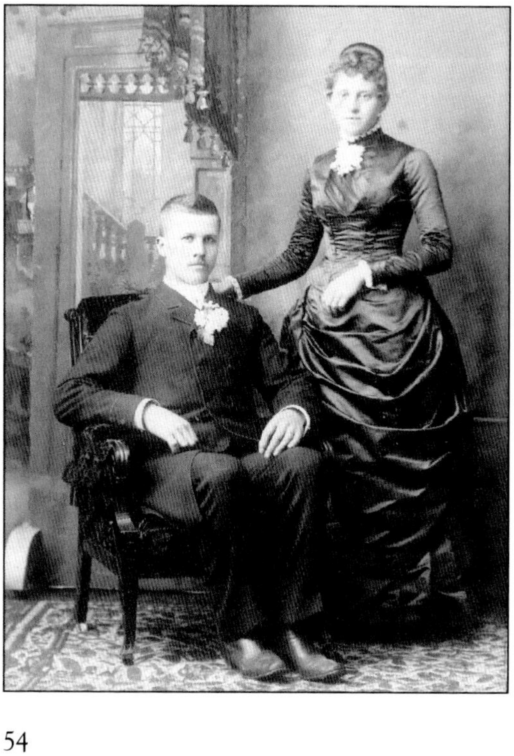

Charles Bremer married Christine Ruthardt on October 4, 1887. As was customary for couples at this time, the groom sat for the wedding photograph and the bride would stand to show all the work that went into the dress. Christine, born in Alpine Township to Philip Ruthardt and Lisetta (Baumhoff) Ruthardt, made this dress. The tucks in the skirt and the lace at the cuff and collar make this a very beautiful wedding gown. Long dark dresses were the fashion, so that the bride could wear the dress for fancy occasions for years to come.

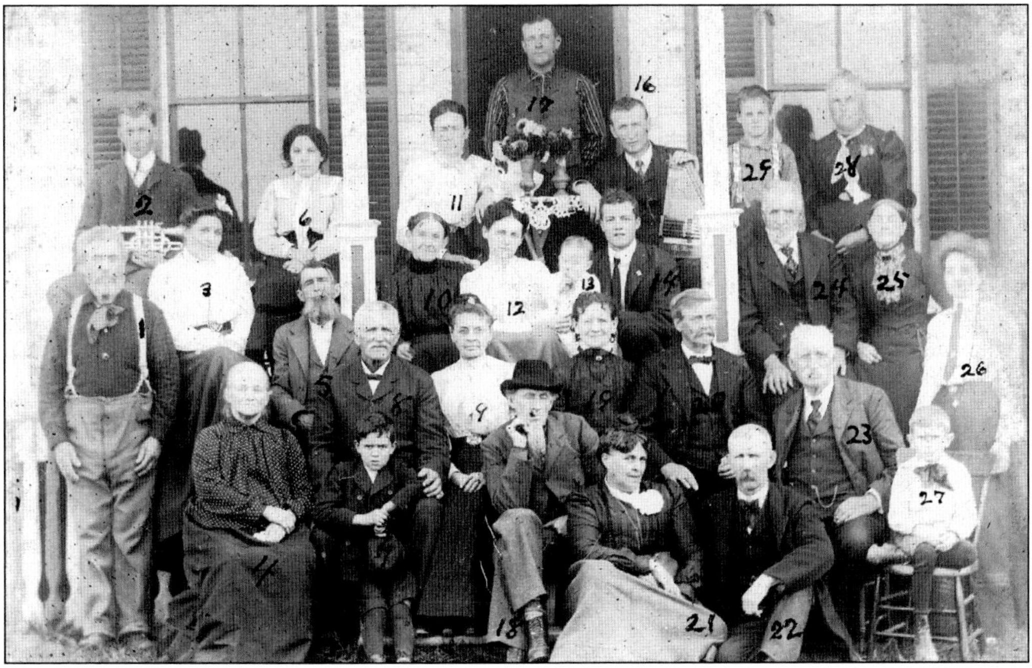

The back of this photograph states that on September 21, 1902, Ephraim and Matilda Brown had a reunion at their home of 35 years, which they had "bought and cleared and improved from a wilderness and reset to a wilderness of fruit trees from which we have harvested and sold over 8,000 bushels of fruit this season." They labeled the photograph as follows: Edward Malloy (1), Clarance Munger (2), Leula Dray (3), Melvina Hoag (4), Arnold Hoag (5), Iva Dray (6), Hary Dray (7), Fred Reiter (8), Charlott Reiter (9), Lucy Williams (10), Mrs. Frank Benson (11), Eva Forester (12), Fred Forester (14), John Williams (16), Robert Brooks (17), Edgar Morris (18), Matilda Brown (19), Ephraim Brown (20), Deloria Munger (21), Wareham Munger (22), Darwin Babcock (23), Deloris Babcock (24), Cordelia M. Babcock (25), Matie Babcock (26), Deraymont Babcock (27), Ella Niron (28), and George Niron (29).

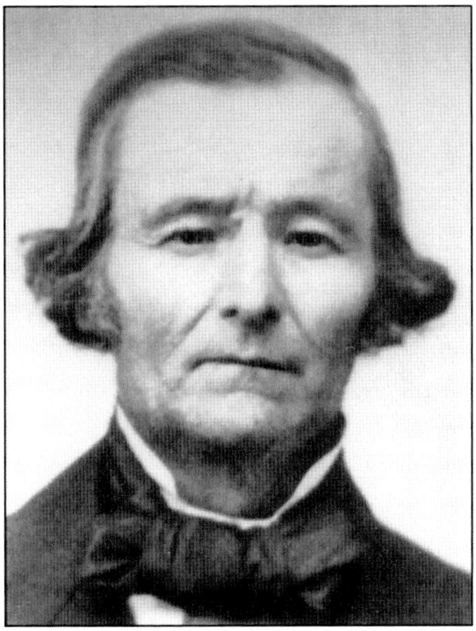

Bela Chase was born in New Hampshire in 1802. He married Orilla Miller and lived in New York, where son Abel was born. In 1851, Bela and Orilla Chase purchased their land in section 16 of Alpine Township.

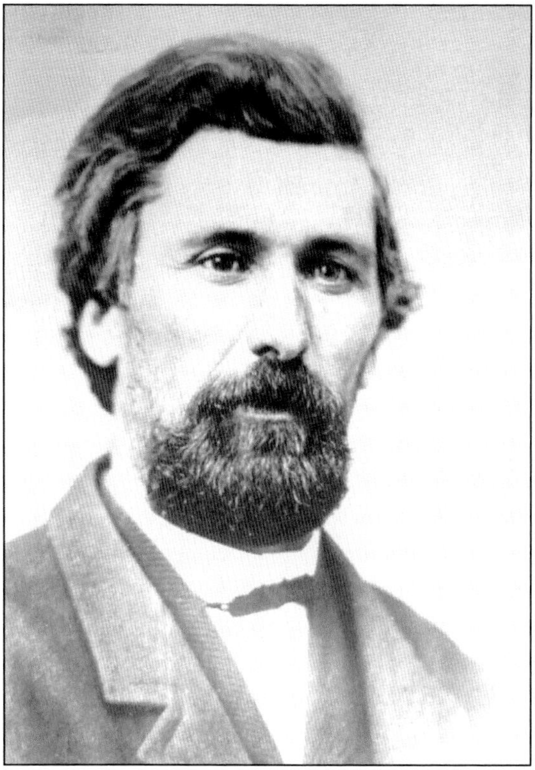

The land that Bela Chase had secured was "patented" to his son Abel Chase and his wife, Rebecca Jane (Herrick) Chase. Abel and Rebecca's son Charles H. and his wife, Mary (Schindler) Chase, bought this farm. Charles was Alpine Township's supervisor from 1904 to 1909. Abel and Rebecca also had a daughter, Minnie Chase.

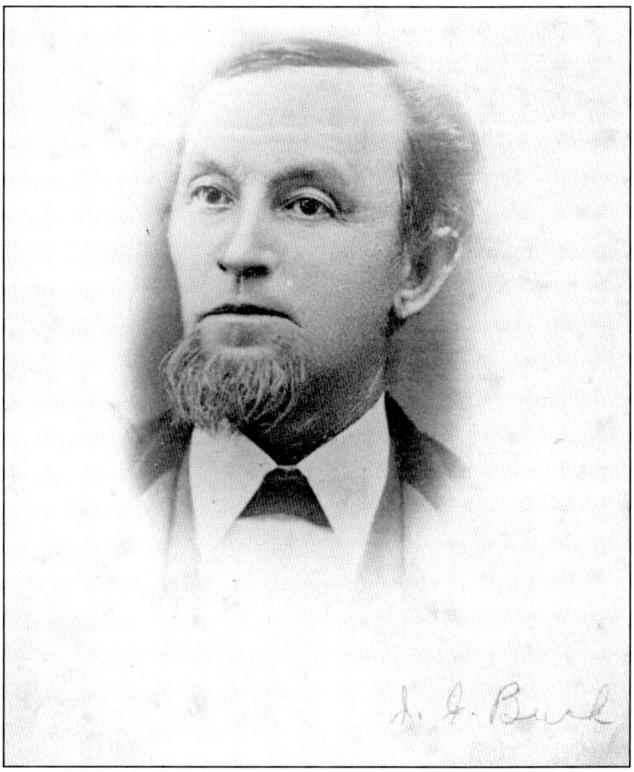

Judson James Buck, son of Elijah Sherman Buck, was born in New York in 1820. He purchased land in Alpine Township with gold. At first, Hiram Myers lived in the log cabin with Buck. Buck married Amelia Wheeler, and they had four children: Cory, Justine, and twins Wilis and Wallis Buck. It is said that Judson Buck never ran a debt and never drank alcohol.

True to form, John Ransom Coffee sits for his wedding photograph as Sarah (Keas) Coffee stands. His suit is vested and the overcoat is buttoned only at the top. Sarah has a black wedding dress with a tight fitted bodice. She has a pleated skirt under the full, folded overskirt that is pulled together in the back.

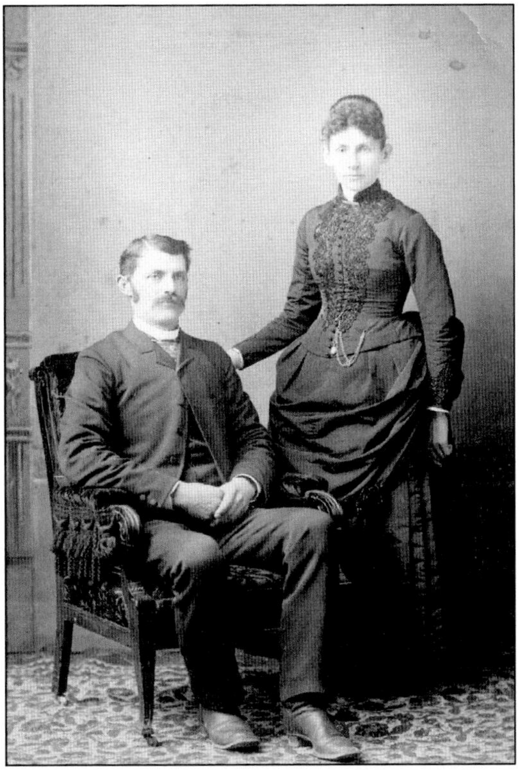

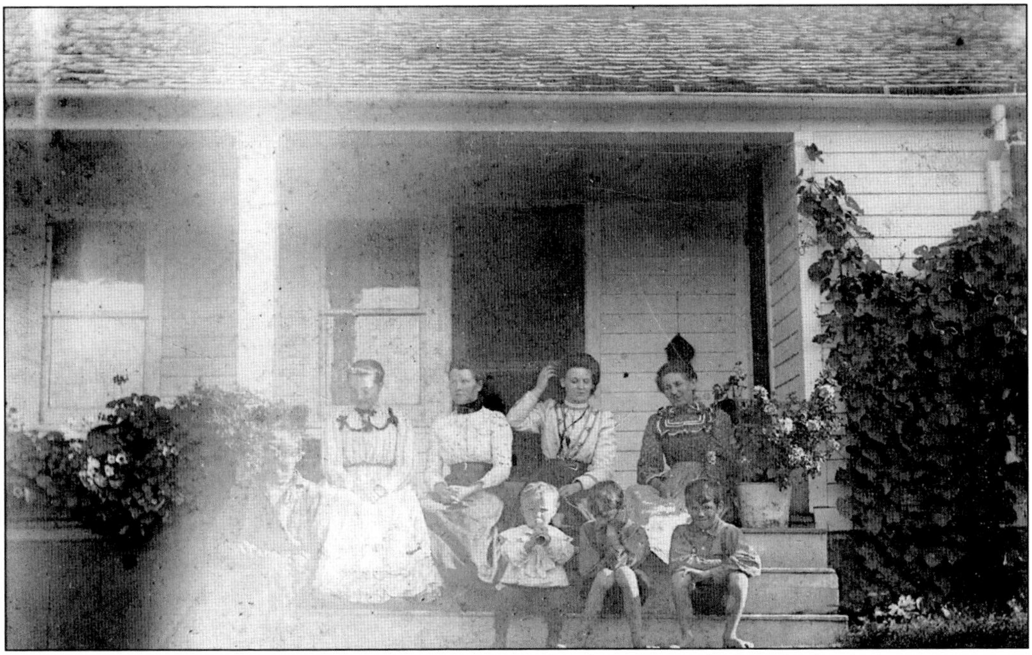

At the Coffee home on Fruit Ridge Avenue, south of Seven Mile Road, the ladies are out on the porch with the children enjoying a visit. From left to right are (first row) Floyd Harrison, Will Coffee, and John C. Coffee Jr.; (second row) John R. Coffee, a Mrs. Savage, Bertha Coffee, Emily Raisch, and Sarah Coffee.

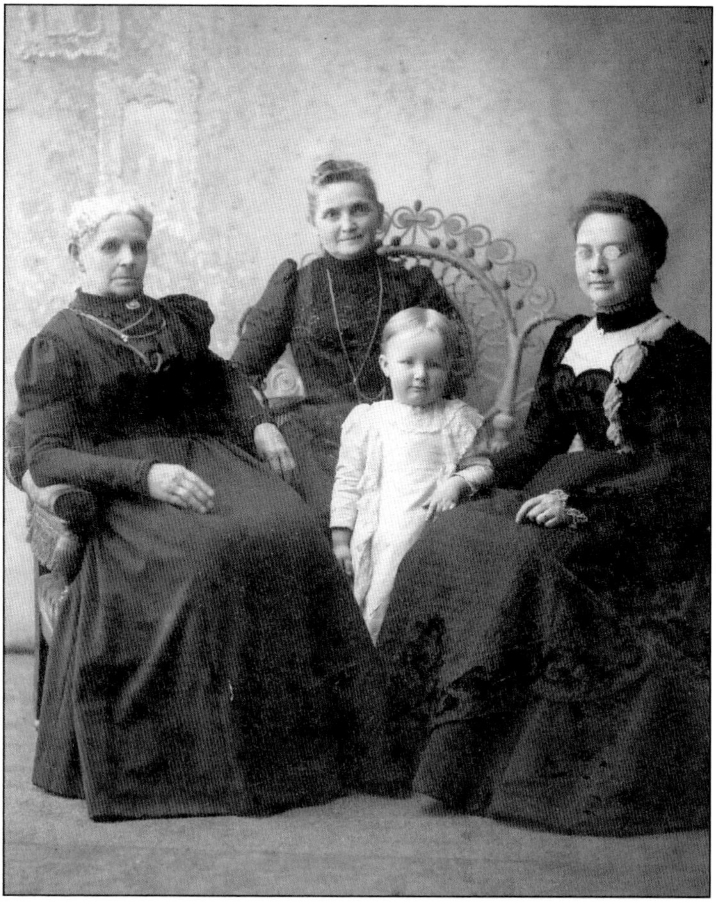

Four generations of the Coffee family are pictured here: grandmother Marinda (Gooding) Coffee, mother Sarah (wife of George Dole), and daughter Georgie (wife of Frank Gould) with son Vivien Gould, born in 1897.

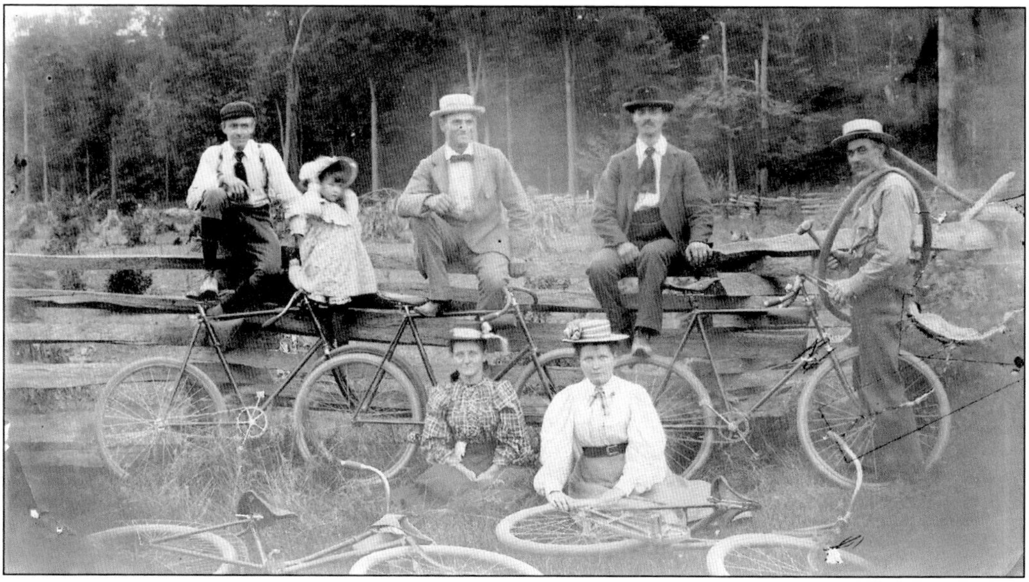

Bertha and Watson Coffee are on an afternoon of bicycling with Mertie and Eugene Willenson. It looks like someone has come along with an extra tire and tools to fix things.

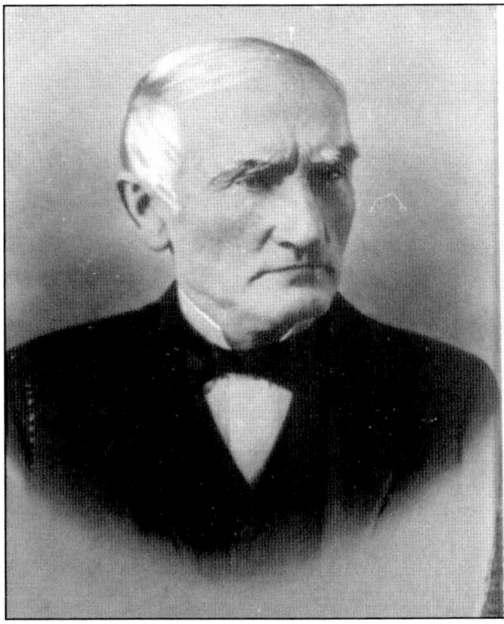 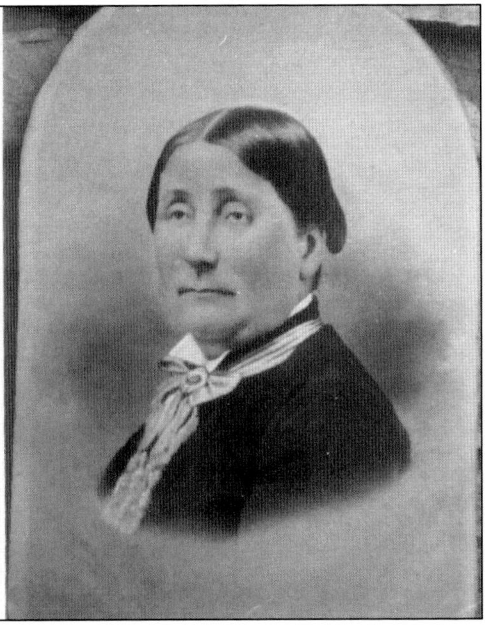

Casper Cordes and Mary Ann (Marten) Cordes had 10 children: Theresia, Frederick, Paulina, Anna, Sophia, Julius, Josephine, Louise, Amelia, and Theodore. Theresia married Joseph Berles, Frederick married Rosina Meyer, Paulina married William Pulte, Anna married Herman Leitelt, Sophia married Charles Schmidt, Julius married Abbie Thome, Josephine married August Brogger, Louise married Michael Thome, Amelia married Charles Wahlfield, and Theodore married Mary Glowasky.

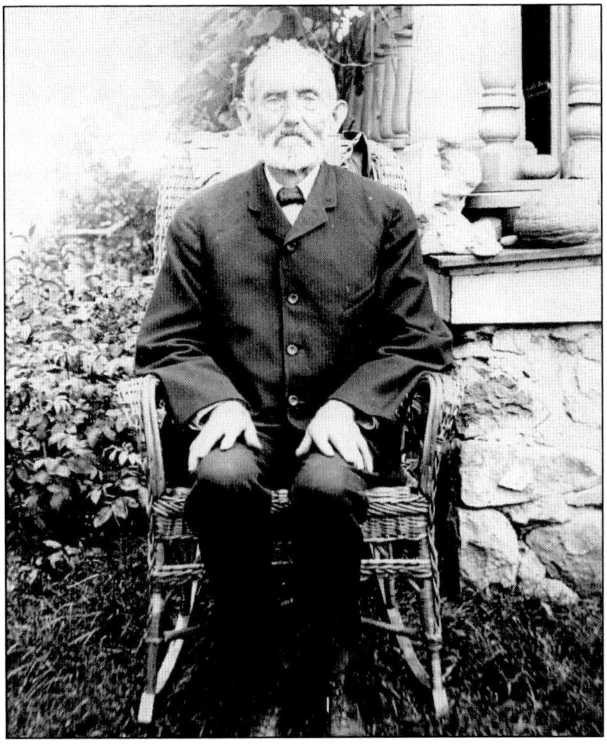

Eberhard Cordes sits in a wicker chair outside his home. He had married Theresa Berles, and they had 11 children: Mary, Anna, Edward, Julia, Caroline, Henry Clement, William, Louise, Richard, and Alfred. Mary married Anthony Hammerschmidt, Anna married Frederick Host, Julia married Joseph Thome, Caroline married Frank Jost, Clement married Mary Thiel, and Alfred married Helen Rauser.

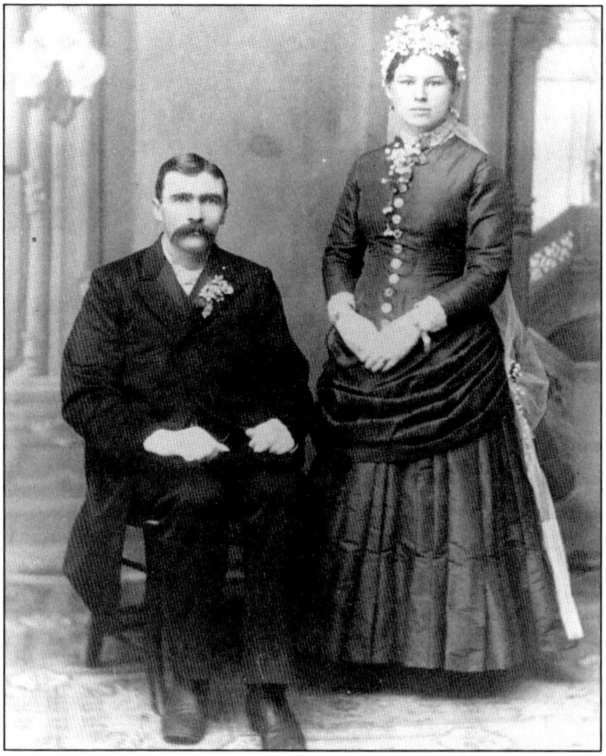

Joseph Cordes married Augusta Meyer, daughter of August Meyer and Frances (Frank) Meyer, in 1881. Augusta stands with a very beautiful dress and headpiece. They had six children: Otto, Edwin, Eugena, Caroline, Clarence, and August. Edwin married a woman named Otilla, Caroline married Clarence Lamoreaux, Clarence married Mary Abraham, and August married Mildred Krantz.

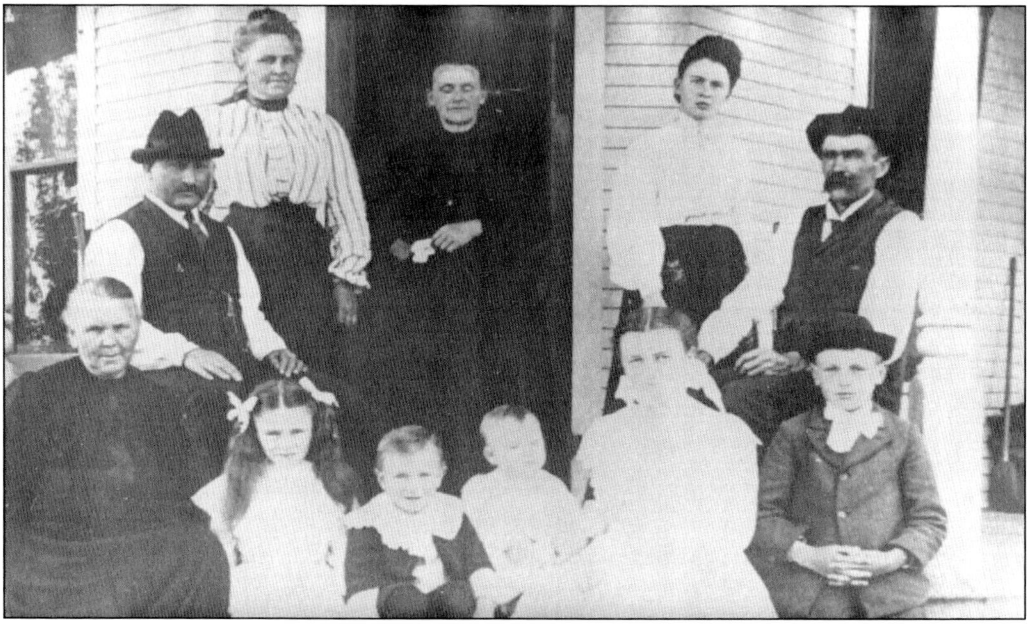

This picture of the Cordes family has them seated on their front porch in 1906. This house went down in the 1965 Palm Sunday tornado. Pictured are, from left to right, (first row) Francesco Meyer, Melinda (Klein) May, August Cordes, a Klein baby boy, Caroline (Cordes) Lamoreaux, and Clarence Cordes; (second row) Charles Klein, Katie (Meyer) Klein, Augusta (Meyer) Cordes, Edwina Cordes, and Joseph Cordes.

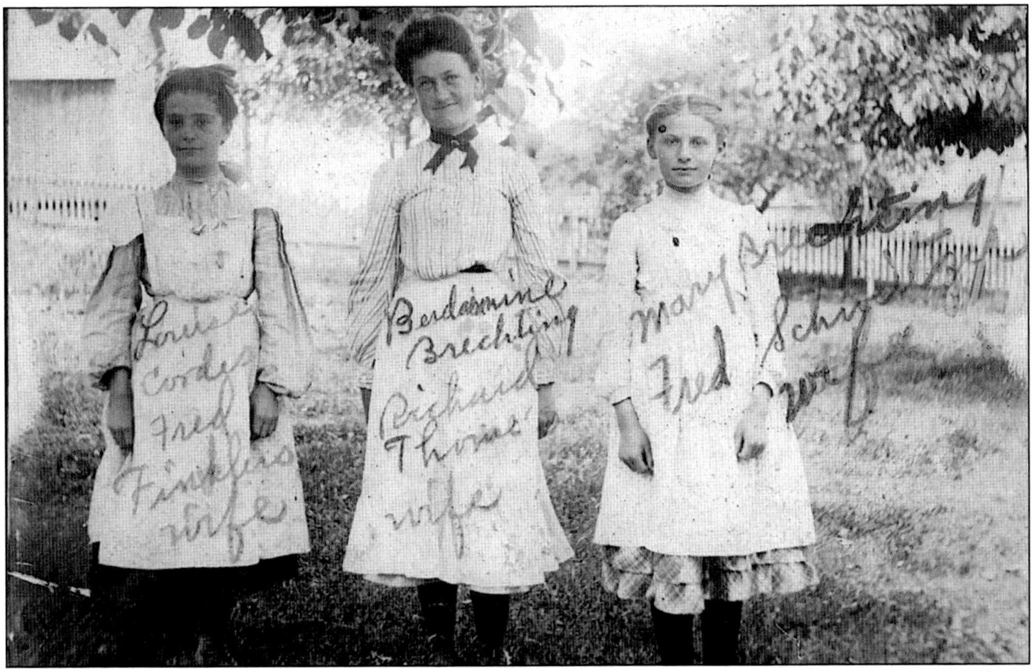

Here are three lovely young ladies in the yard. From left to right are Louise Cordes, who later married Fred Finkler; Bernadine Brechting, who would become Richard Thome's wife; and Mary Brechting, who would live on Alpine Avenue as Fred Schweitzer's wife.

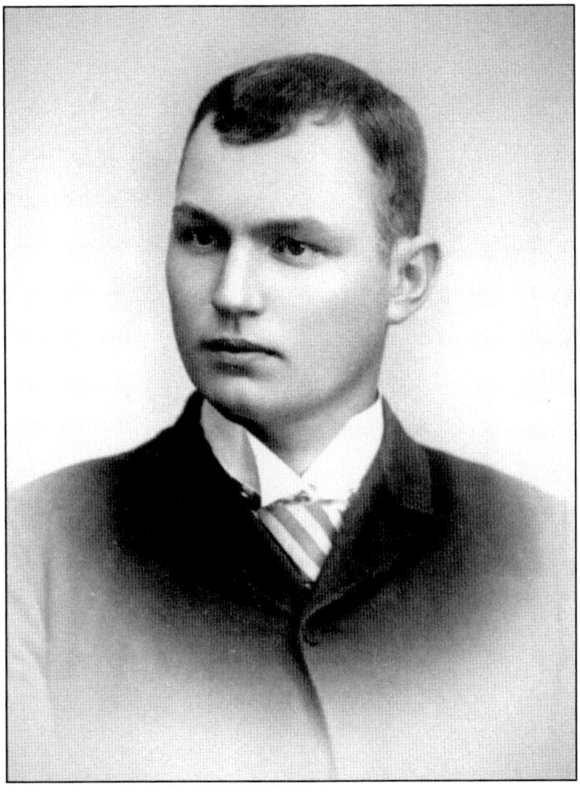

Charles Courtade served as supervisor of Alpine Township from 1923 to 1925, before his untimely death from diabetes complicated by pneumonia.

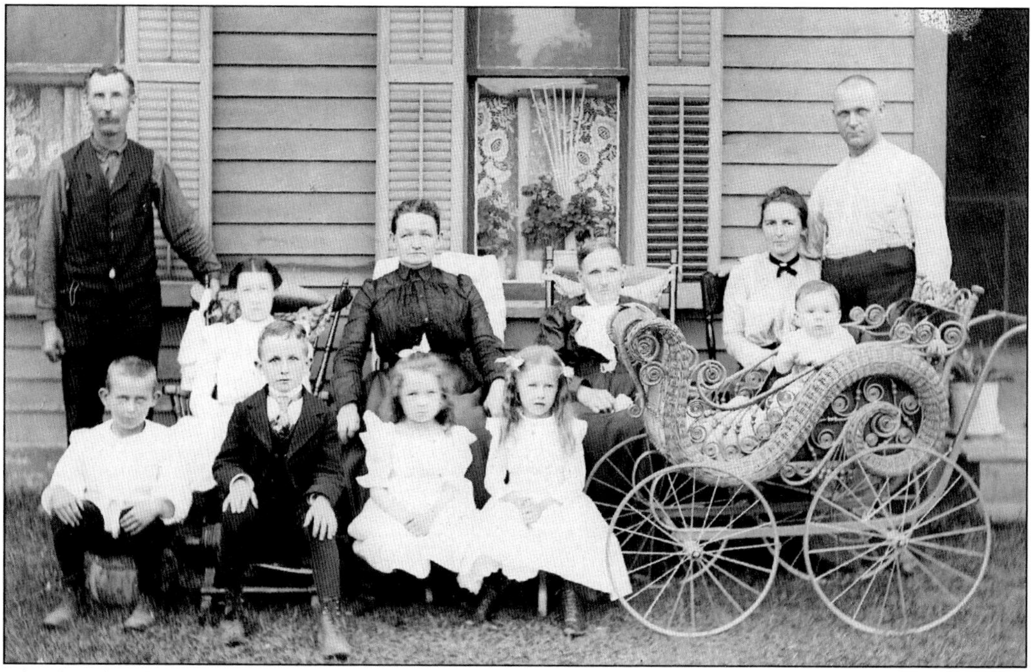

The family of Ken Cranmer is seated on their front porch on Eight Mile Road. The baby sits up in a very fine buggy.

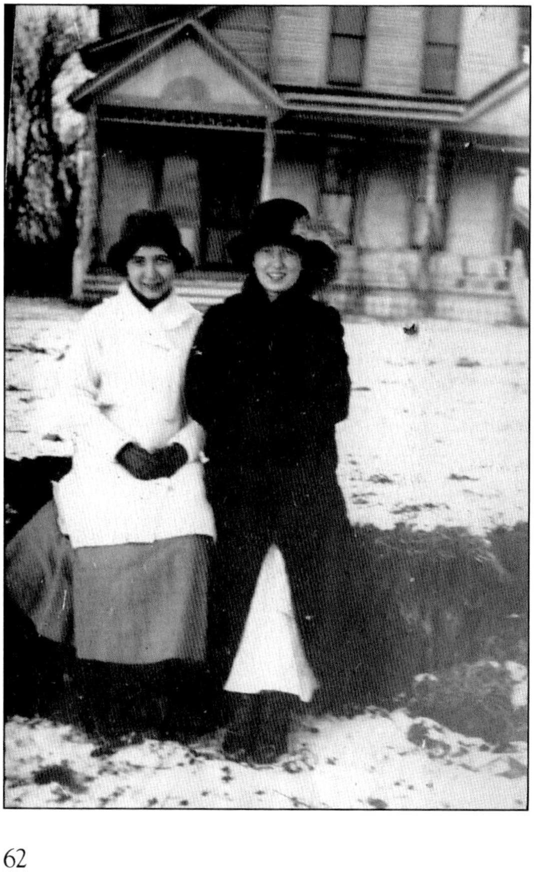

Friends Mildred Cranmer (left) and Lucille Saur sit for a picture looking as if they are ready for the winter weather.

Luella and Cameron Cranmer sit for their picture in the wooded area of their farm on Eight Mile Road.

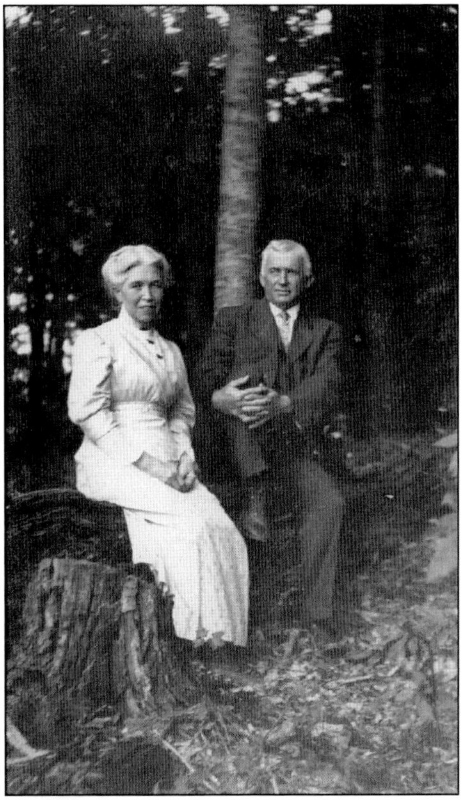

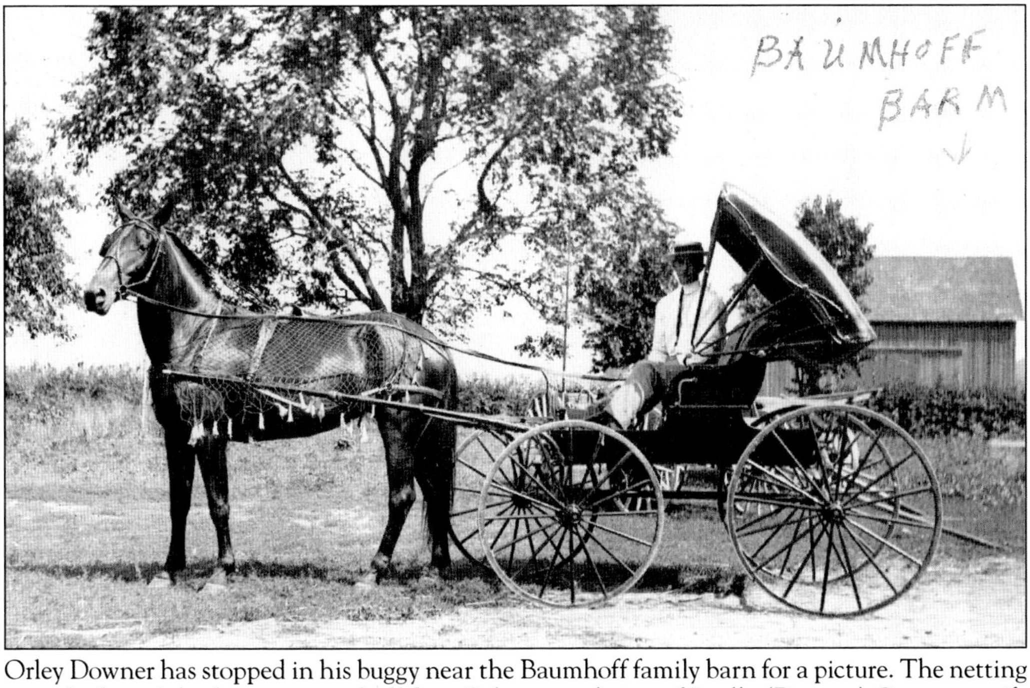

Orley Downer has stopped in his buggy near the Baumhoff family barn for a picture. The netting over the horse's back was to ward off flies. Orley is a relative of Luella (Downer) Cranmer, wife of Cameron Cranmer.

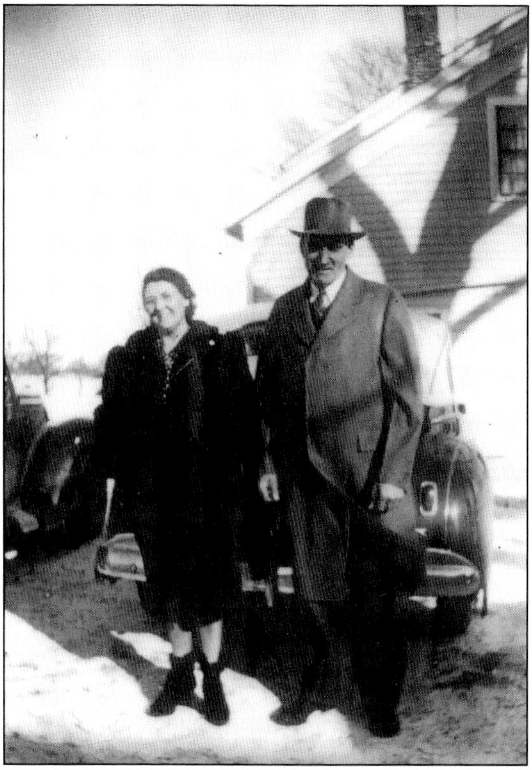

Edwin Dunneback and his wife, Theresa (Lothschutz) Dunneback, are ready to go out in the winter weather. One of their barns was the center for dances, hayrides, and many wedding receptions from the 1940s to the early 1960s.

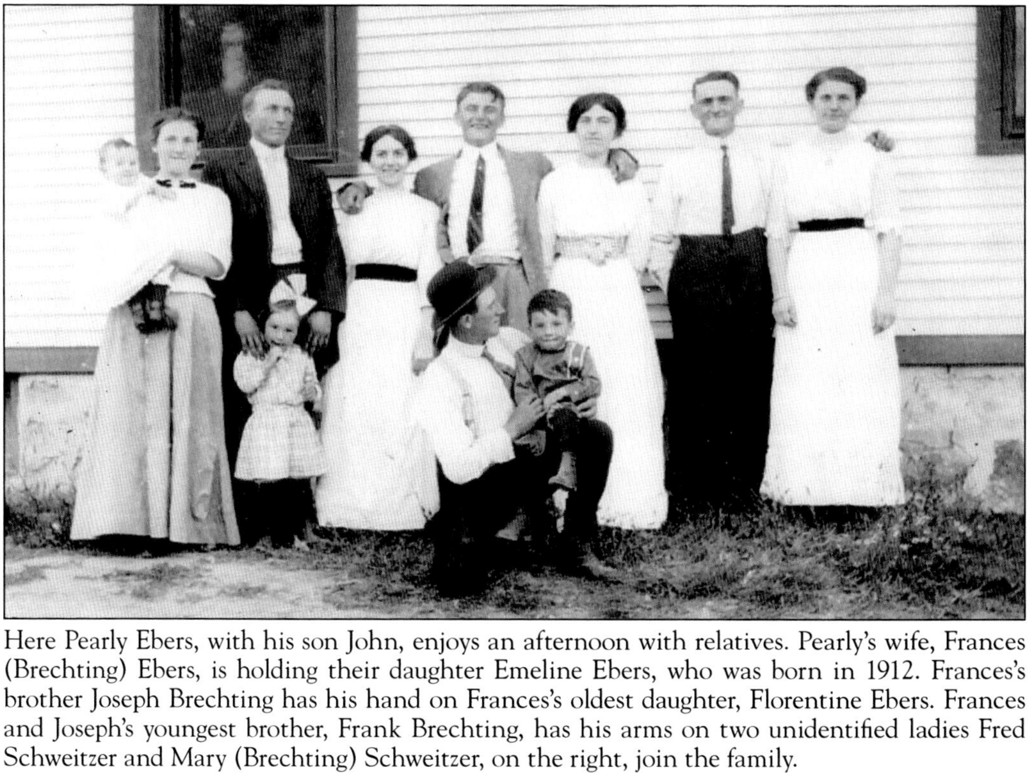

Here Pearly Ebers, with his son John, enjoys an afternoon with relatives. Pearly's wife, Frances (Brechting) Ebers, is holding their daughter Emeline Ebers, who was born in 1912. Frances's brother Joseph Brechting has his hand on Frances's oldest daughter, Florentine Ebers. Frances and Joseph's youngest brother, Frank Brechting, has his arms on two unidentified ladies Fred Schweitzer and Mary (Brechting) Schweitzer, on the right, join the family.

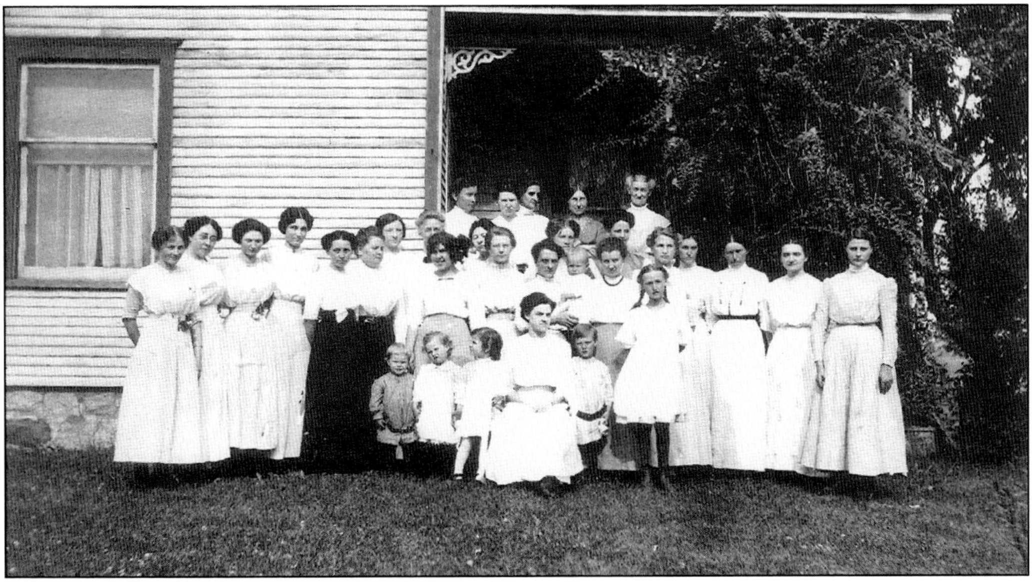

The back of this photograph states that this "miscellaneous shower" for Vernie Ebers, daughter of Frank Ebers, was on Saturday, June 21, 1913. "The maybe bride was entertained in the living room, which was decorated with fish and fishing tackle. Played the game The Bride Packed Her Truck and in it she gets Archie's socks, etc. Louise got the ring (which meant she could be the next bride) and Hattie M. got the thimble (destined to be an old maid) that was baked in the 'hope' cake."

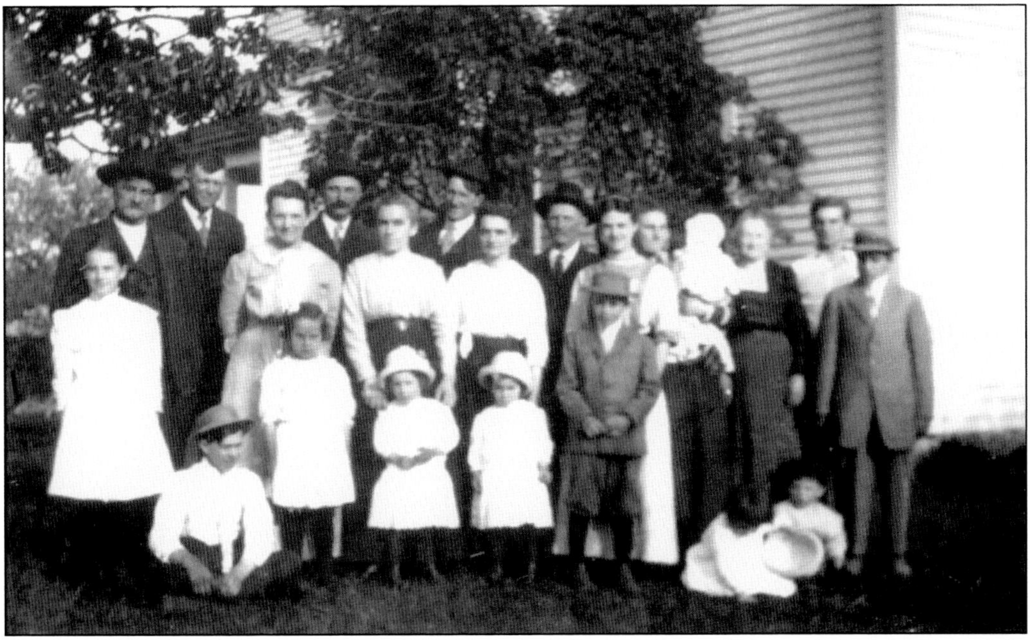

At this Ebers and Alberts family gathering, from left to right are (first row) Walter Ebers, Lila Ebers, twins Ethlyn and Evelyn Alberts, Avery Ebers, John Ebers, and Florentine; (second row) Violet Ebers, Anna Ebers, Emma (Schindler) Alberts, Louise Schindler, Vernie Ebers, and Edward Alberts; (third row) Frank Ebers, Ed Schindler Jr., John Alberts, Pearly Ebers, John Ebers, Frances (Brechting) Ebers with the baby, Mary Ebers, and Richard Alberts.

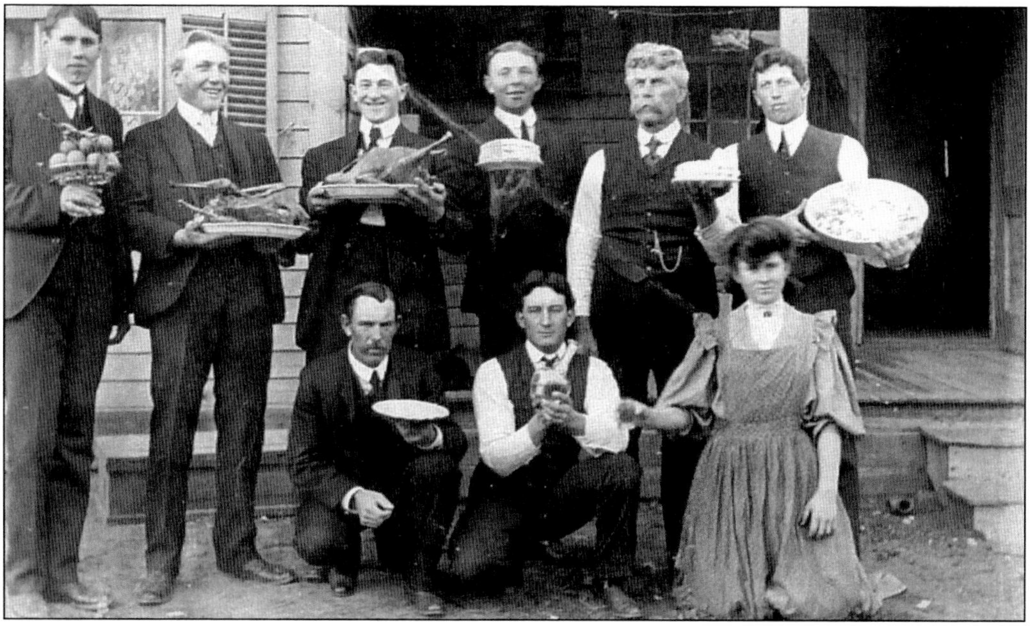

Four young men from Alpine Township went to California to visit their old neighbor John Herbert Snyder Jr., standing second from the right. John had married Eva Catherine Rusche in Alpine Township. She died shortly after they moved to California. They had lived on Bristol Avenue, across the road from her parents. Here, standing from left to right, are Edward Platte, Joseph Brechting, Pearly Ebers, and Charles Steinbrecher. On the far right is John Snyder's son Herbert "Roy" Snyder. The three in front are unidentified.

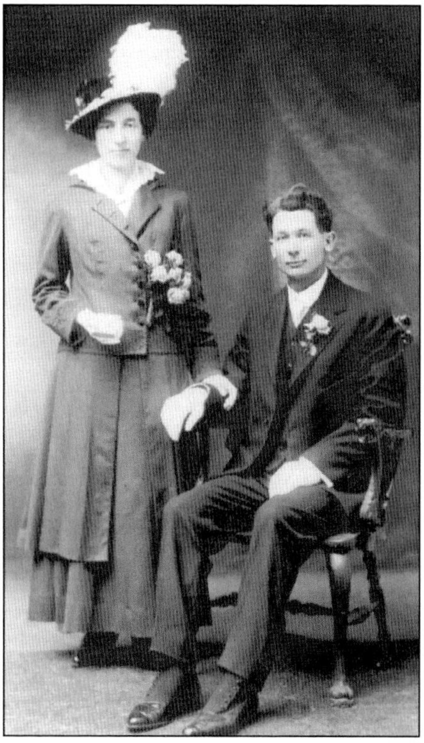

John Jacob Heinbeck married Magdalena "Lena" Bissot at Holy Trinity Catholic Church on November 11, 1914. Magdalena is wearing a tailored suit, ruffled blouse, and lovely hat with a feather plume.

In 1843, Maria Theresia (Flucht) Henze came to America from Wamge, Germany, with her son John Casper and daughter Mary. Both Maria and her son John had both lost their spouses. After a stormy ship ride of one month to New York, they found that almost all of Maria's favorite dish set was broken. They lived in Detroit long enough for John Casper Henze to marry Anna Elizabeth Bender in the old St. Mary's Church in downtown Detroit. After 1950, all left Detroit for Alpine Township, where they purchased 60 acres from John Platte on Alpine Avenue, north of Four Mile Road in section 35.

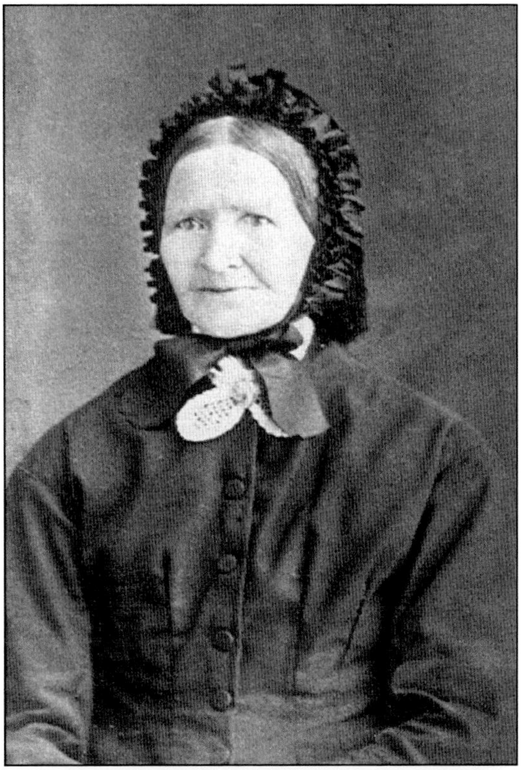

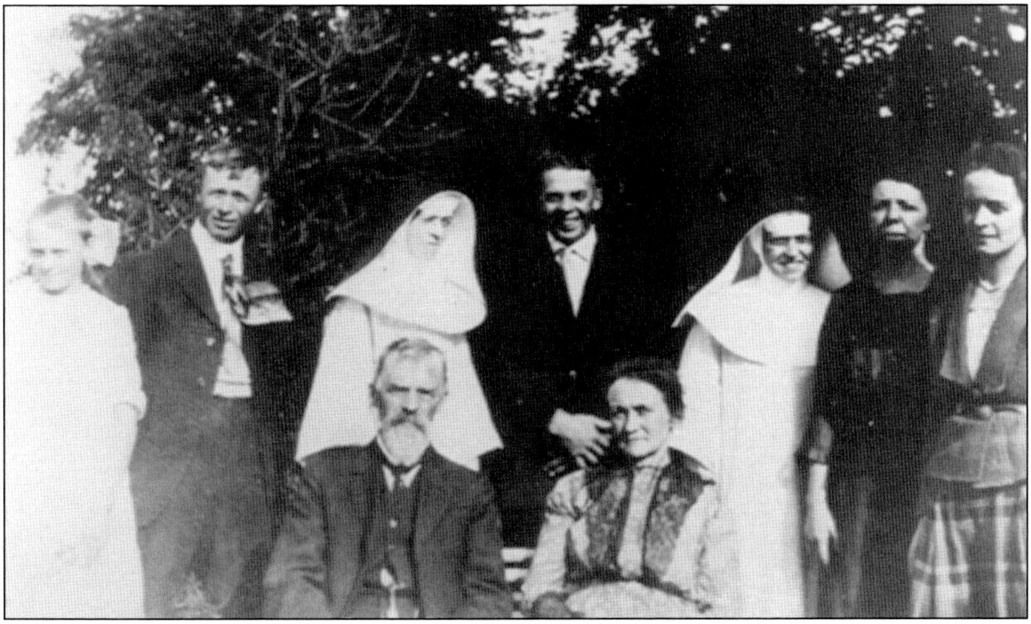

The Henze family stopped for a photograph on this fine Sunday afternoon together. Father Casper Henze and mother Mary Rose (Hahn) Henze are seated. Standing are, from left to right, Mary Rose, Frank, Anna, Karl Clemens, Esther Elizabeth, Irene Louise, and Florentine Henze. Mary Rose married Frank Brechting; Frank married Laura Steffens; Anna took the name Sister Matilda, O.P; and Esther Elizabeth took the name Sister M. Casper, O.P.

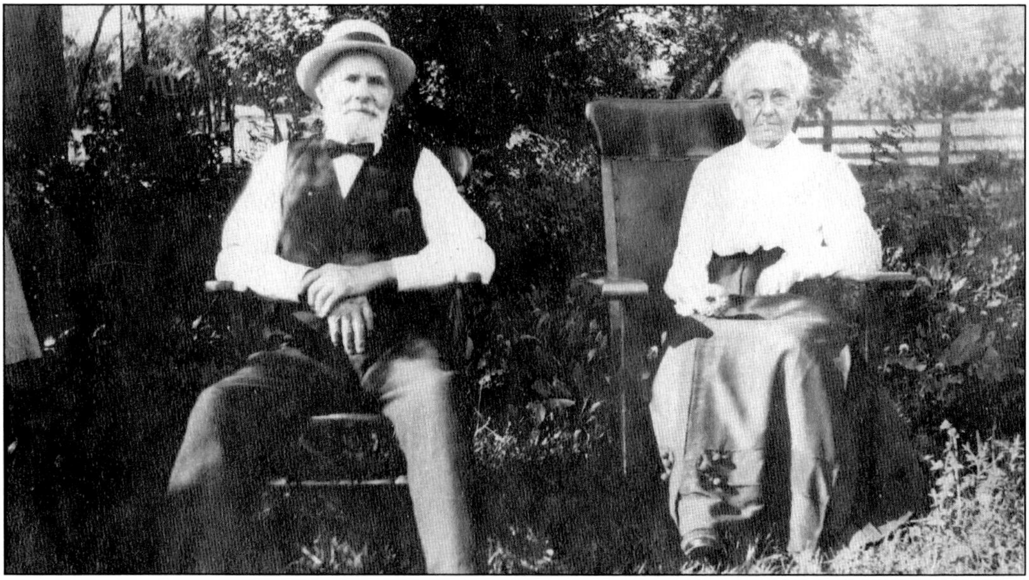

James Hill was born in England. At the age of 16, he started in Canada with his brother, John Hill. James was a mason by trade and found work in Grand Rapids. About 1863, James settled on his father-in-law's farm after meeting his future wife, Mary Ann Snowden, when he was plastering their house. James and Mary Hill sit out in the yard on a fine summer day. Their farm was at Seven Mile Road and Peach Ridge Avenue. Their children were Rowland, Annie, and Carrie Hill. Rowland married Carrie Denison, Annie married Pearly Brown, and Carrie died at the age of 18.

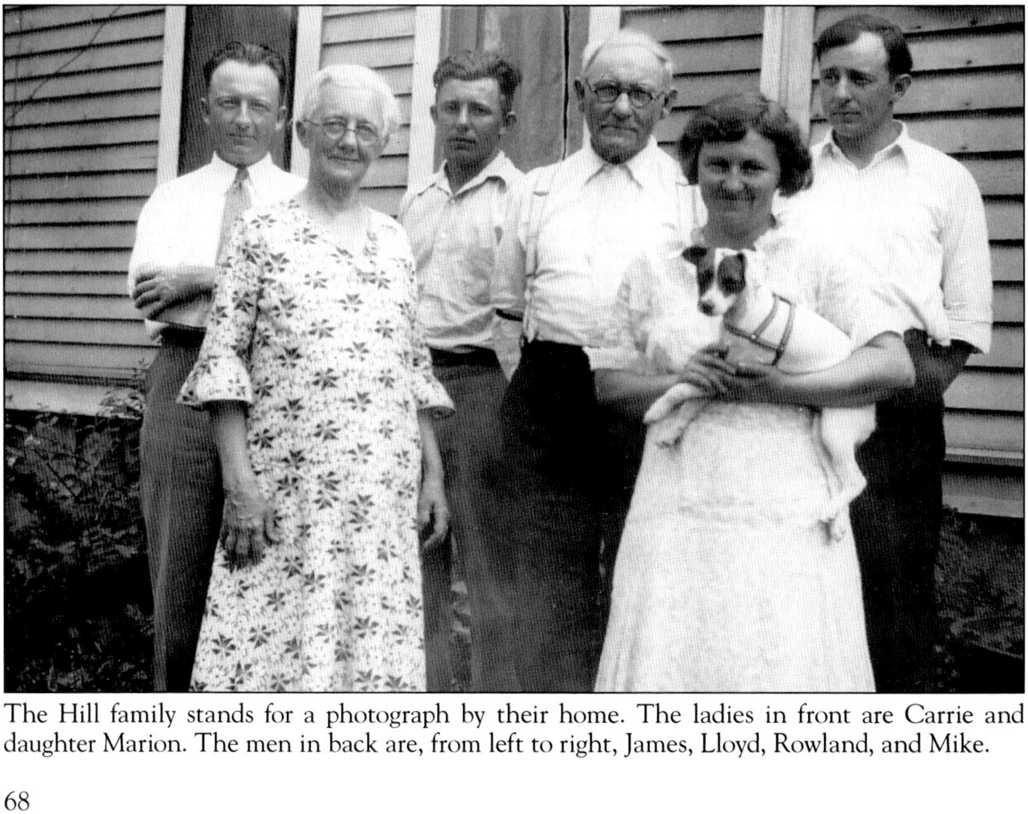

The Hill family stands for a photograph by their home. The ladies in front are Carrie and daughter Marion. The men in back are, from left to right, James, Lloyd, Rowland, and Mike.

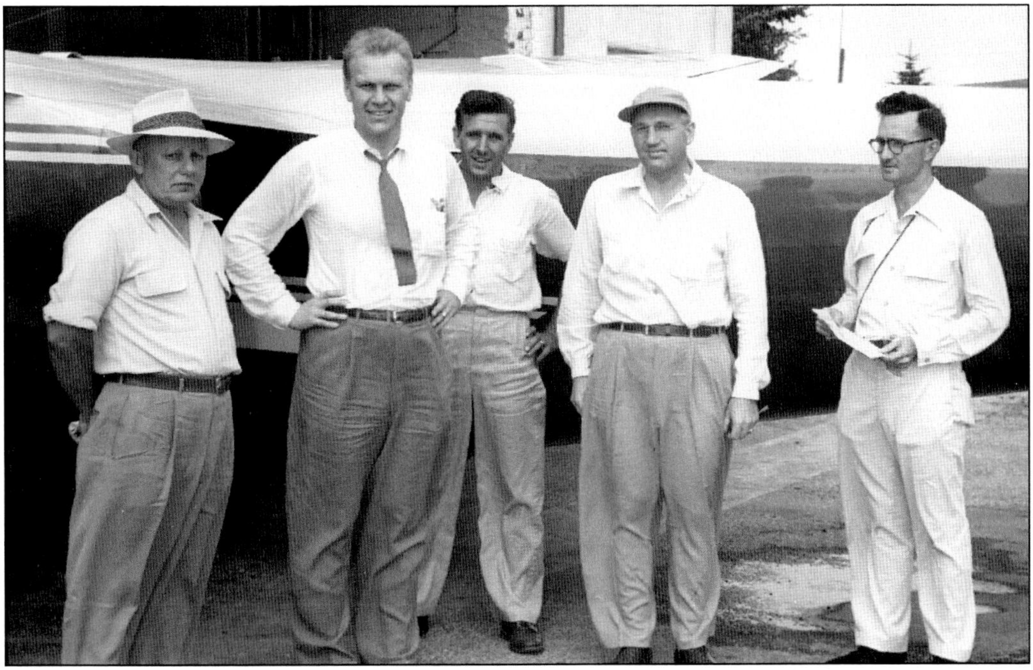

While Lloyd Hill, on the far left, was supervisor of Alpine Township, he had an opportunity to work with state representative Gerald Ford (second from the left), who would become president. These men seem to be at an airport with an unidentified pilot in the middle. Russ Hill, secretary of MSCS, and Wilber Kellogg, district soil specialist, are on the right. The late president Gerald Ford grew up in Grand Rapids and lived the longest life of any American president to date.

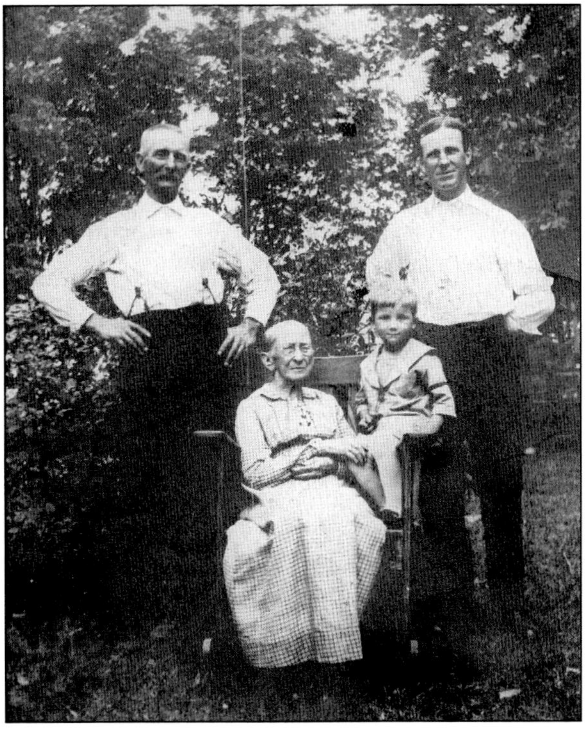

Four generations of the Hills family who lived on Alpine Avenue and Seven Mile Road are seen here: Lemira (Colton) Hills; Henry C. Hills (left), who married Melva Mae Rogers; Terry L. Hills, who married Alvena M. Gerken; and Harold C. Hills, who was born on March 8, 1915.

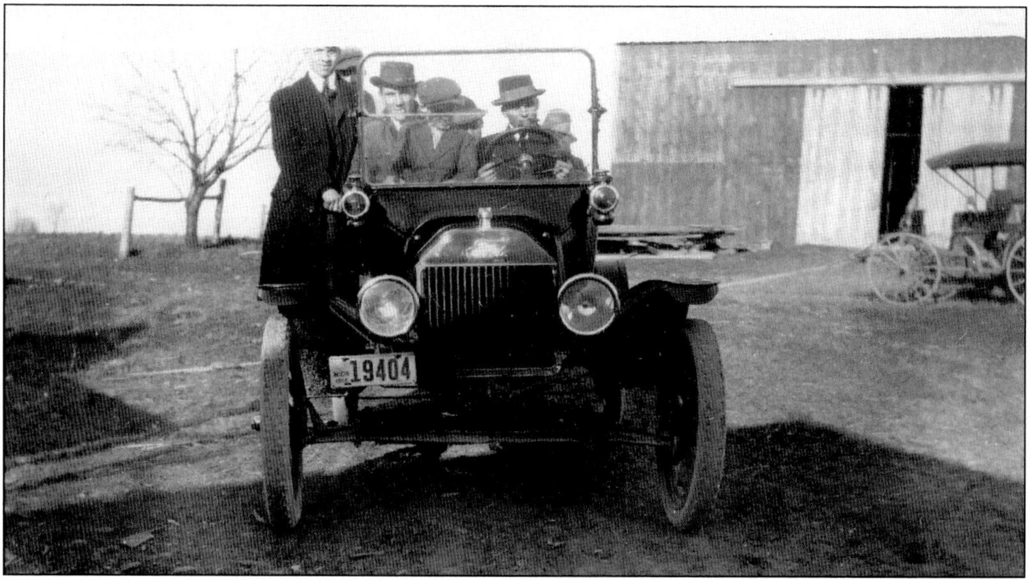

Joe Kline, with his brothers and son Ray Kline, seems to be having fun in a new vehicle, with an older one in the background.

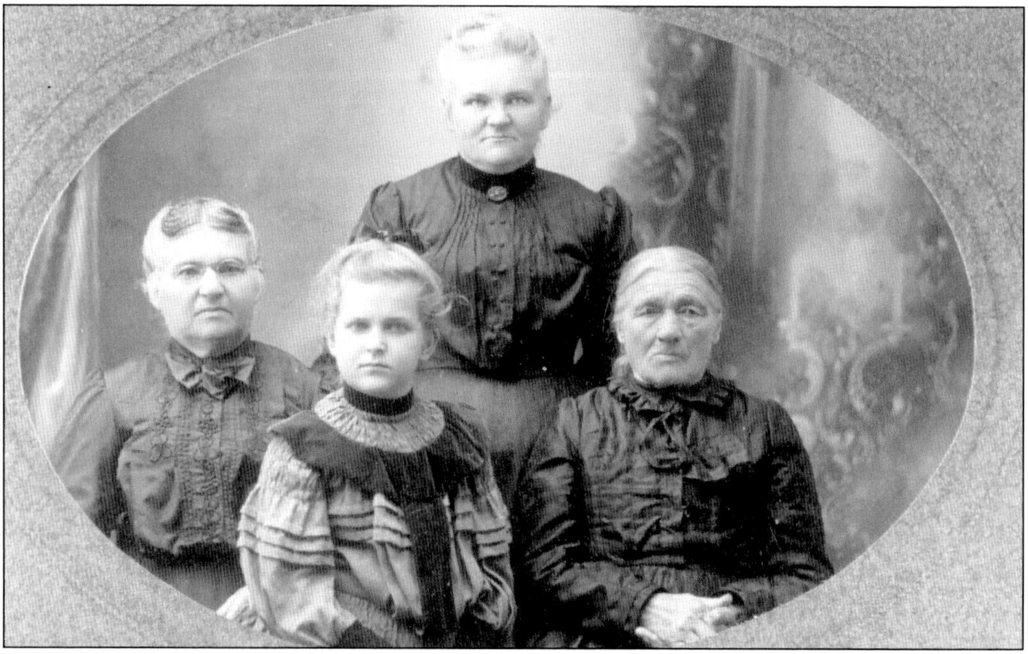

Margaret Klenk is seated on the right with her three daughters. Matilda Ritz is standing. Lizzie Schaefer is on the left with Rose Vogel in the middle.

Delia (Caywood) Johnston stands by a very ornate chair in her dress with a full skirt. A full-sleeved white blouse can be seen under her black top. The skirt and top were usually two pieces. She uses a hoopshirt to keep her black skirt full.

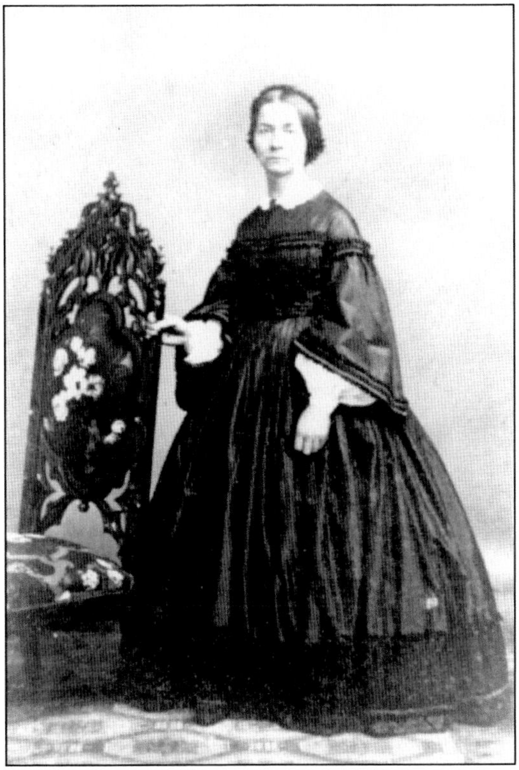

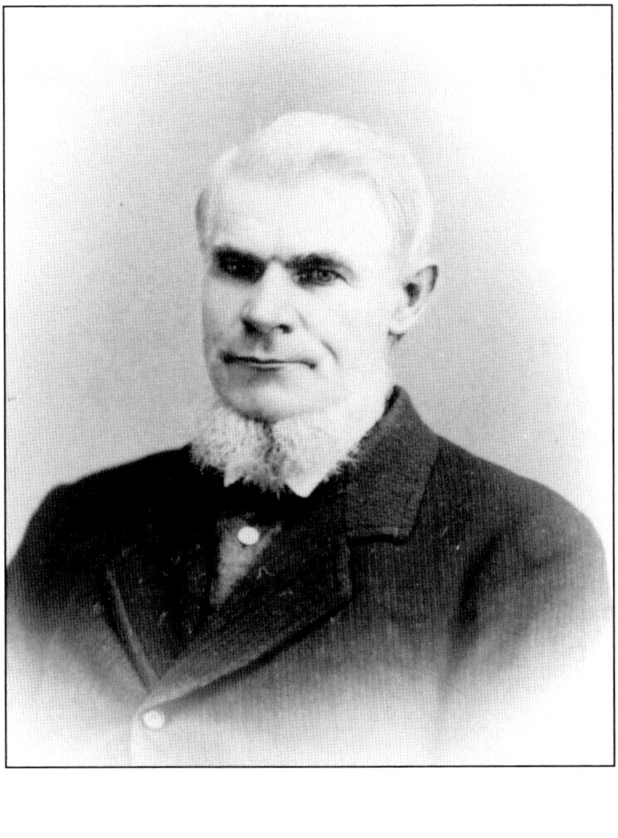

Luther Johnston married Delia Caywood in 1850. They had three daughters: Mary, Ida, and Julia. Julia married Charles Sawyer. Luther married a second time, to Anna Harron of New York. Their farm was on Peach Ridge Avenue, north of Four Mile Road. He was known for his Durham shorthorn cattle. The 1881 *History of Kent County, Michigan*, states, "His herd of 25 exhibits some of the best samples of the breed to be found in the country, several of which have taken premiums above all competitors."

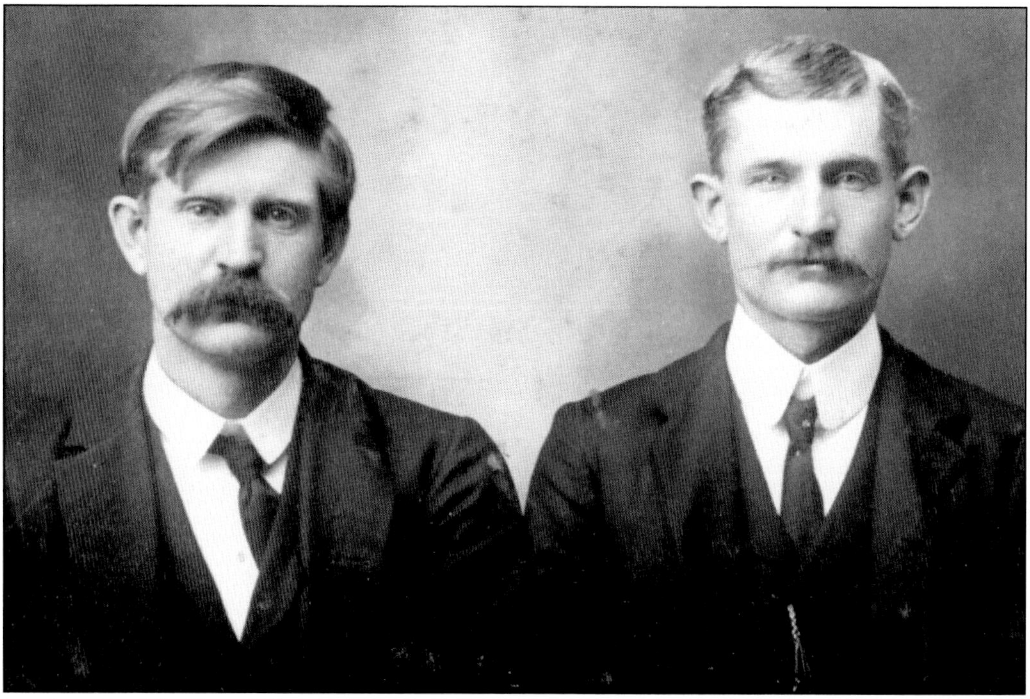

Brothers Fred (left) and Philip Klenk both farmed in Alpine Township.

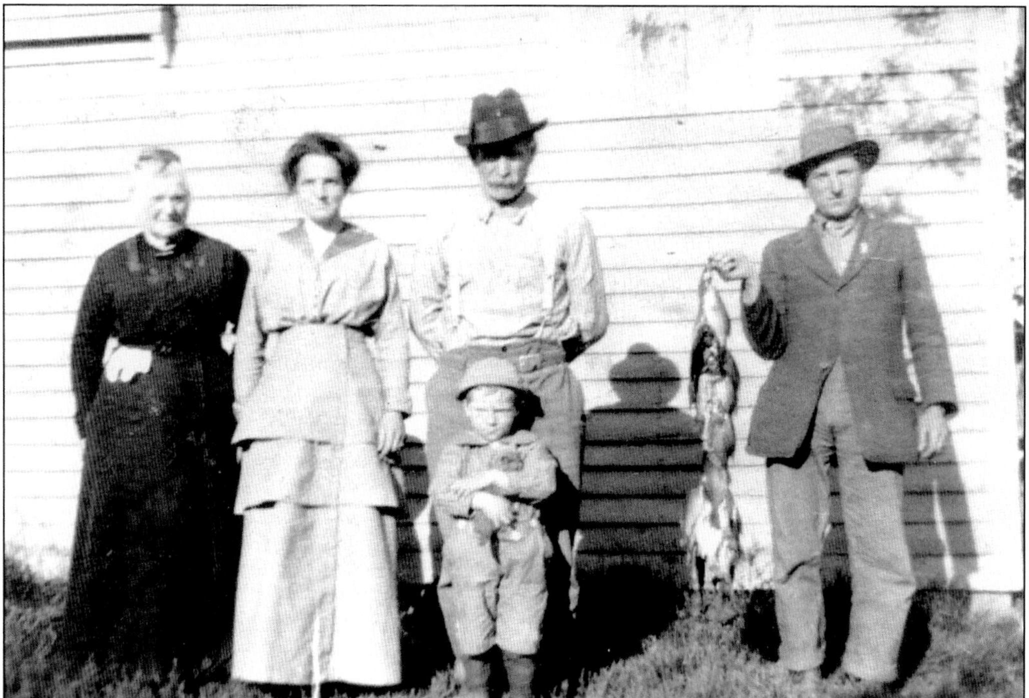

Fred Klenk must have taken this picture of his mother, Margaret (Fahling) Klenk; his wife, Julia (Vogel) Klenk; his son Harold Klenk; and his brother Philip Klenk. It looks like an unidentified friend has caught their dinner.

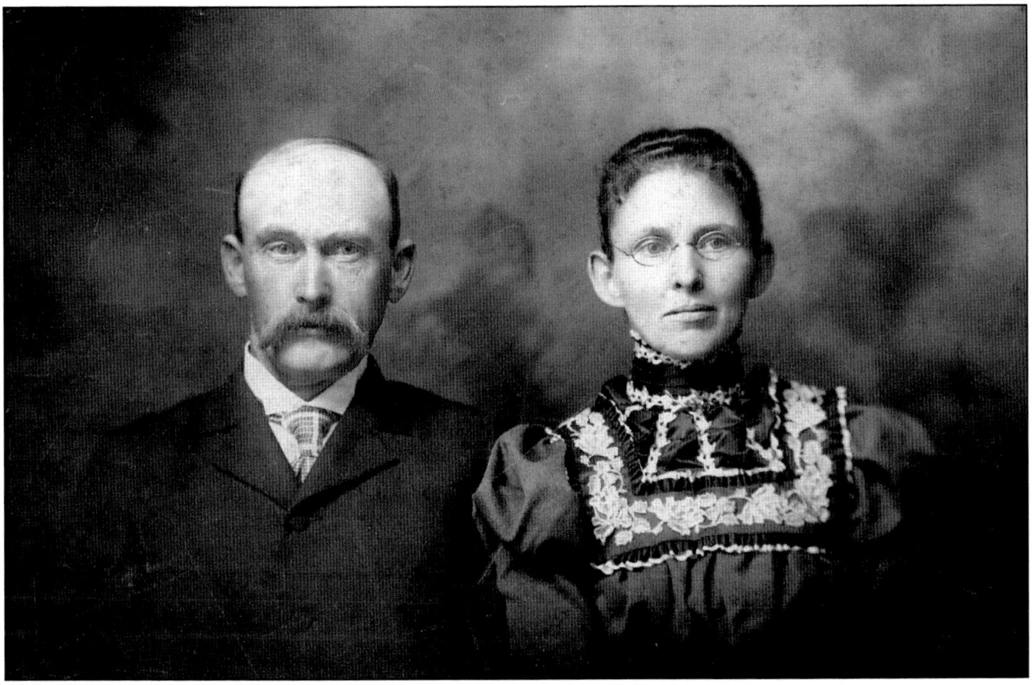

Fred Baumhoff married Annie (Hills) Baumhoff. He was born in Missouri and came to live with the Ruthardt family in Alpine Township. Annie was the daughter of Aaron Hills and Lemira (Colton) Hills.

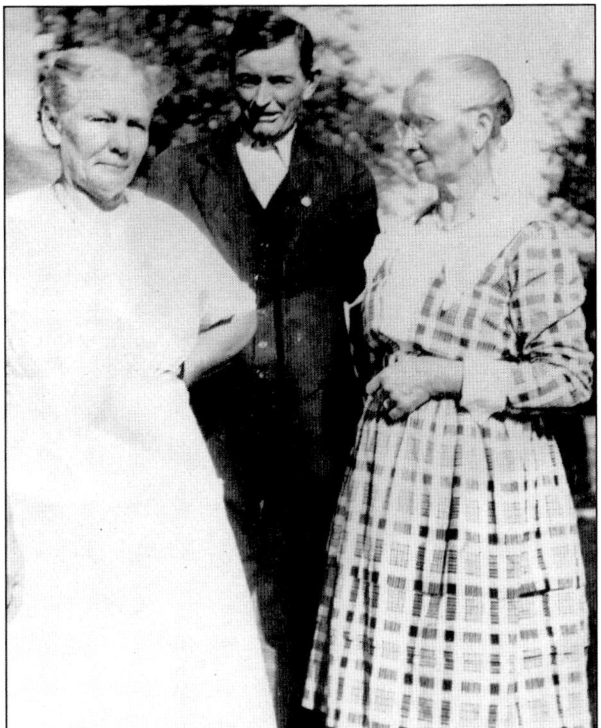

Charles Morse stands with his wife, Emma, on the right, and Emma's sister Sarah on the left. It looks like a bright sunny day. Charles and Emma's farm was on Six Mile Road and Peach Ridge Avenue.

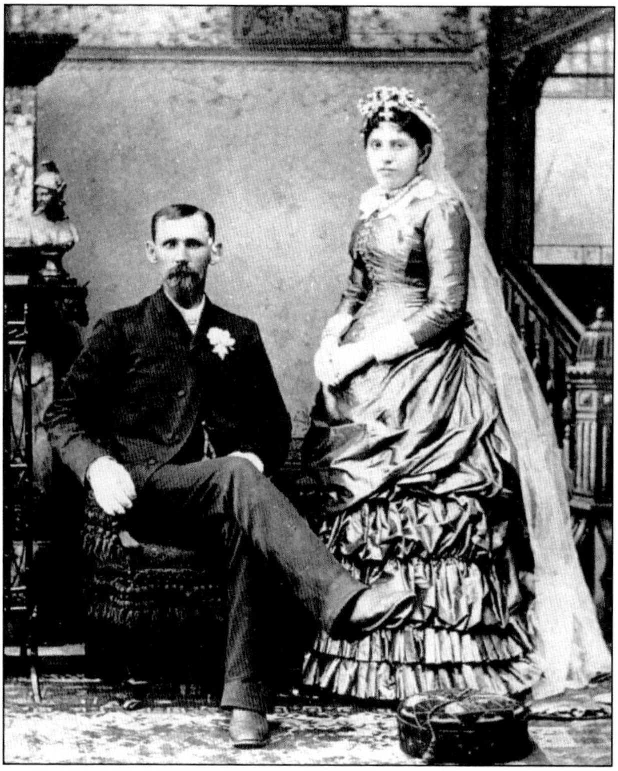

Joseph Platte married Catherine Albert on May 20, 1884. Her dress of silk satin shines with many tucks, and she has a full-length veil. A seamstress would wonder how many yards of material went into a beautiful dress like this. Both are buried at Holy Trinity Parish Cemetery.

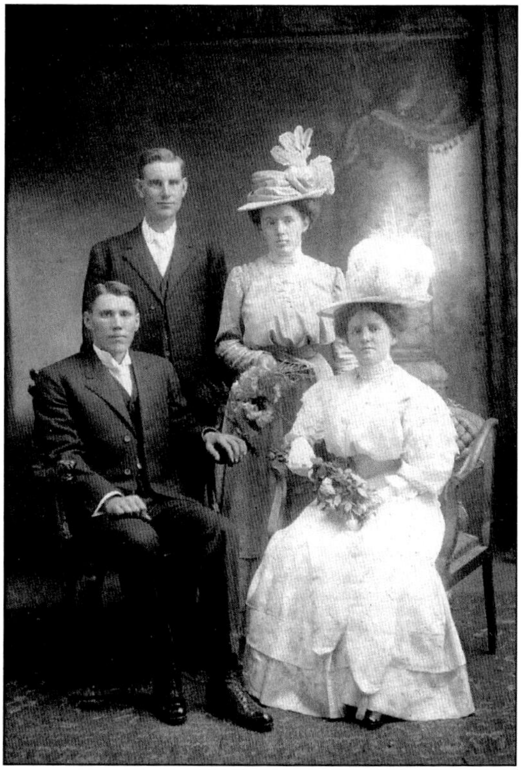

Edward Platte, son of Joseph and Catherine Platte, married Wilehmina Thome in November 1908. Rolland Stoddard and Edith Platte stood up for them. The ladies are now dressed in white with lovely hats, and the wedding couple is seated for this picture.

On May 23, 1903, Will Rasch purchased a farm in Alpine Township at the Adam Lachman estate auction. Will's only son, Robert G. Rasch, bought the farm one year before he married Elizabeth Dietrich in 1918. Robert's oldest son, Herman, bought the farm in 1944, when he married Bernadette Brechting. The Centennial Farm is still being run by the family.

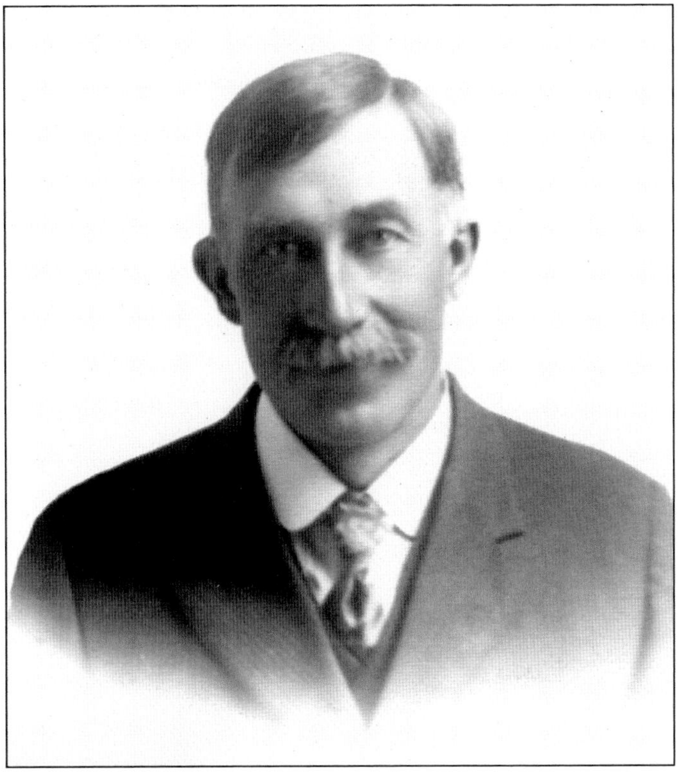

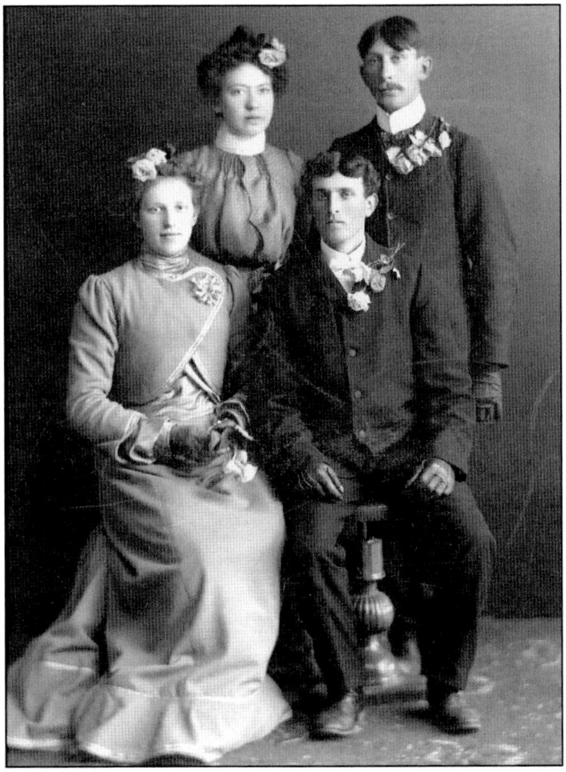

In 1901, Melanie Alt, daughter of Marcus Alt and Josephine (Hoffman) Alt, married John Rothenthaler. John was cutting wood when a tree fell on him and killed him in 1923. This was the same year Melanie gave birth to their 12th child.

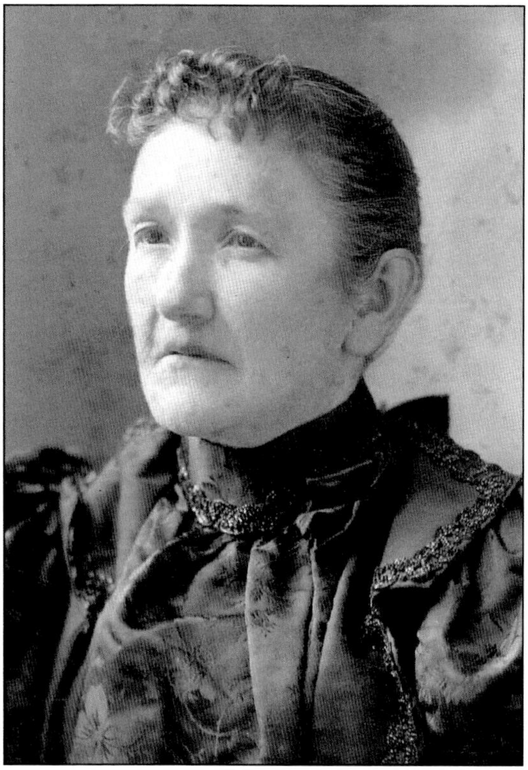

Mary (Rusche) Ebers, daughter of Anthony and Rose Rusche, had her portrait taken in Grand Rapids in a very beautiful high-neck dress. The top of these dresses had many parts. Mary married John Ebers, son of Henry Ebers and Christine (Warthy) Ebers. They had one son, Pearly, who married Frances Brechting in 1908. They lost their infant daughter Lillian in 1883.

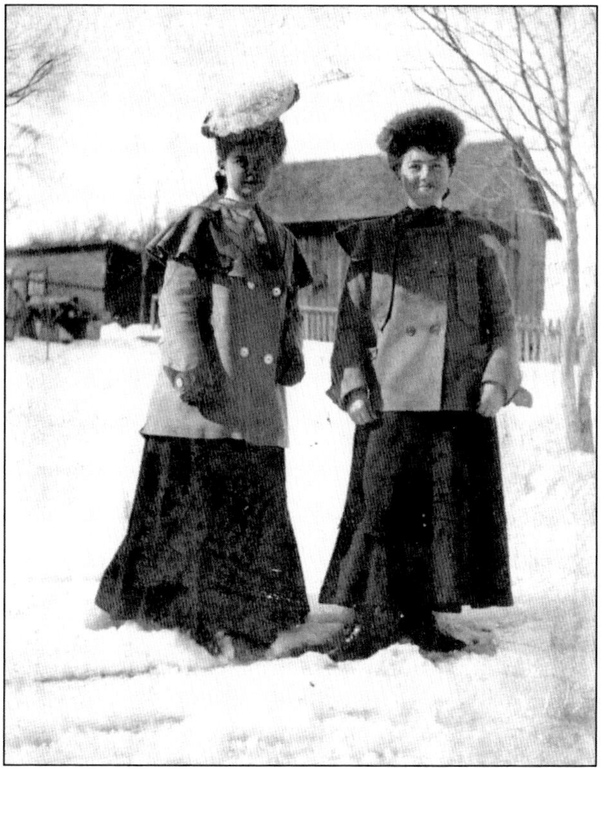

The wind seems to be blowing the snow around for Frances Rusche (left) and Trace Cordes. They will stay warm with their long skirts, hats, gloves, coats, and scarves.

Eva Christine (Nagel) Ruthardt was the second wife of George Michael Ruthardt and mother of William, who married Bertha Baumhoff and after her death, Libbie Dohrn; Salome, who married Robert Baumhoff; and Frederick, who married Emma Kellogg.

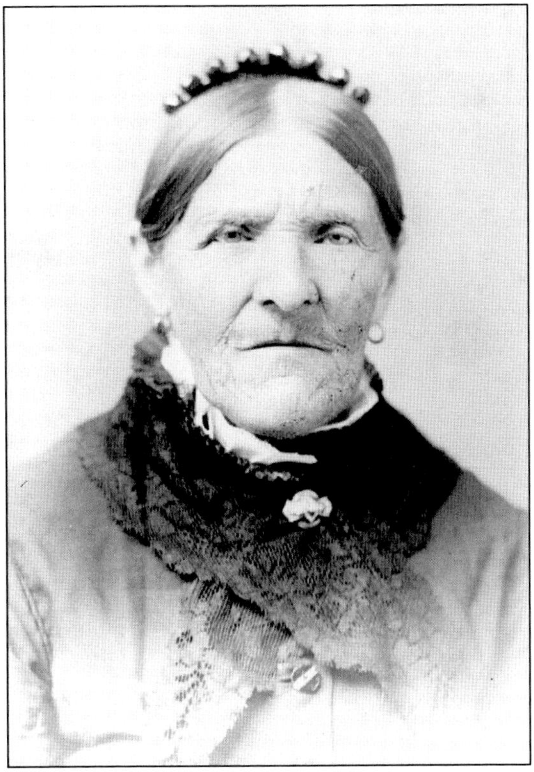

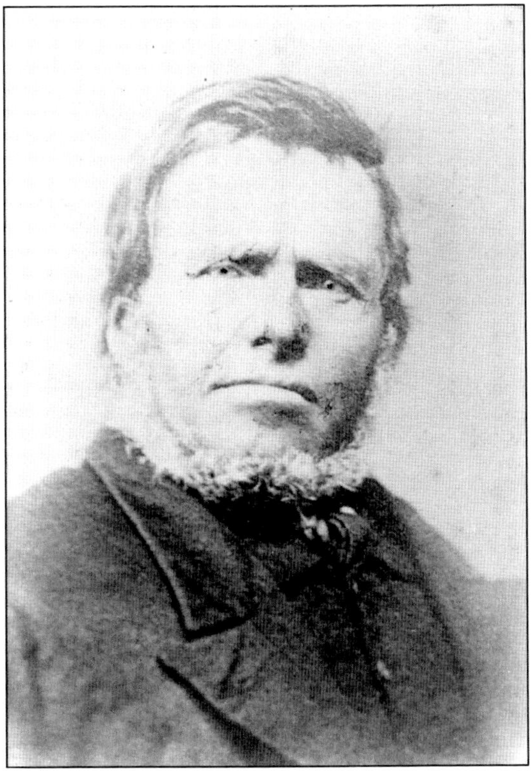

George Michael Ruthardt first married Rosena Thonhimer in Baden, Germany. She gave her husband five children but passed away in 1845 in Germany. George came to America in 1846 with his son Philip. In 1847, George married Eva Christina Nagel. They had three children. He was a farmer and a tanner by trade.

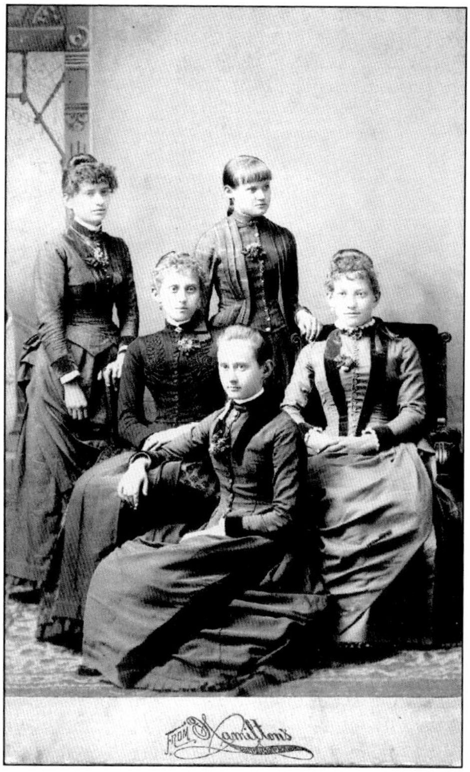

Philip Ruthardt and Lisetta (Baumhoff) Ruthardt had five daughters: from left to right, (first row) Mary Augusta; (second row) Christine and Emma Christine; (third row) Louise Salome and Lisetta Rosina. Louise Salome married Frank Niehouse, Lisetta Rosina married Charles Dietz, Christine married Charles Bremer, Emma Christine married Perl Richmeyer, and Mary Augusta married John Corporon.

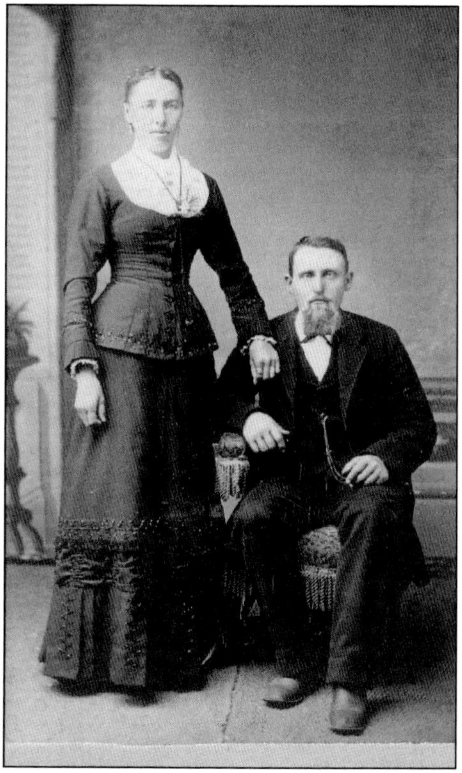

Salome Ruthardt married Robert Baumhoff, brother of Fred Baumhoff. She stands to show the beauty of her handmade wedding outfit. Her two-piece "dress" has a white inlay and the decoration on the blouse matches that of the skirt.

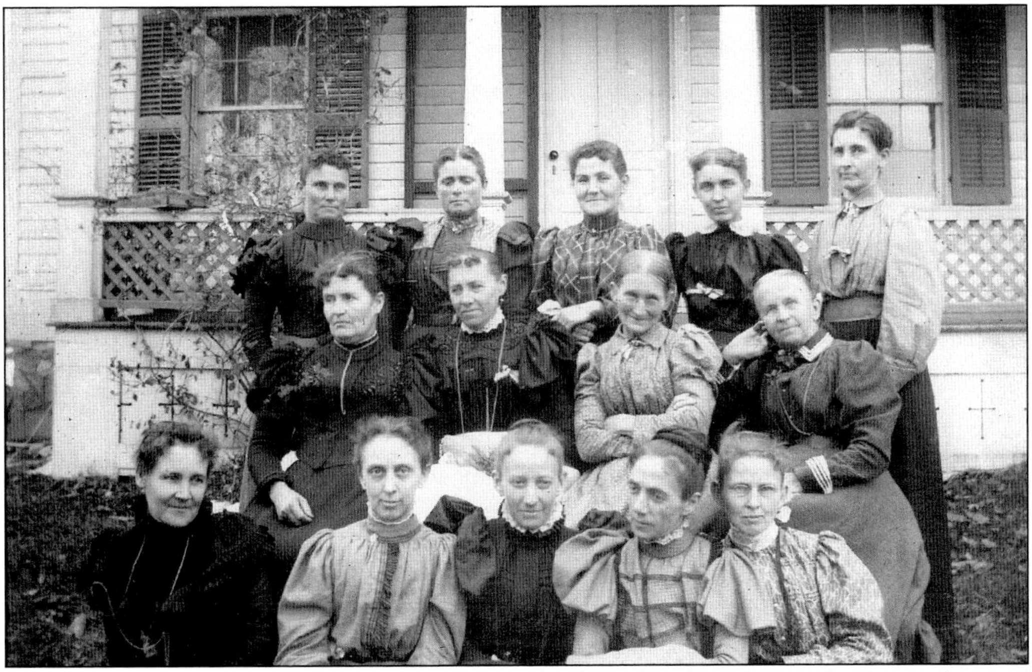

Libby Ruthardt, standing in back on the left, and Salome (Ruthardt) Baumhoff, seated second from the left in the middle row, enjoy a get-together with their friends and family at the Ruthardt home.

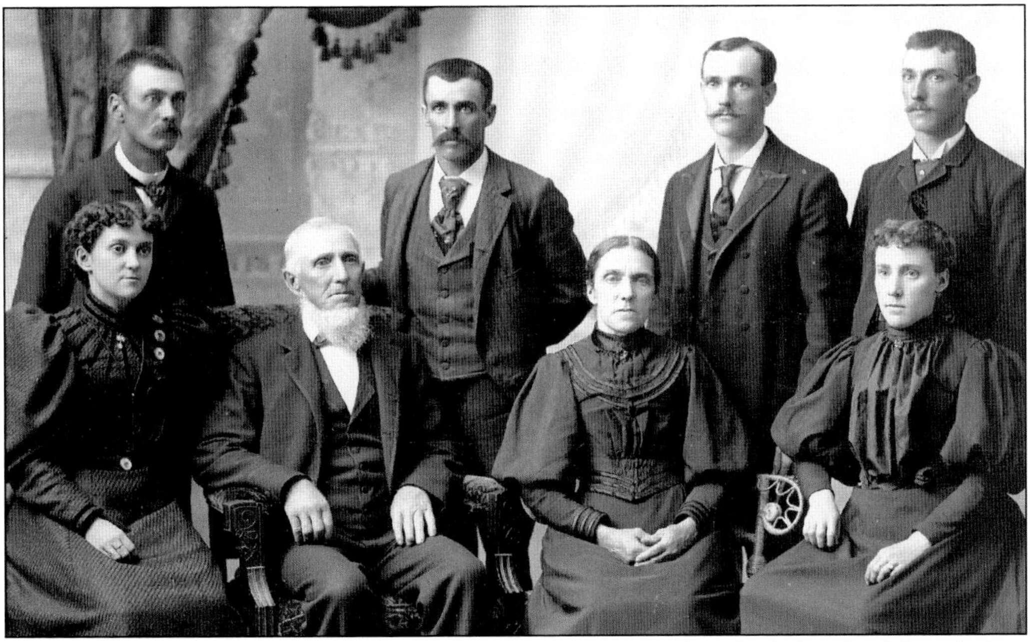

Ferdinand Scheidel is seated here with his wife, Catherine (Vierheilig) Scheidel, and their children. From left to right are (first row) Annie, Ferdinand, Catherine, and Carrie; (second row) Lewis, John, Charles, and Peter. Lewis married Alice Williams, Charles married Lissetta Greiner, Peter married Eva Catherine Steffens, Annie married Phillip Fritz, and John married Rose Wilkelm.

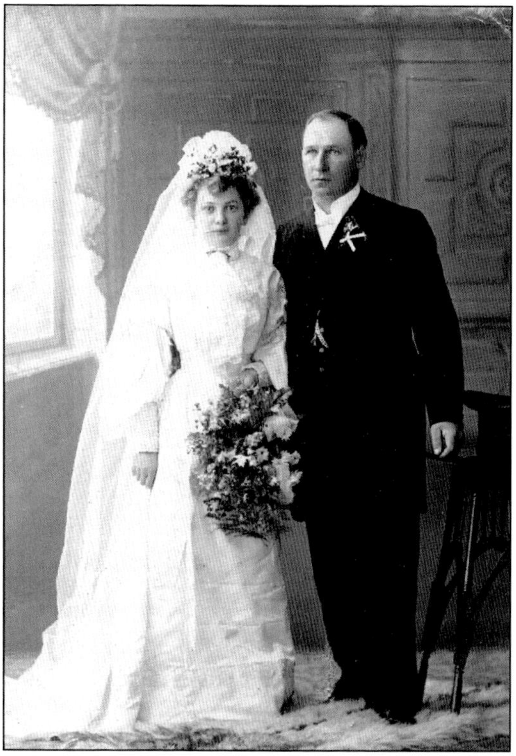

This is the June 1904 wedding picture of Joseph Schindler and Anna Hausmann. Joseph Schindler was the son of Ferdinand and Franziska (Bergmann) Schindler. Franziska was the daughter of Karl and Mary (Hockeborn) Bergmann of Mildenau, Bohemia. Ferdinand was the son of Joseph and Maria Anna (Nase) Schindler. Ferdinand had sailed to America at the age of 17 with his older brother, Ed Schindler Sr. Sometime after the 1860 census was taken, Ferdinand returned to the old country and married Franziska. They left Bremen, Germany, aboard the USS *Union* and came to New York on November 22, 1869. They had six children: Charles, Joseph, Edward, Mary, Louise, and Fredrick.

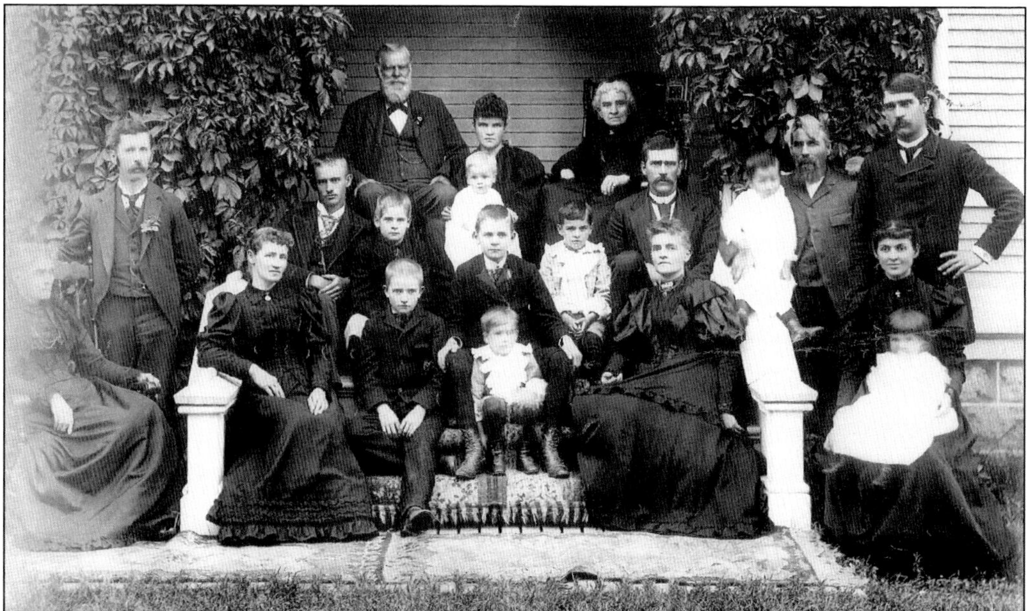

In 1891, Sherman M. Pearsall and Catherine (Bailey) Pearsall celebrated their 50th wedding anniversary with family and friends. They are seated in the back with their children and grandchildren.

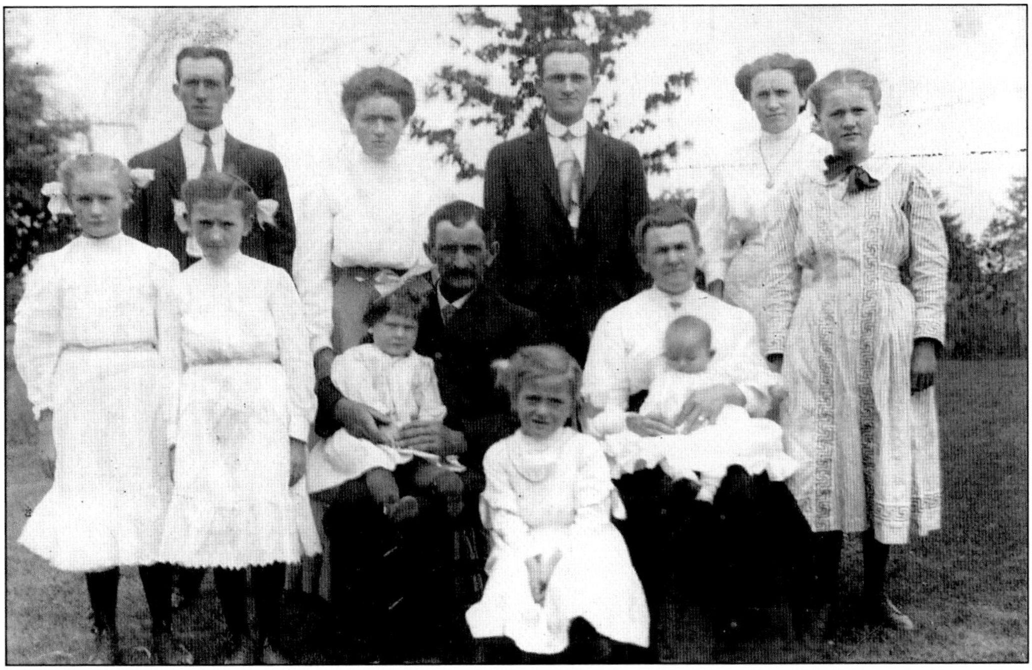

The Nicholas Schweitzer family looks as if they are all dressed up for Agnes's baptism. From left to right are (first row) Veronica, Louise, Nicholas holding Clara, Nettie, and Matilda holding Agnes; (second row) Joe, Theresa, Fred, Rose, and Minnie. Theresa married Joseph Cordes, Rose married Nick Pitsch, Minnie married Frank Antor, Veronica married William Scheidel, Louise married Frank Chicklin, Clara married Frank Grantkowski, Nettie married Chester Seamon, and Agnes married Howard Sonke.

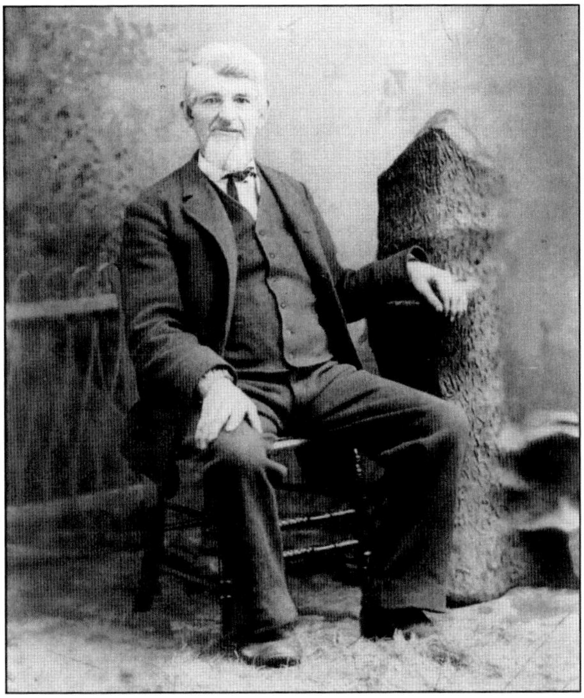

Peter John Thome, born in Dautweiler, Germany, in 1822, was a steamboat navigator on the Grand River from Grand Rapids to Grand Haven. He blew the first steam whistle ever heard in Grand Rapids. Thome married Gertrude Snyder/Schneider. Their farm was on Baumhoff Avenue, north of Four Mile Road. They donated the first two acres of land for the first Holy Trinity Catholic parish cemetery after he bought the land in 1847.

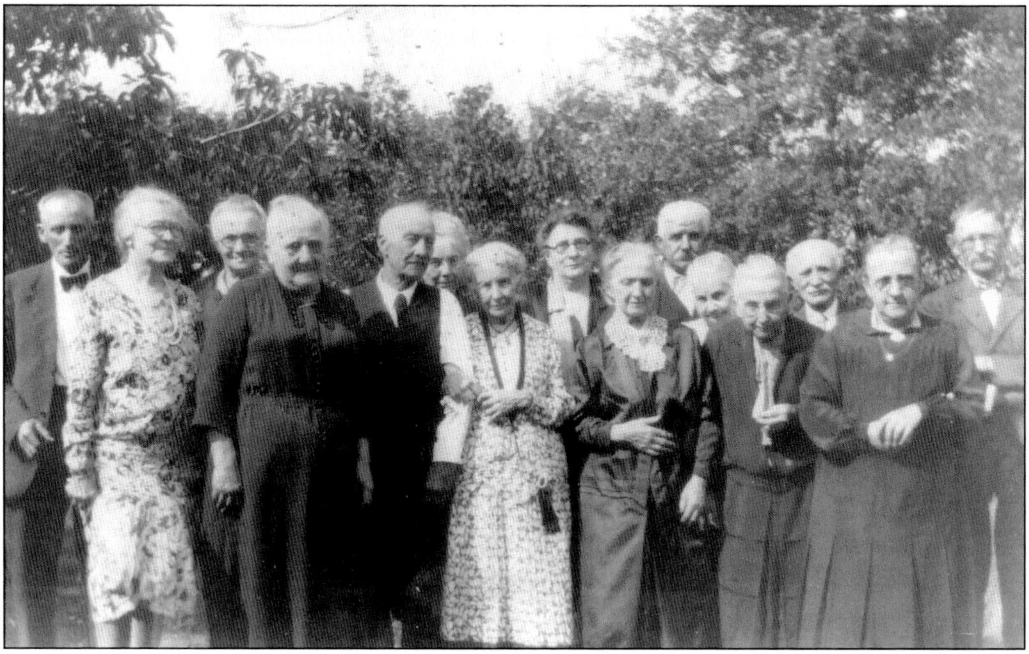

In 1933, Louise (Cordes) Thome and Michael Thome, fourth and fifth from the left, celebrated their 50th wedding anniversary with their family. From left to right are Theodore Cordes, Veronica (Thome) Friar, Julia (Cordes) Thome, Louise and Michael Thome, Mary Ansorge, Katherine (Thome) Ansorge, holding on to her brother Michael Thome, Amelia Wahlfield, Pauline Pulte, Charles Wahlfield, unidentified, Anna Leitelt, William Pulte, Josephine (Cordes) Brogger, and August Brogger.

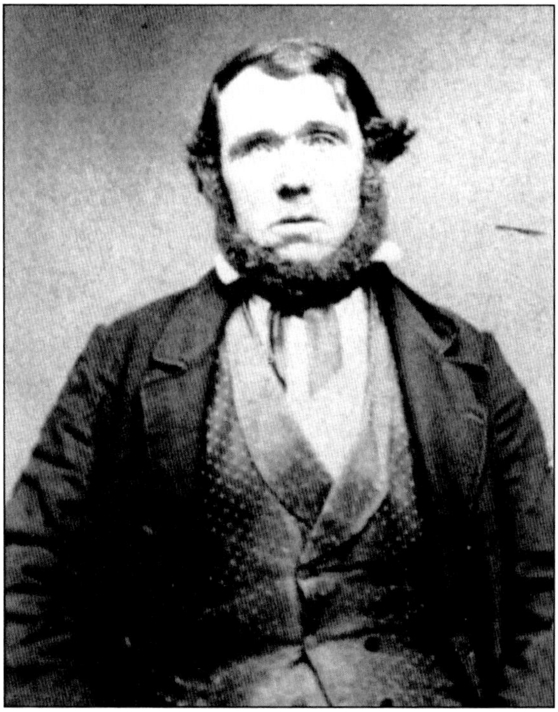

Andrew Vierheilig was born in 1803 in Oerlenbach, Germany. He moved to Alpine Township and purchased property on section 22, where he lived with his wife, Katharina.

Rev. A. B. Toms and his wife, Mary (Davenport) Toms, were married September 4, 1864. Before they left their home in Connecticut, they had three children: Edwin, Oscar, and Electa. In 1844, he had purchased a farm near the corner of Nine Mile Road and Vinton Avenue. Their granddaughter Alice "Kitty" Toms became a doctor and married Walter Vinton.

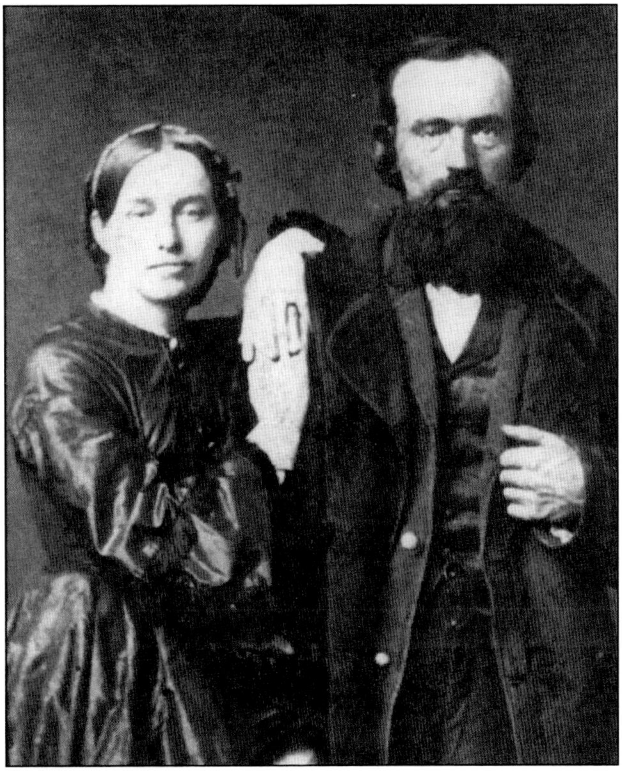

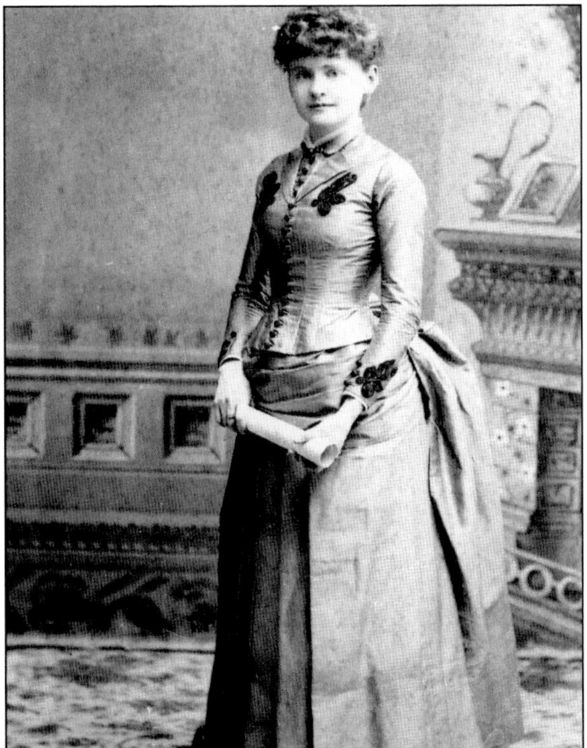

Alice "Kitty" Toms was the granddaughter of Rev. A. B. and Mary Toms, who came to Michigan from Connecticut. She was the area's first known female physician. In 1892, Kitty married Walter Vinton, the son of Porter Vinton Sr. and Elizabeth (Staley) Vinton. Dr. Vinton obtained her license in 1903 and ran a hospital in her home.

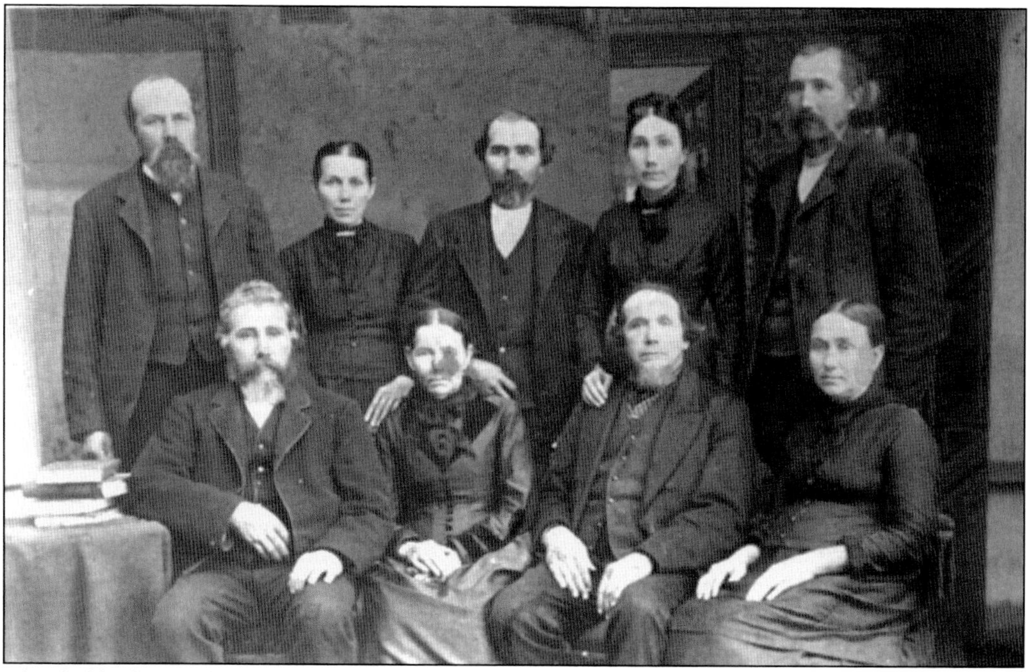

Theobald John Umlor and Salome (Host) Umlor raised these children at their farm in section 20 on Stage Avenue and Six Mile Road. From left to right are (first row) John B., Anna, Joseph, and Mary; (second row) Michael, Lena, Theobald, Theresa, and Adam. Michael married Mary Magdalena Schoenborn; Lena married Michael Thome; Theobald married Katherine Dohm; Theresa married Frank Nash; Adam married Apolonia Wunech, then Jane Wunech; John B. married Mary May, then Elizabeth Schneider; Anna married William Brakel; Joseph married Cordelia Neekeson; and Mary married Jacob May.

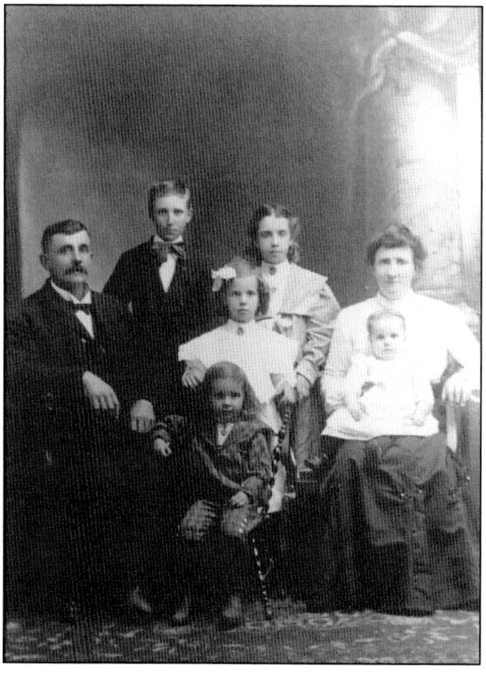

In 1906, Charles Wahlfield and Amelia (Cordes) Wahlfield brought their family to sit for a family photograph. Clockwise from the left, Ed, Frances, Freda, and Carl are between their parents, while Wilma is held by her mother. Their home was on Alpine Avenue at Alpine Church Road.

John Jacob Vogel Sr. married Mary Miller in 1858. They had Jacob, who married Cecilia Rusche; Christine, who married Fred Davenport; Fred, who married Minnie Ruehs; Julia, who married Fred Klenk; Carl "Charley," who married Otellia Schumacher; and Philip, who married Rose Klenk.

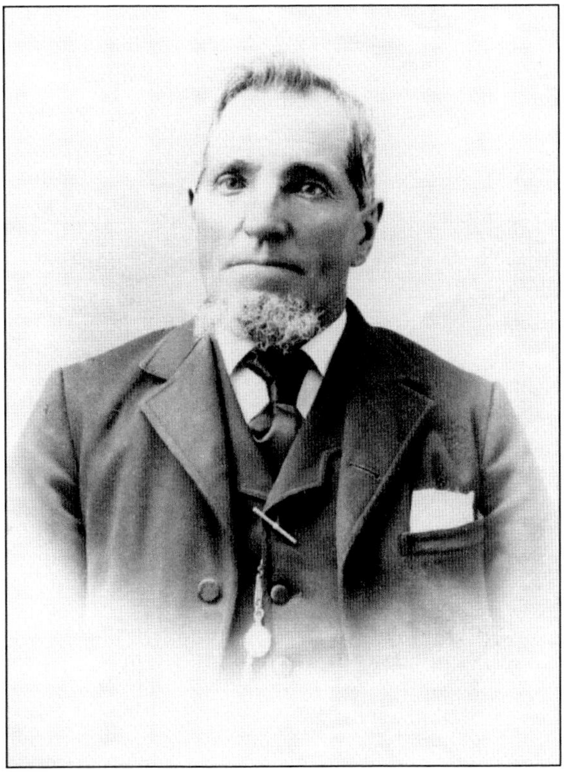

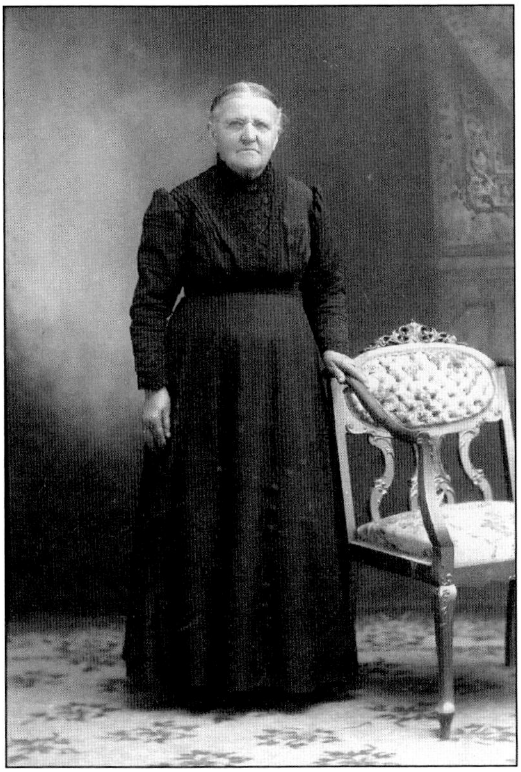

When Mary Vogel passed away in 1917, she had been a resident of Alpine Township for almost 60 years. She came to America with her grandparents when she was eight years old. They started in Ohio, as many people did when they came down the Erie Canal. Then they moved to a farm in Allegan County. Mary married John Jacob Vogel Sr. in 1858. They had six children, listed above.

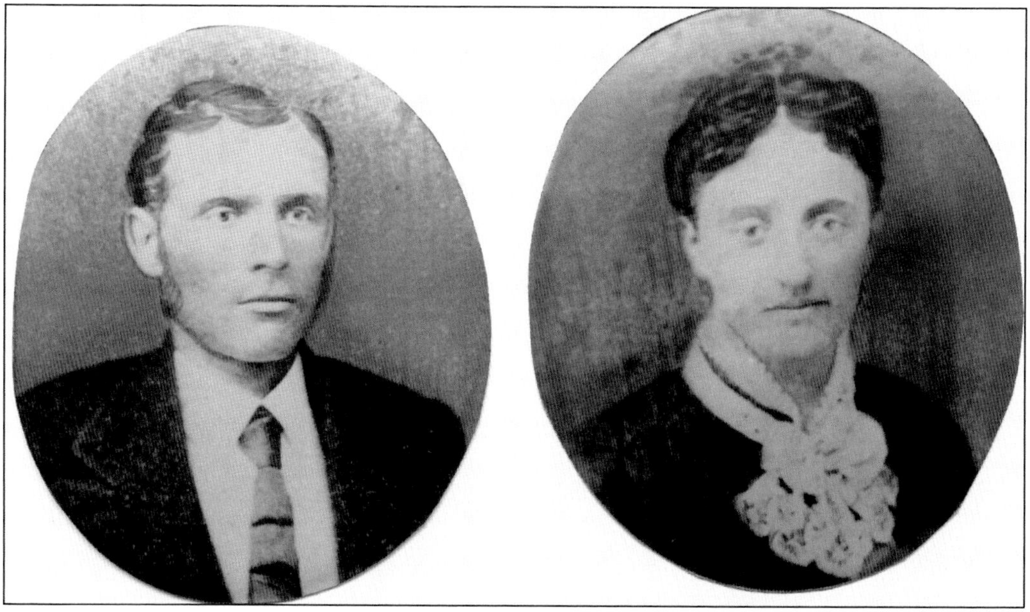

This is Alexander Hamilton Withey, son of Levious Withey and Charlotte (Rice) Withey, and his wife, Celia Ellen Watkins, daughter of John Watkins and Anne (Hoyle) Watkins, who owned a farm in section 11 of Alpine Township. Alexander became a representative for Farmers Handy Wagon Company in Saginaw. Celia was one of three sisters who died during childbirth. Celia's mother, Anne Watkins, kept a very sad diary that tells of her first daughter, Maria Watkins, who married Samuel Mead, son of Clark and Betsy Mead, of Alpine. Maria died in childbirth with her daughter, Ruth. Her second daughter, Celia Withey, died giving birth to her second son, Johny. Mary Watkins married Edgar Stage and died giving birth to son George.

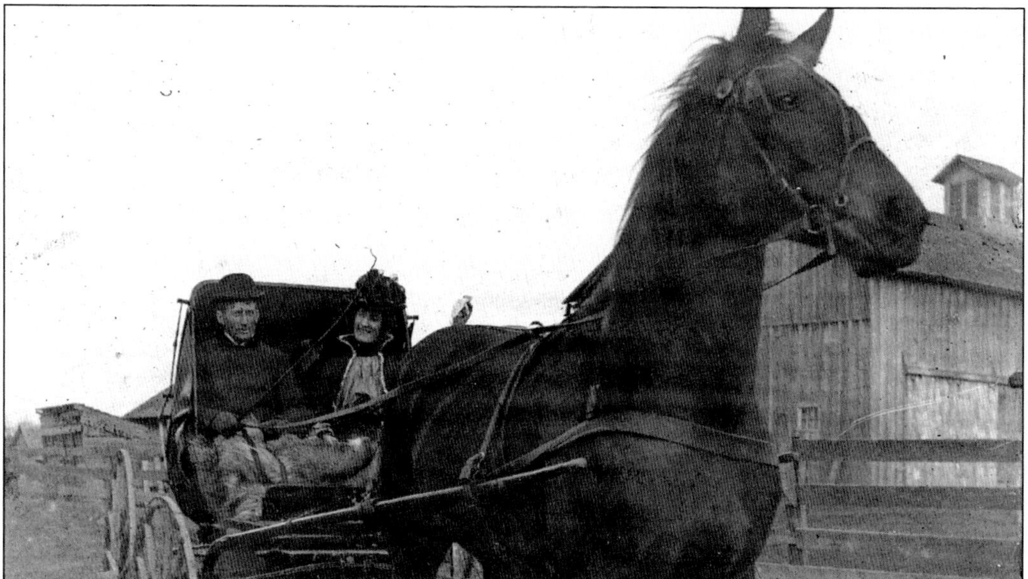

Gottfried Gork Jr. and his wife, Emma (Johnson Maves) Gork, were married in February 1904. This picture shows the pride people had in their good horses. They are on their farm pictured on page 50 of this book.

Five

WORKING

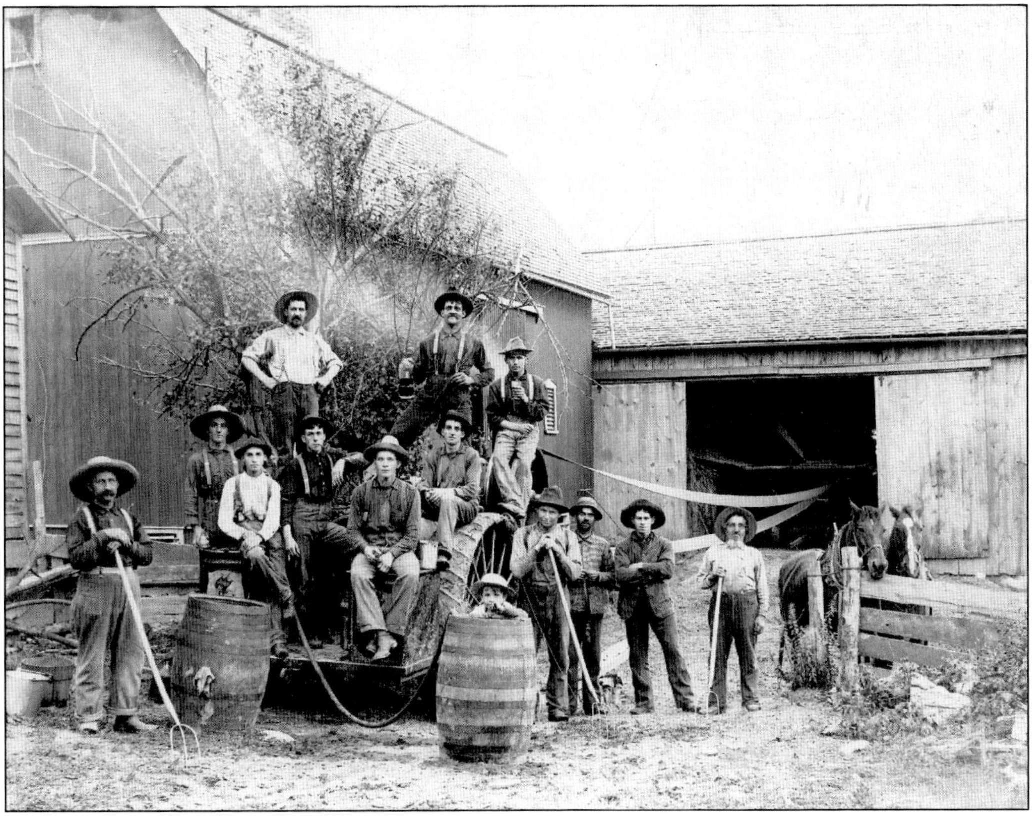

As farms were cleared and fields tilled, the annual thrashing of grains was done by crews. Thrashing was a big event on any farm. Here on the Vogels' farm are Jake and Philip Vogel, Frank Rusche, John Ebers, Joe Gorbert, Charles Vogel, Phil and Fred Davenport, Jacob Vogel, other unidentified threshers.

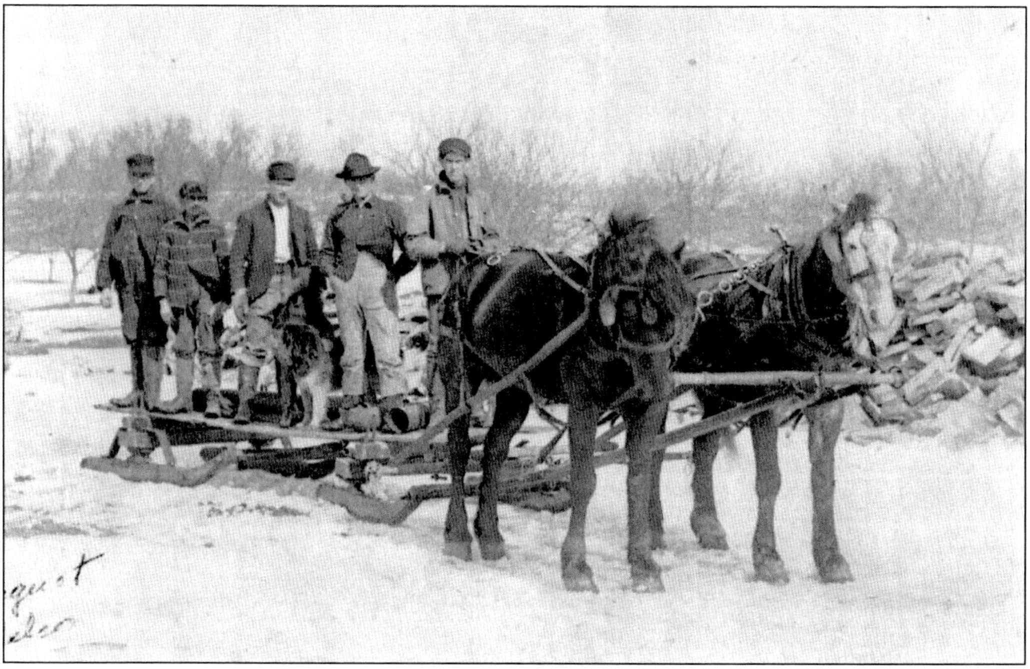

Enoch Armock and his work crew go out with a flatbed sleigh and a good team of horses.

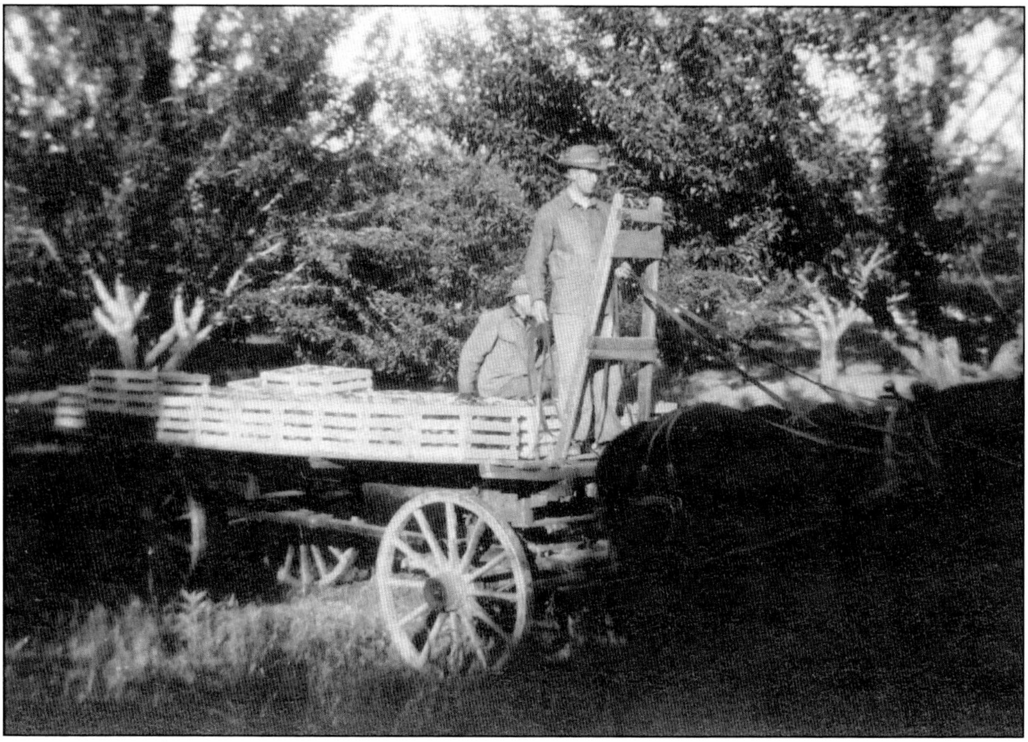

Ken Brown is hauling crates in the orchard. Alpine Township is part of the area called the Ridge. It is a hilly area in western Michigan that is ideal for growing fruit with Lake Michigan to the west.

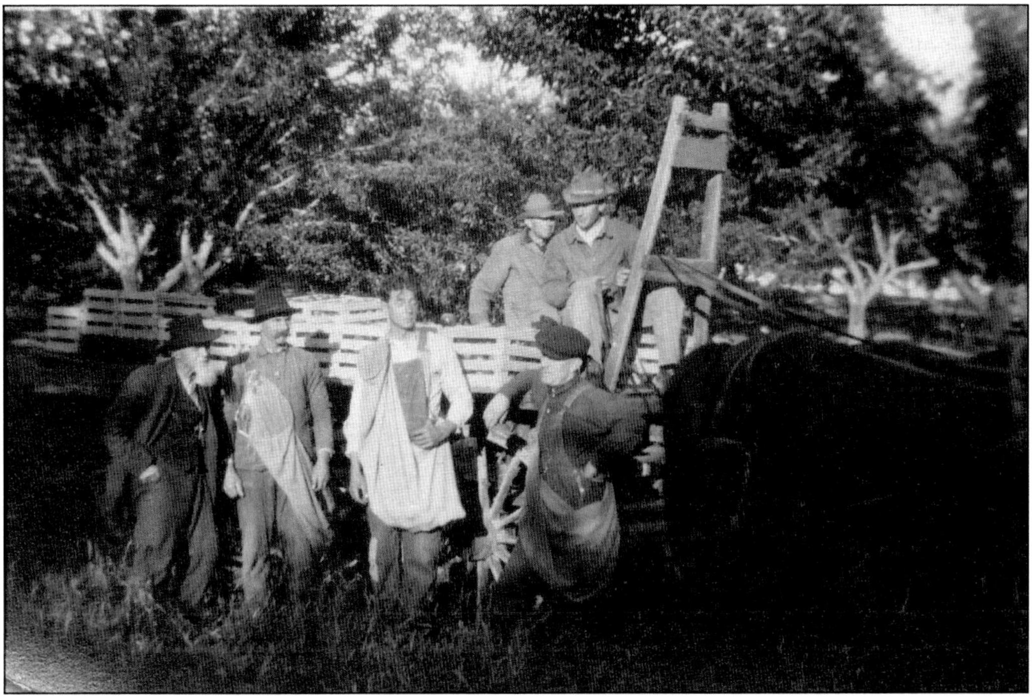

This apple-picking crew, on the Ken Brown farm, was kind enough to stop for a picture. The crew members have picking sacks around their necks that they empty into the wooden crates on the wagon.

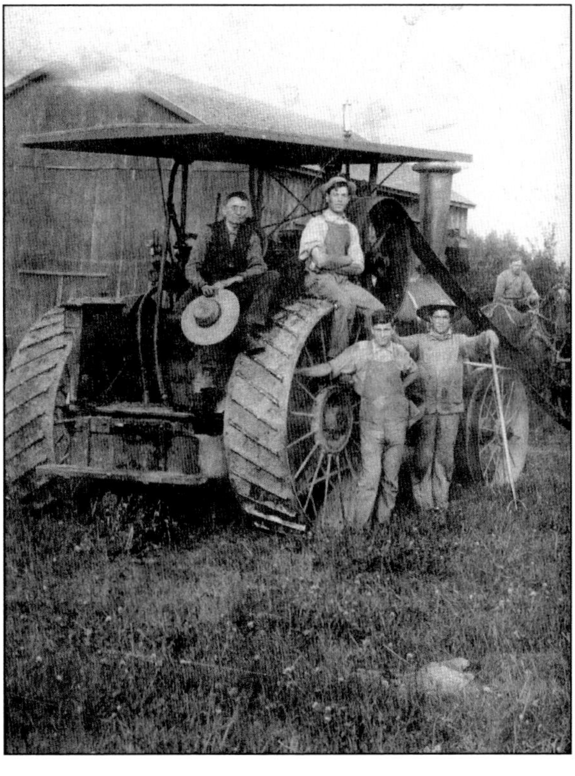

This is a threshing machine working on the Chase family farm.

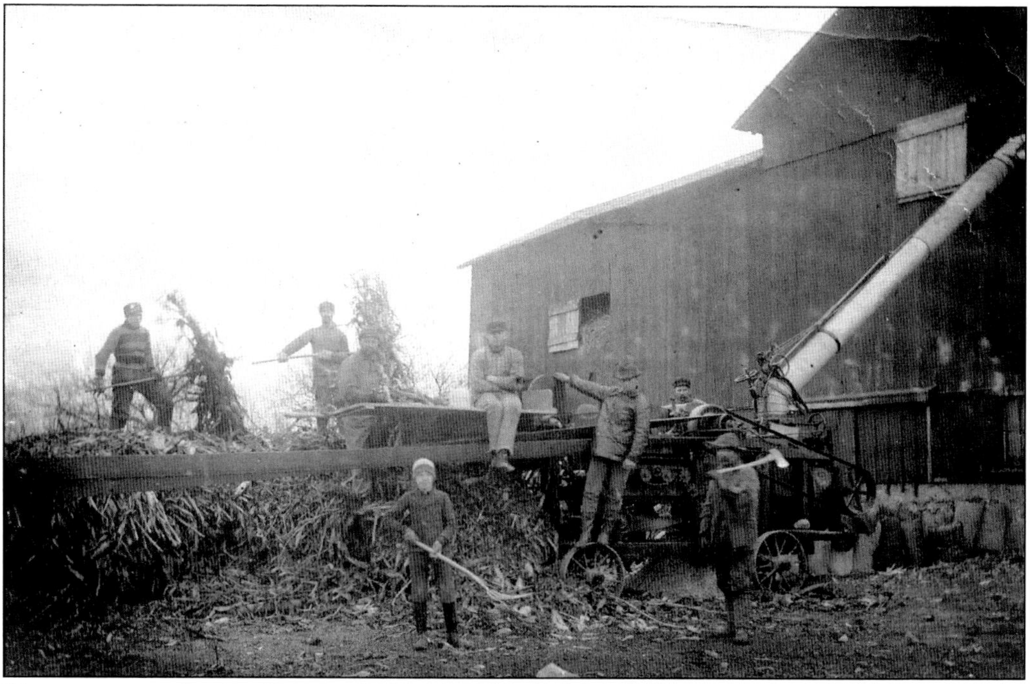

These men stop for the photographer as they fill the barn with corn at the Coffee farm on Fruit Ridge Avenue.

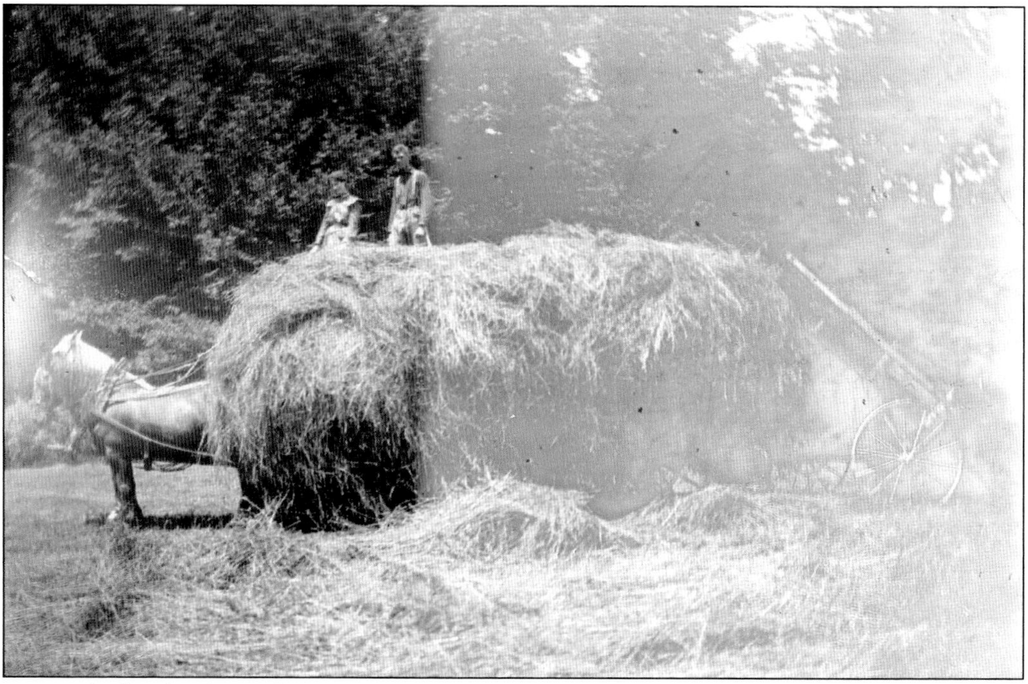

Notice the hay loader in the rear in this photograph as two people in the Coffee family start the ride to the barn on top of the load of hay pulled by a team of horses.

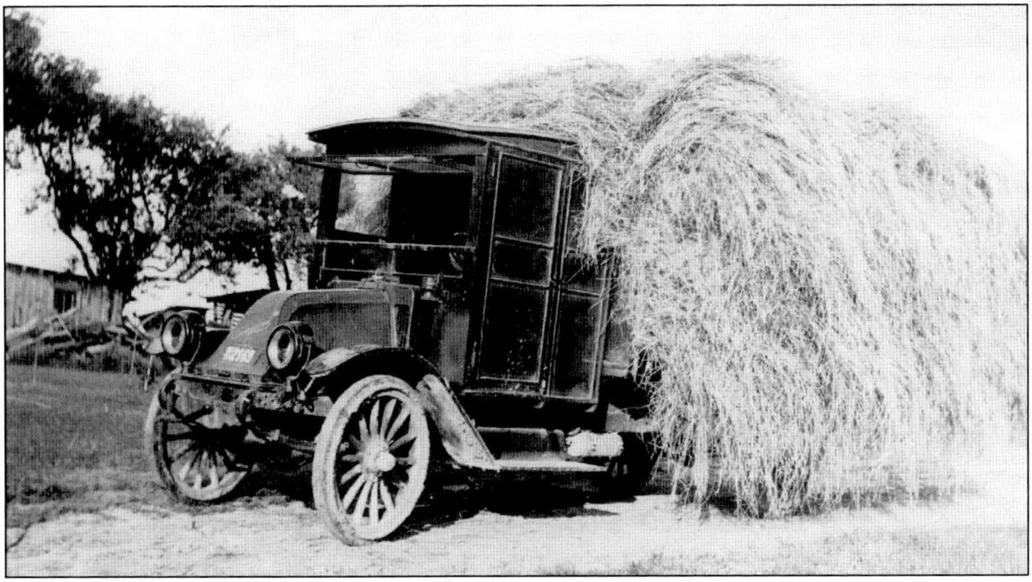

The Coffee farm truck is hauling a load of hay around 1919.

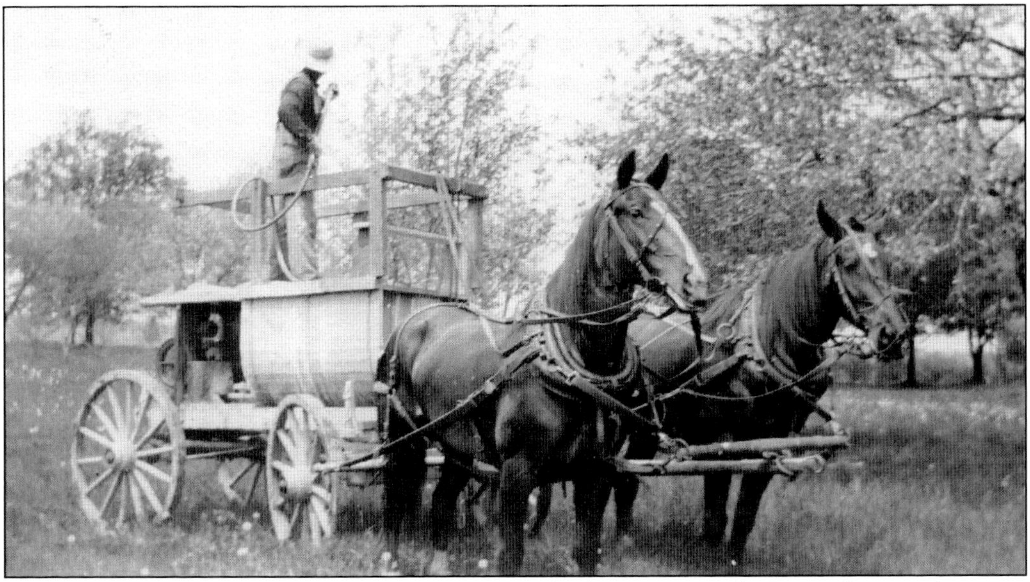

The grower stands high on the wagon as he sprays the fruit trees on the Bettes farm, with a team of horses pulling the wagon.

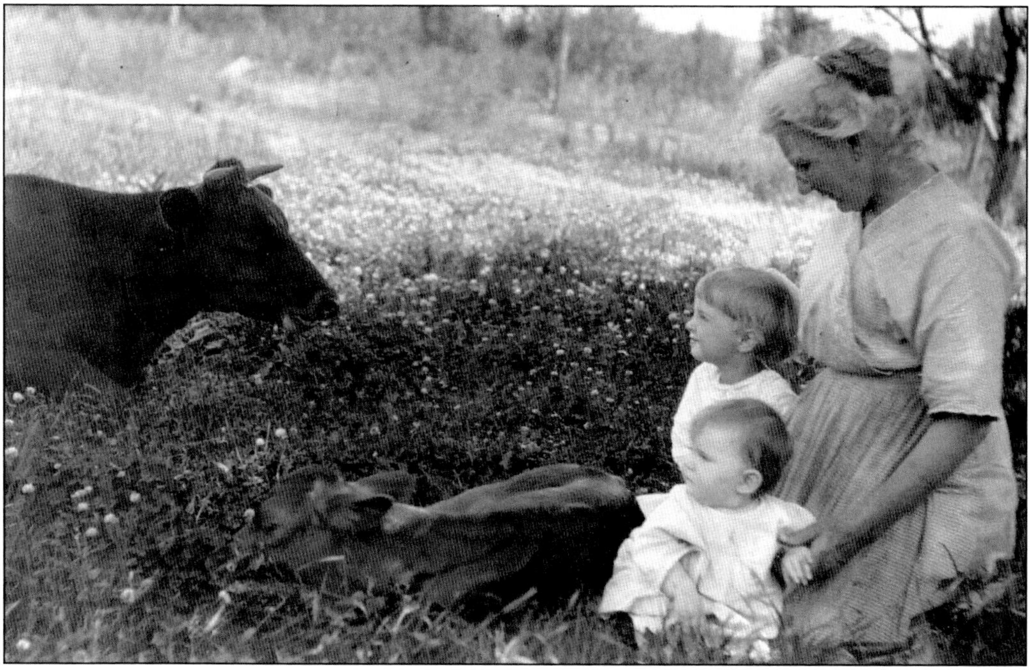

Grandma Sarah (Gooding) Coffee was known for being good with animals. Here she sits with two grandchildren, Maurine and baby John Coffee, in a field with a cow and a calf.

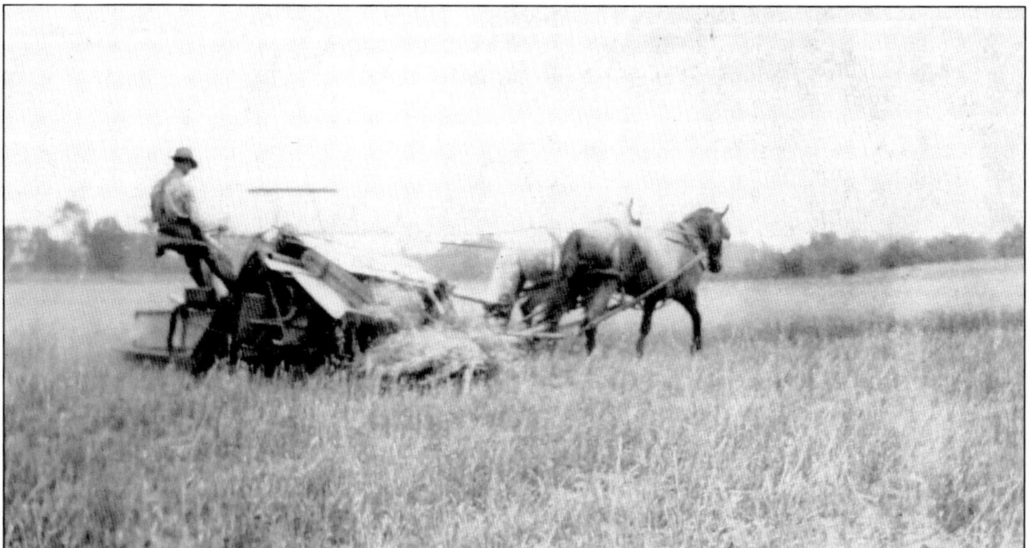

Watson Coffee has a team of horses to help him run the binder in his field on Six Mile Road and Hendershot Avenue. The bundles are set up to dry before they are brought into the thrashing machine.

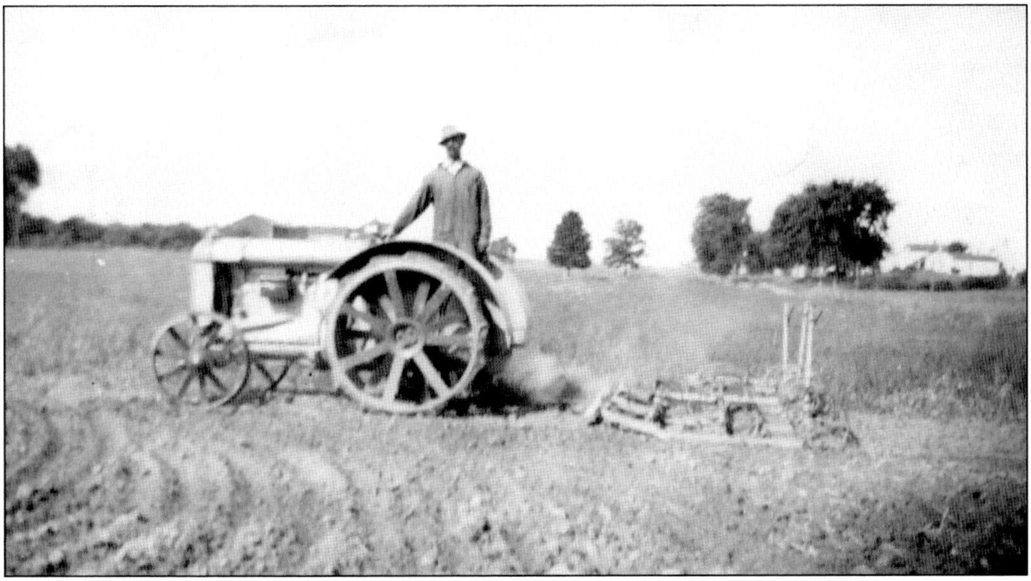

Watson Coffee is seen dragging his field at his farm on Six Mile Road and Hendershot Avenue. He is using a metal wheeled tractor.

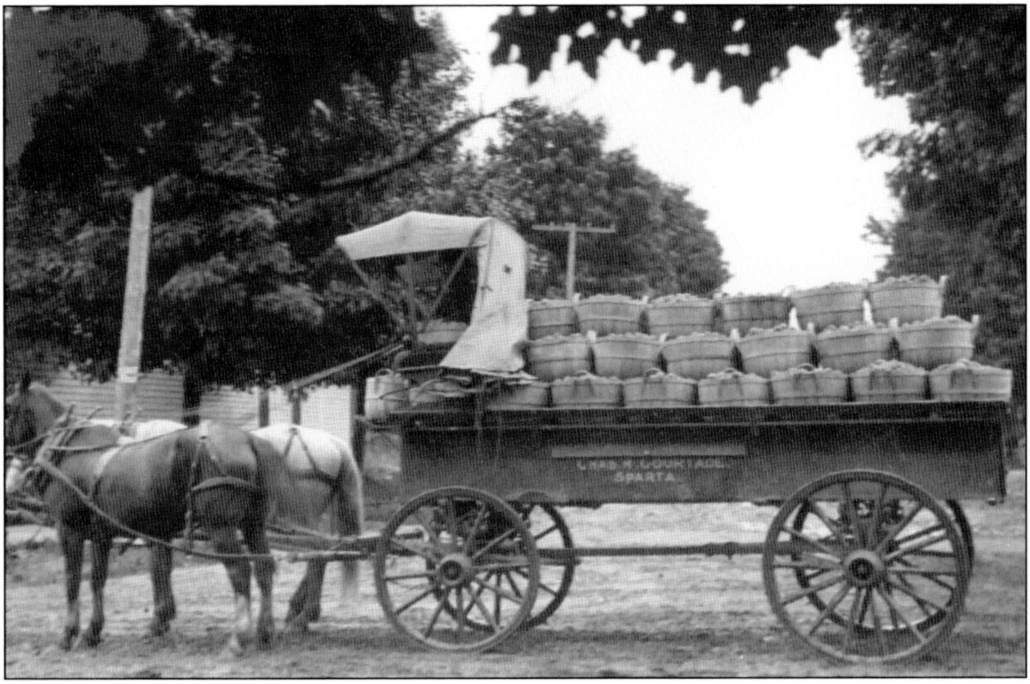

Charles Courtade, seen here with a load of peaches, served as Alpine Township supervisor from 1923 to 1925.

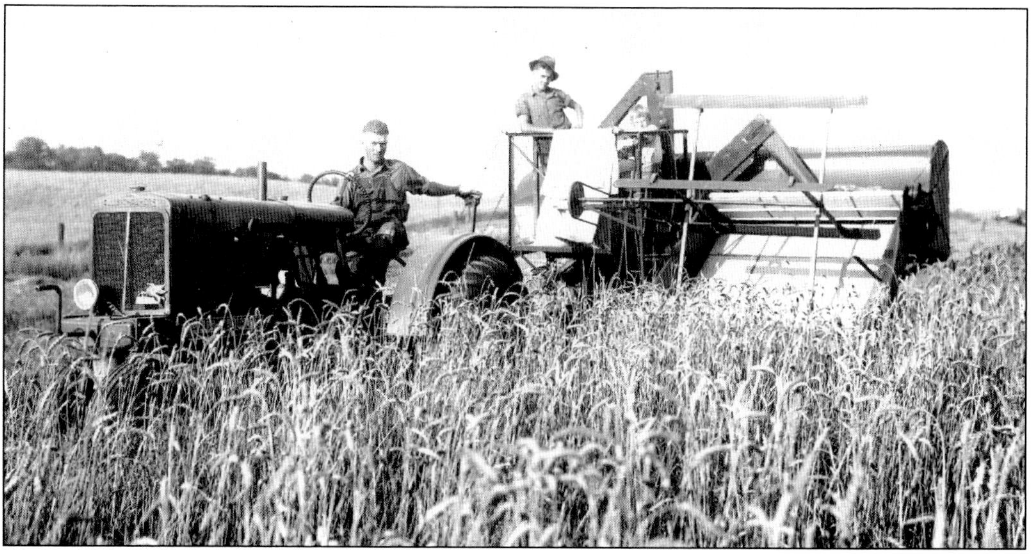

In 1937, Ken Cranmer and Carl Momber work with the Cranmer family combine that was said to be the first in Alpine Township. Other farmers were not sure it would work on the hills.

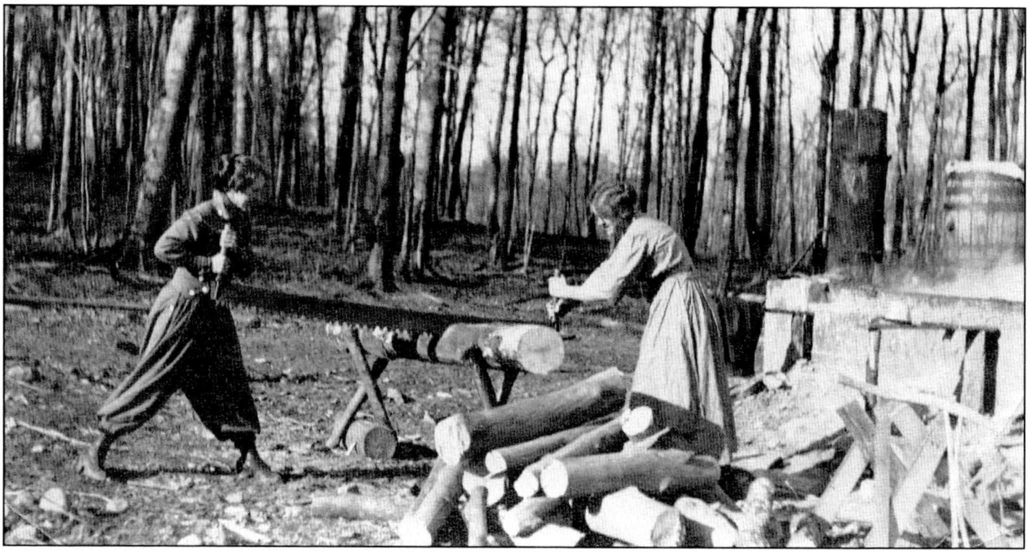

In 1912, Altie (left) and Mildred Cranmer are out cutting wood for the boiling down of maple sap.

Mildred Cranmer carries buckets from the maple trees on the Cranmer farm on Eight Mile Road. The maple trees' sap will be boiled down into maple syrup.

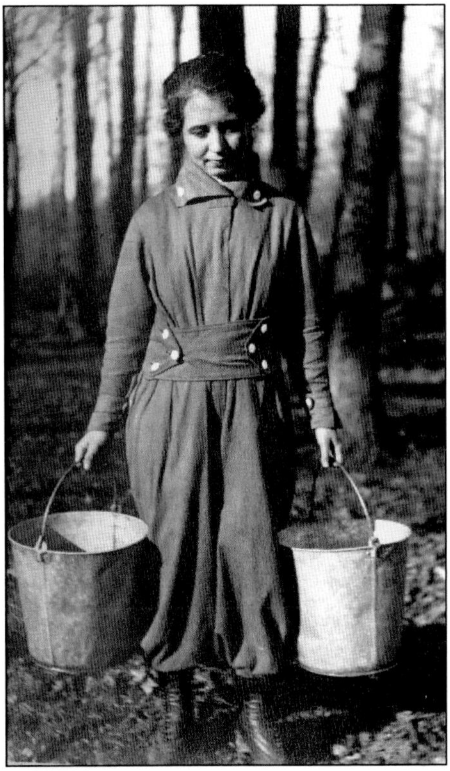

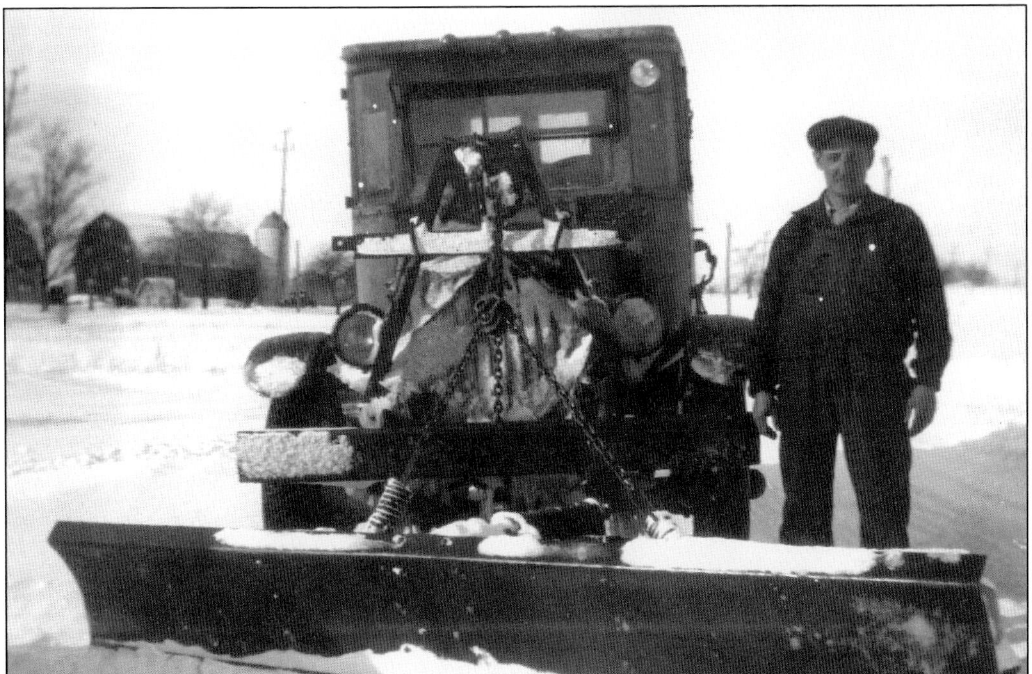

Fred Deiss works to plow the snow off the road. He was employed by the Kent County Road Commission.

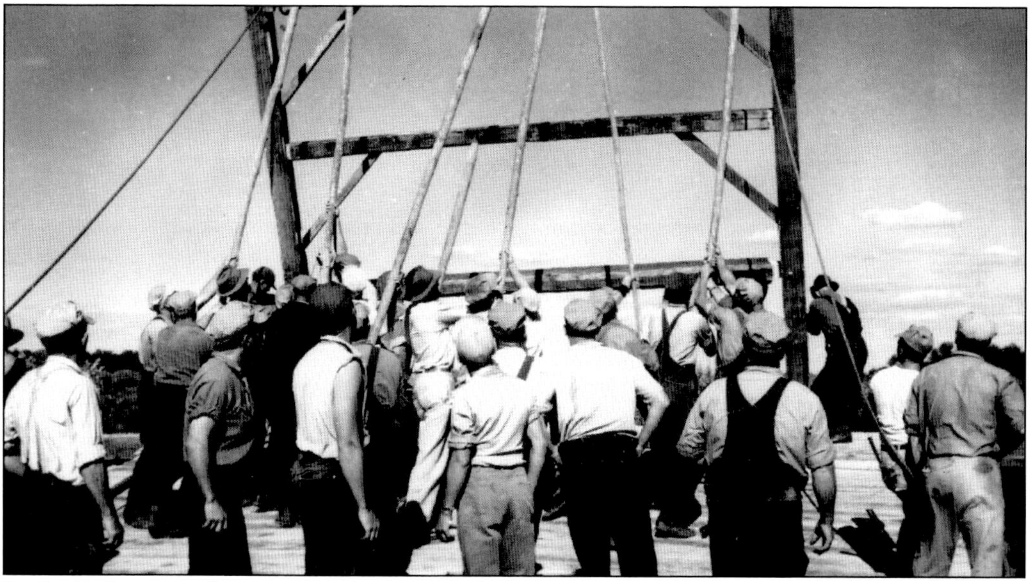

In the Ridge area of western Michigan, people can count on their neighbors in times of tragedy. Here neighbors in Alpine Township get together for a barn raising when the Dunneback family lost their barn to fire. The year before, they had lost their parents in an automobile accident at a train crossing.

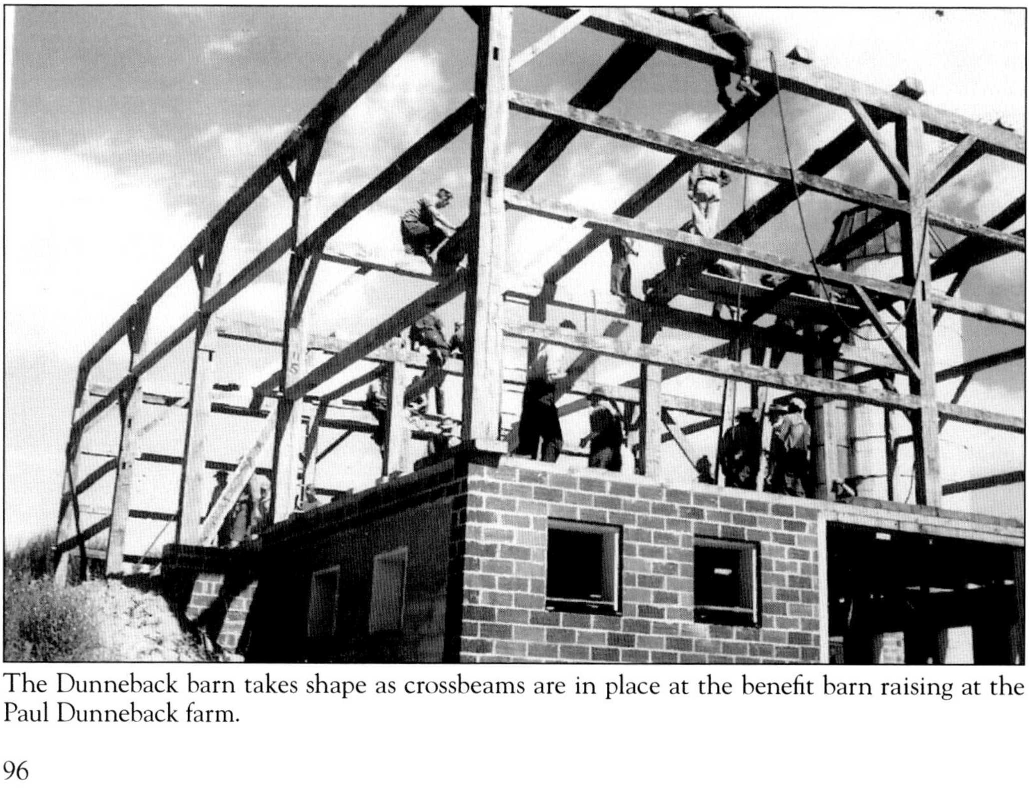

The Dunneback barn takes shape as crossbeams are in place at the benefit barn raising at the Paul Dunneback farm.

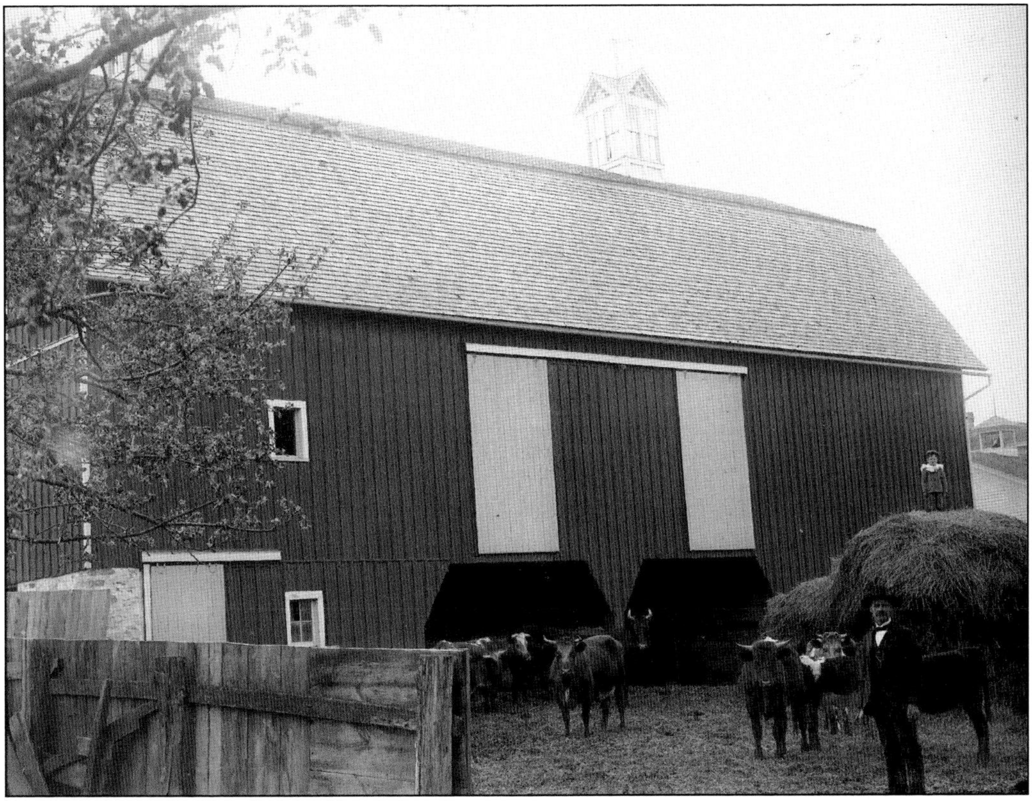

Frank Ebers stands in his barnyard with his cattle. He has put his son Avery out of harm's way on top of the pile of hay.

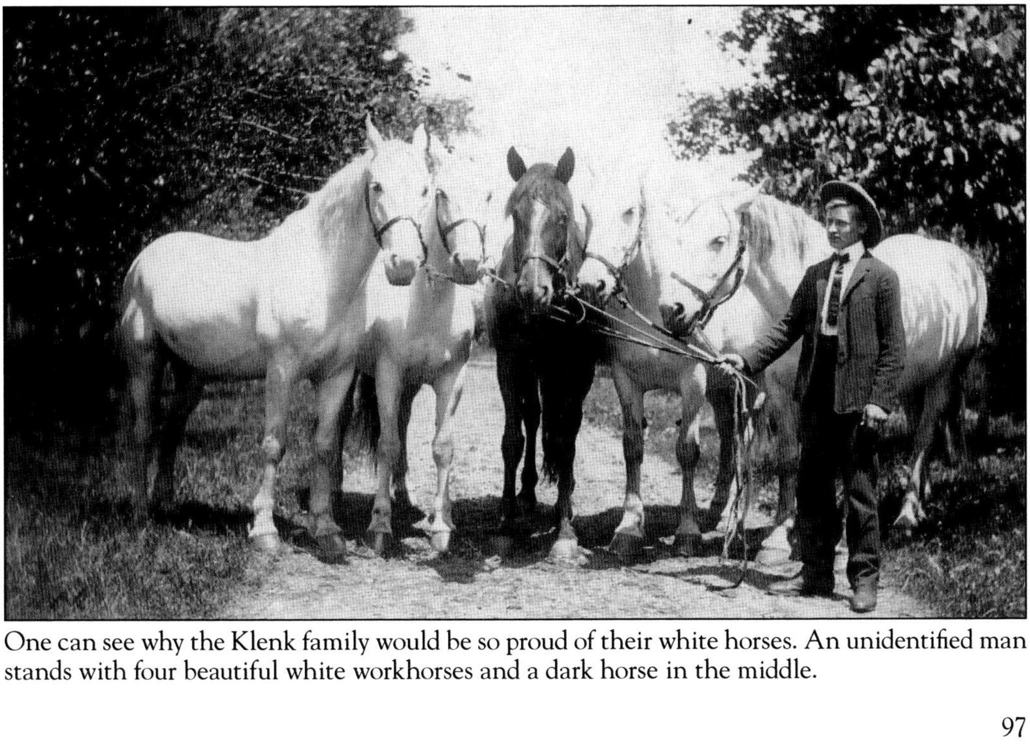

One can see why the Klenk family would be so proud of their white horses. An unidentified man stands with four beautiful white workhorses and a dark horse in the middle.

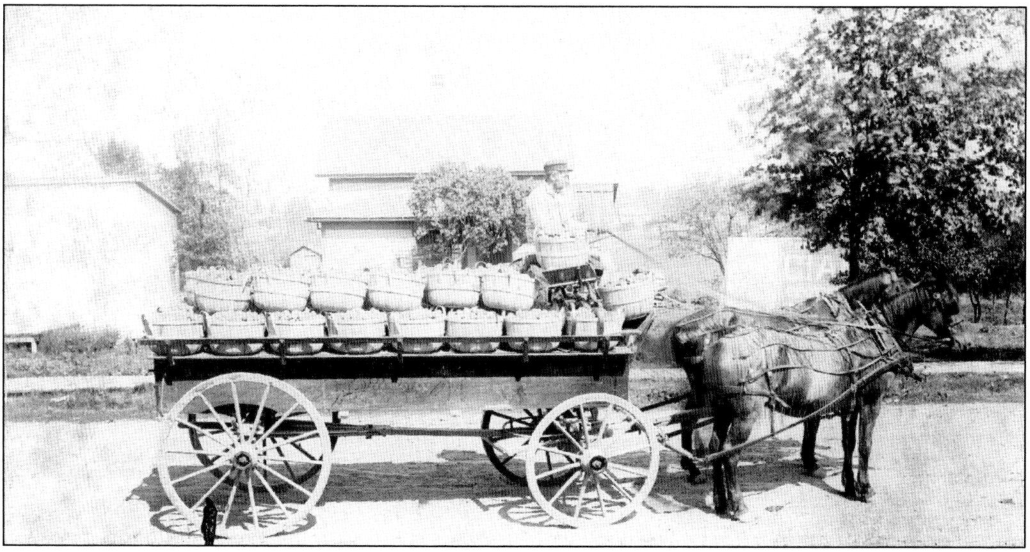

George Klenk goes to market with 54 bushels of potatoes. His horses have netting covering them to ward off flies.

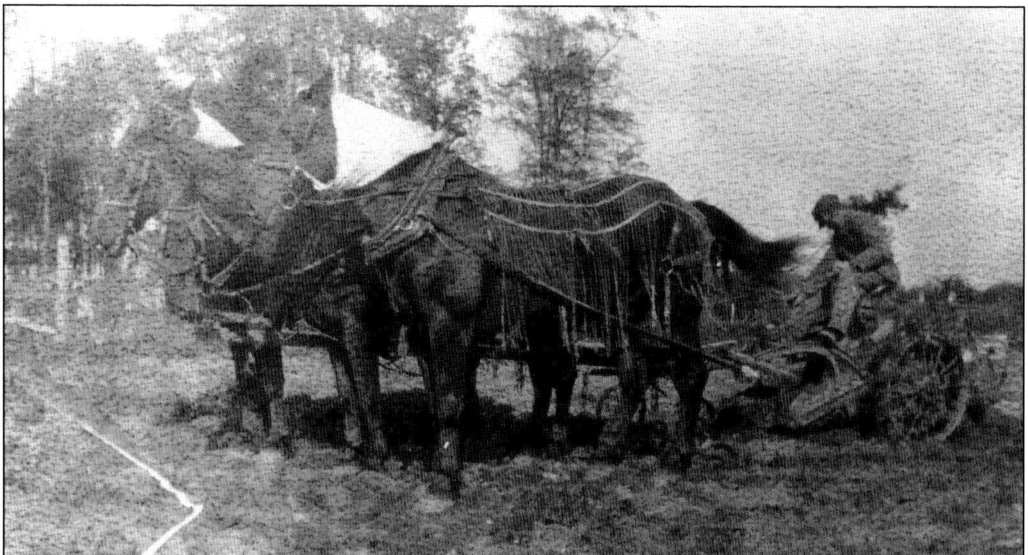

Joe Kline, on Fruit Ridge Avenue, not only has netting on his horses' backs, he also has white scarves on the outside horses' heads to keep the flies away as he plows the field.

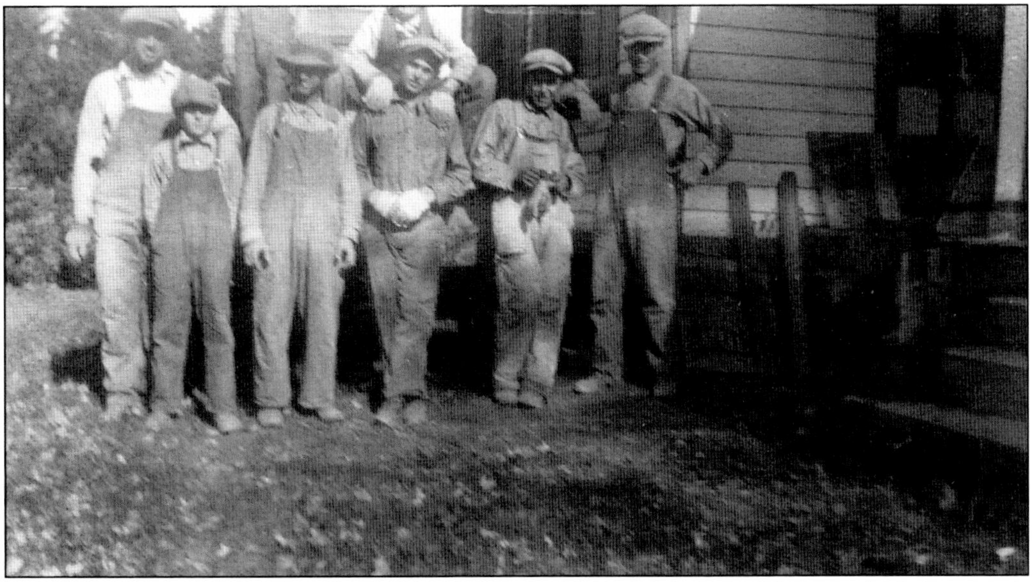
These are the potato pickers on the Kline farm. Ray Kline is the young boy on the left.

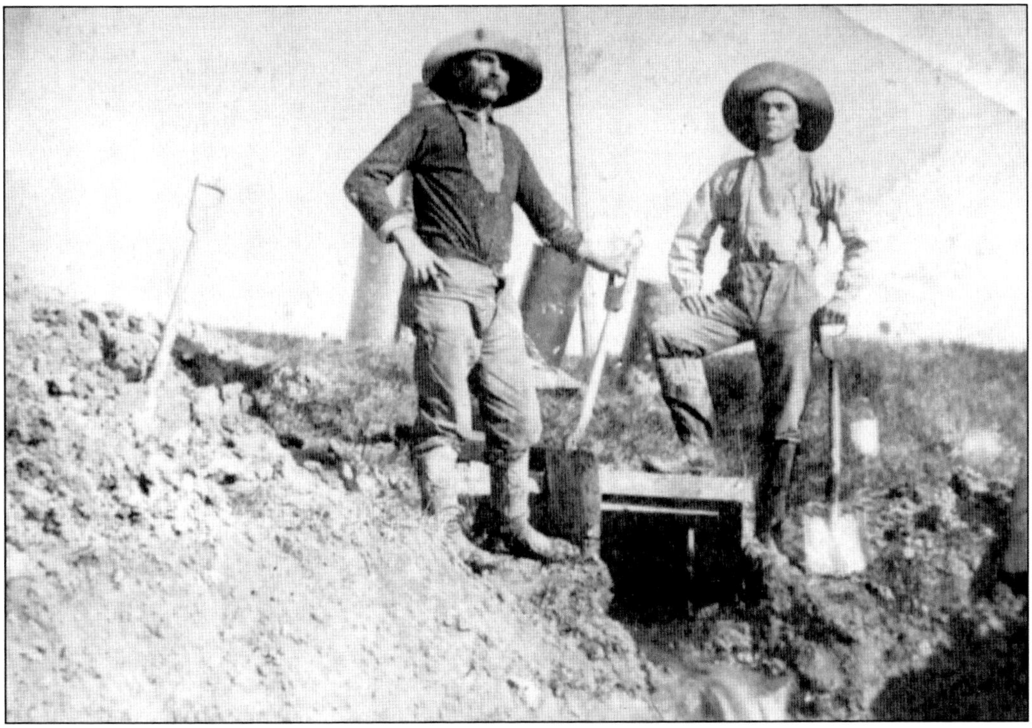
This picture of Henry Stevens, on the left, and Joseph Steffens was taken about 1885 at the bridge over Mill Creek on what is now Michigan 37, north of Eight Mile Road.

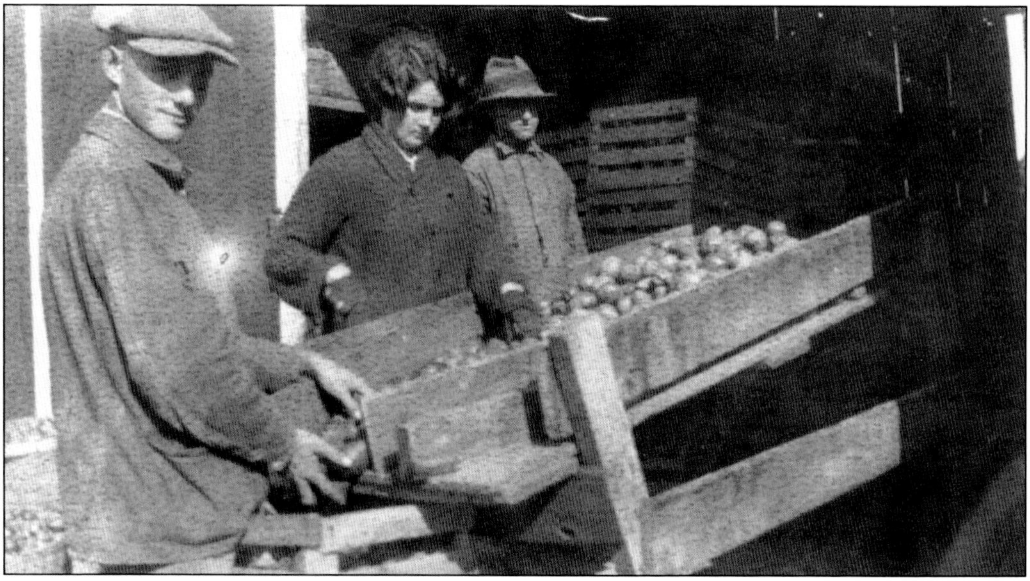

After picking the potatoes, they are sorted by, from left to right, Reynold, Cecilia (Scheidel), and Bill Kline. Then off they go to sell at a market.

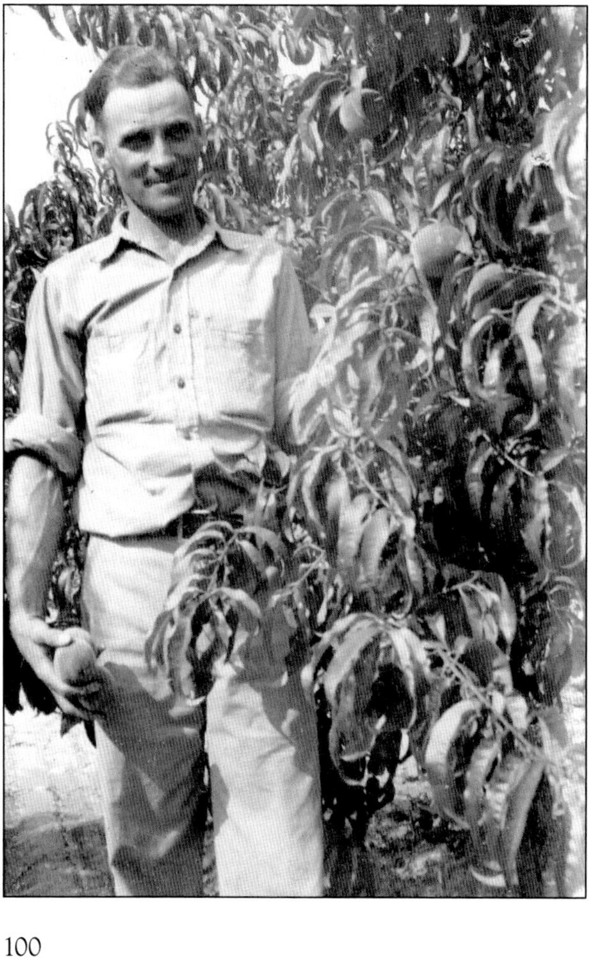

Robert Joseph Kline stands by his peach tree. It looks like the peaches are ready for a pie. Kline married Janet Hahn, who taught at the local Boyd School.

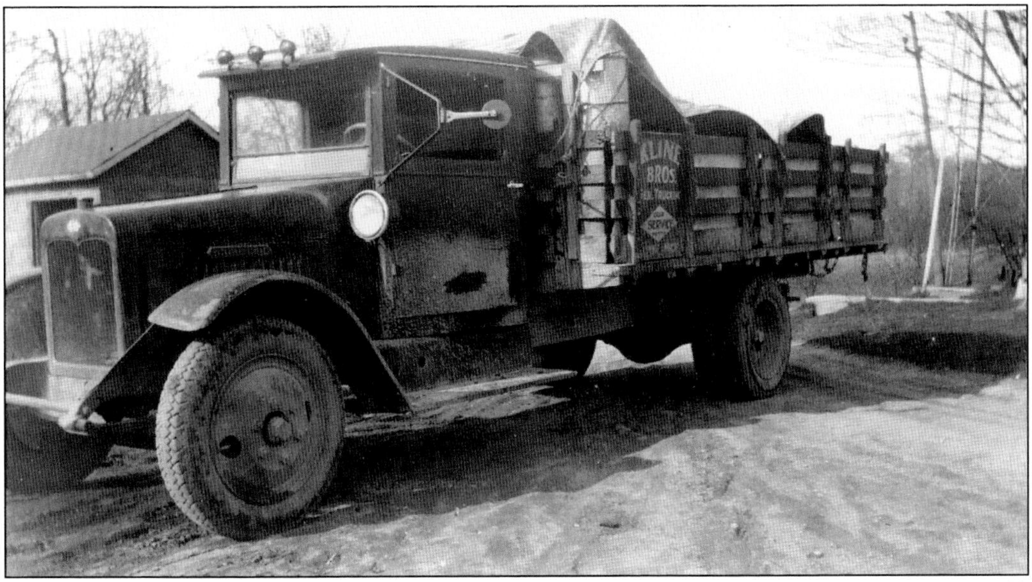

Robert J. Kline and his brother Reynold F. Kline hauled milk for dairy farmers. This is their milk truck parked next to the "milk house" at their farm on Fruit Ridge Avenue.

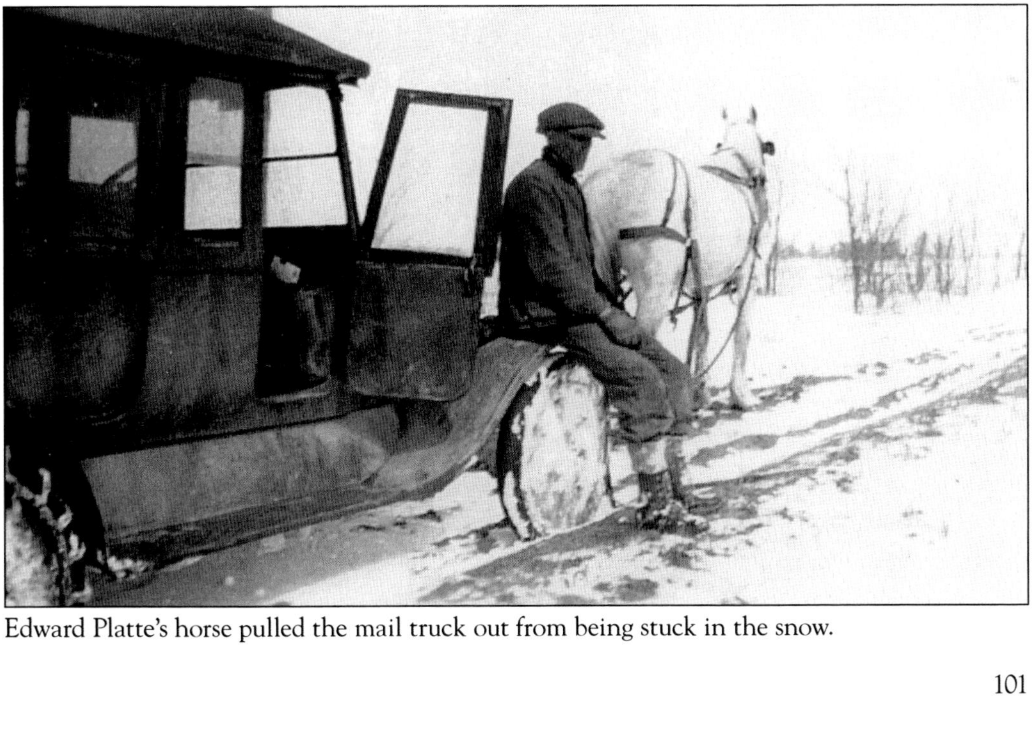

Edward Platte's horse pulled the mail truck out from being stuck in the snow.

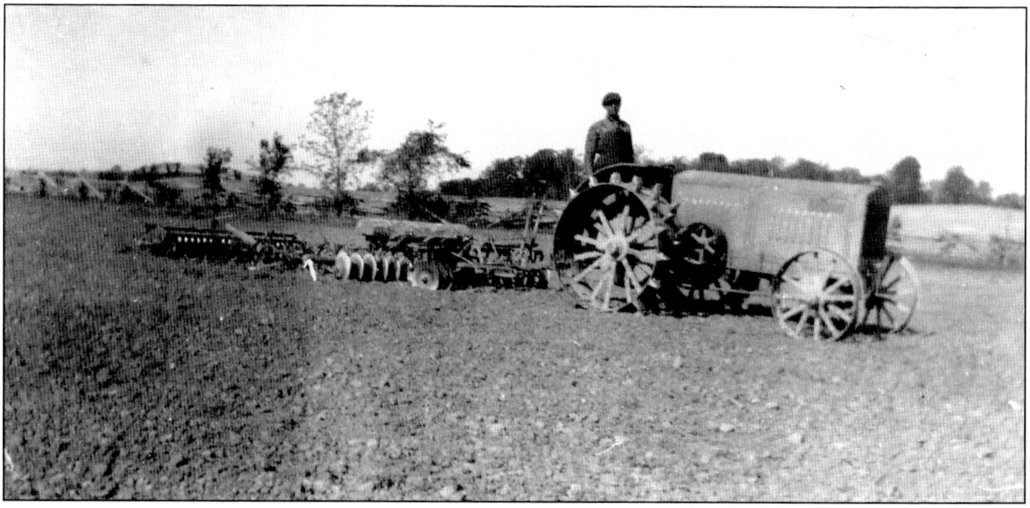

Robert G. Rasch is disking in an area he called "the flats" at the west end of his farm on Stage Avenue. Those metal tires look like they can get through any field of mud.

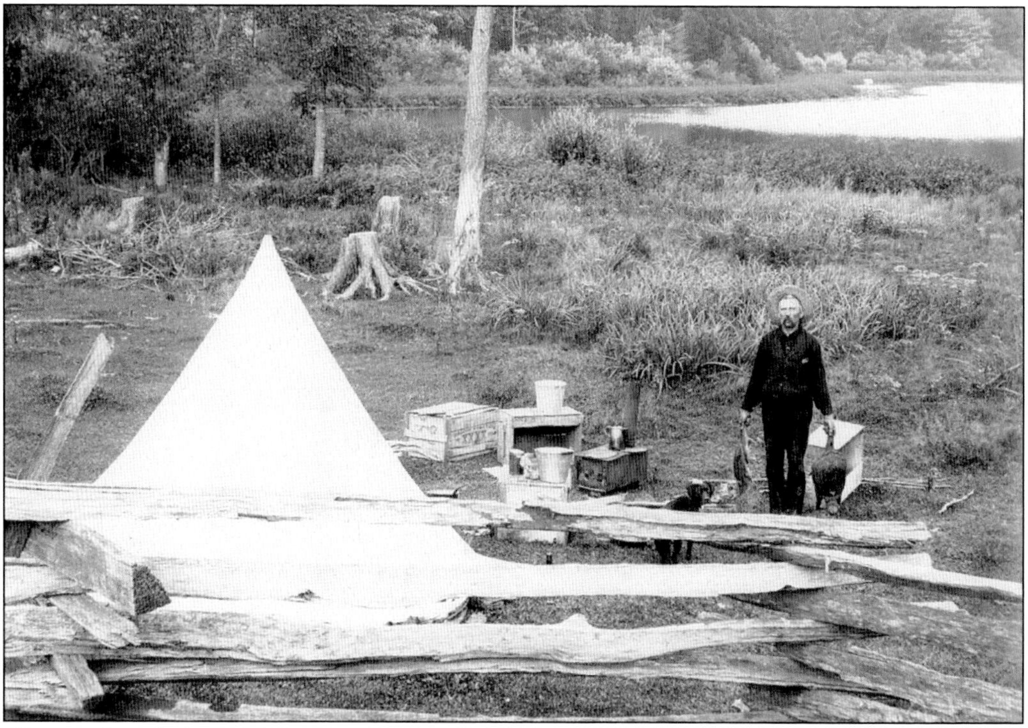

This unidentified man has set up camp on the Ruthardt farm with Baumhoff Lake in the distance. His dog turns to the photographer as the man holds the day's catch of turtles.

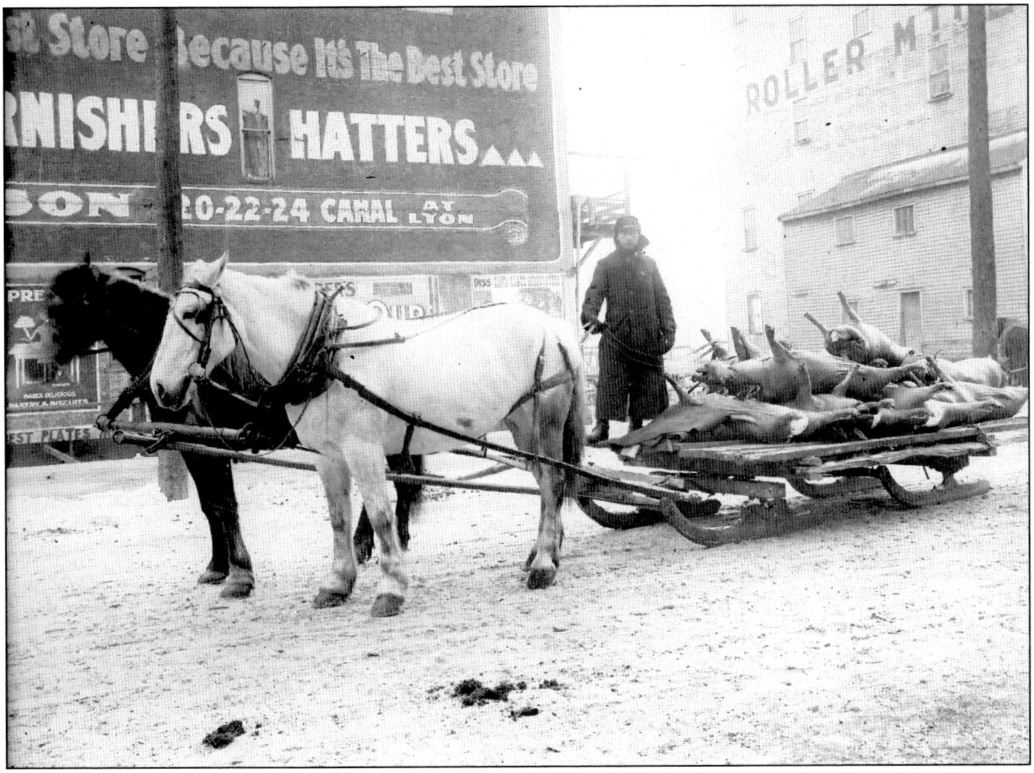

In 1902, Joseph Schindler is taking a load of butchered hogs to the meat wholesale market in Grand Rapids with his team of horses and a sleigh.

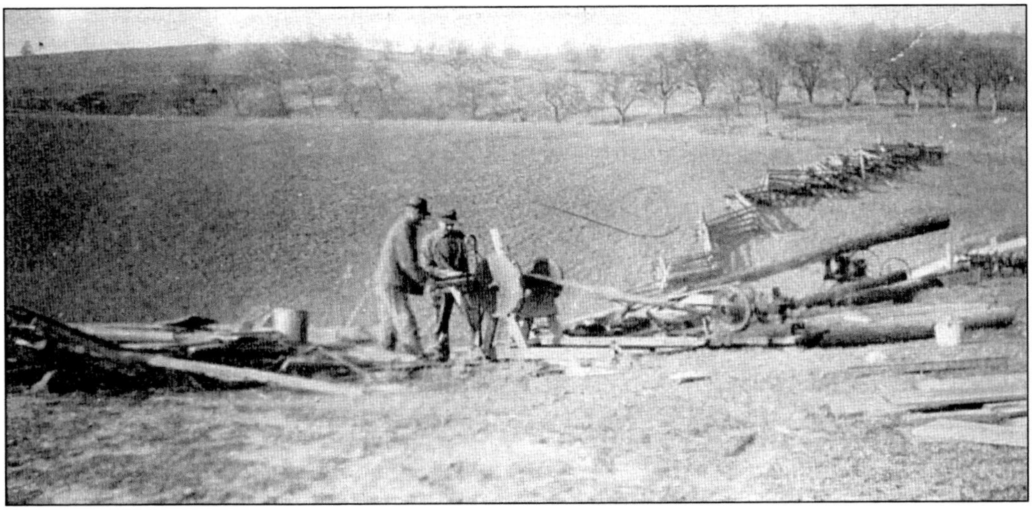

Fred and Joe Schweitzer are working up the hill with a fence. The beautiful rolling hills with an orchard can be seen in the distance.

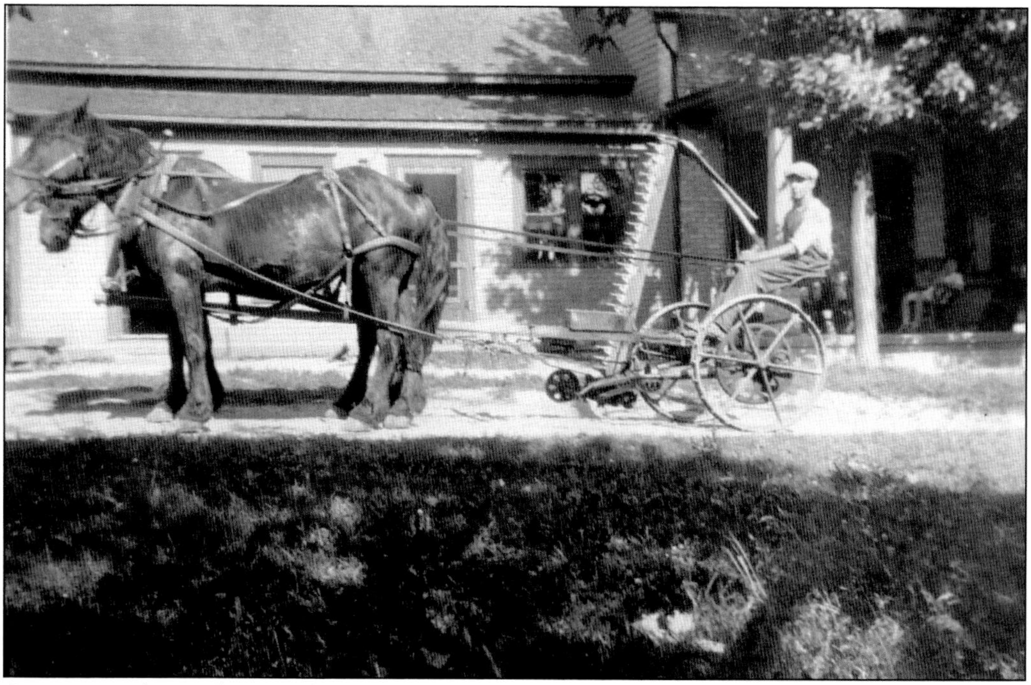

Gustov Vogel is ready to cut hay in his field with a good team of horses.

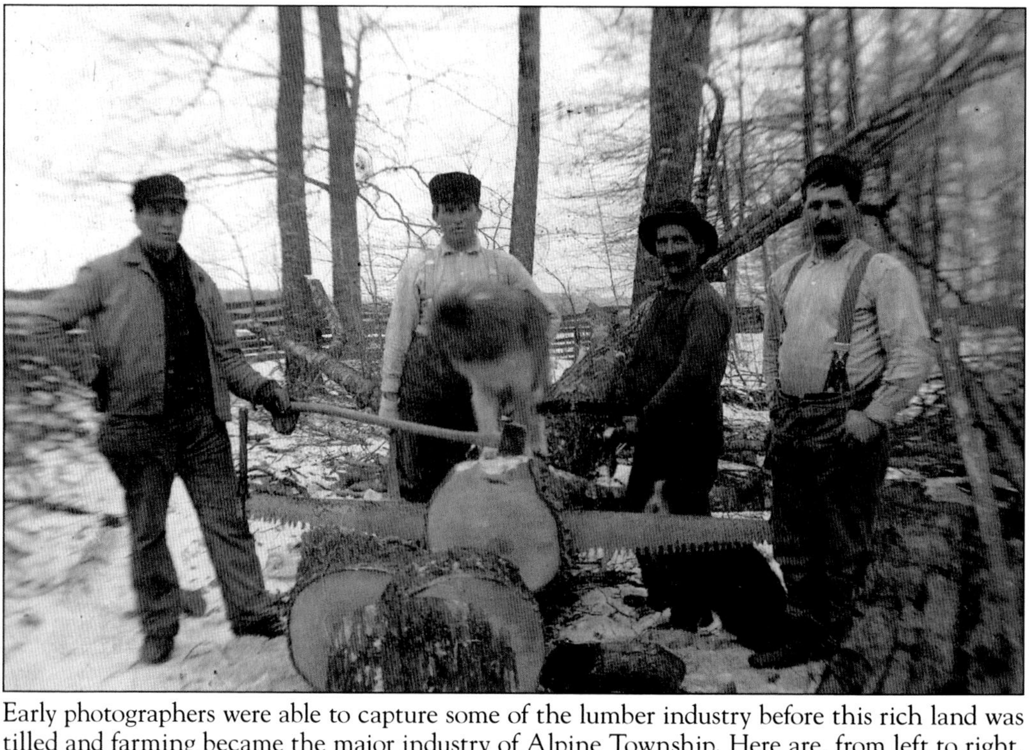

Early photographers were able to capture some of the lumber industry before this rich land was tilled and farming became the major industry of Alpine Township. Here are, from left to right, William O'Toole, Frank Rusche, Porter Vinton, and Jake Vogel with ax and saw, cutting down trees. The dog on the log would not stand still for the photograph.

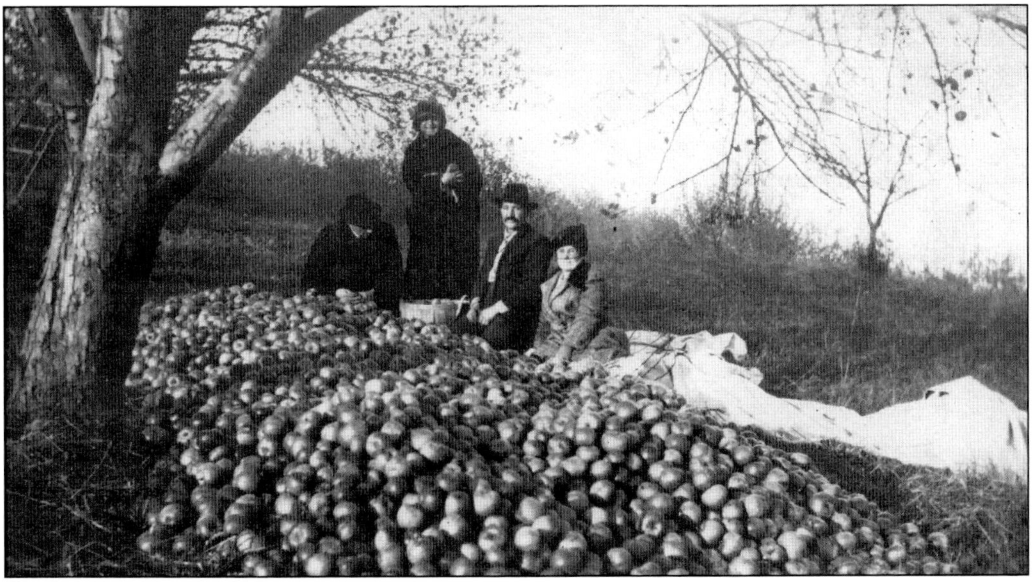

When one did not have baskets or barrels, the apples would be put on the ground. Here the Vogel family picks up some of their harvest.

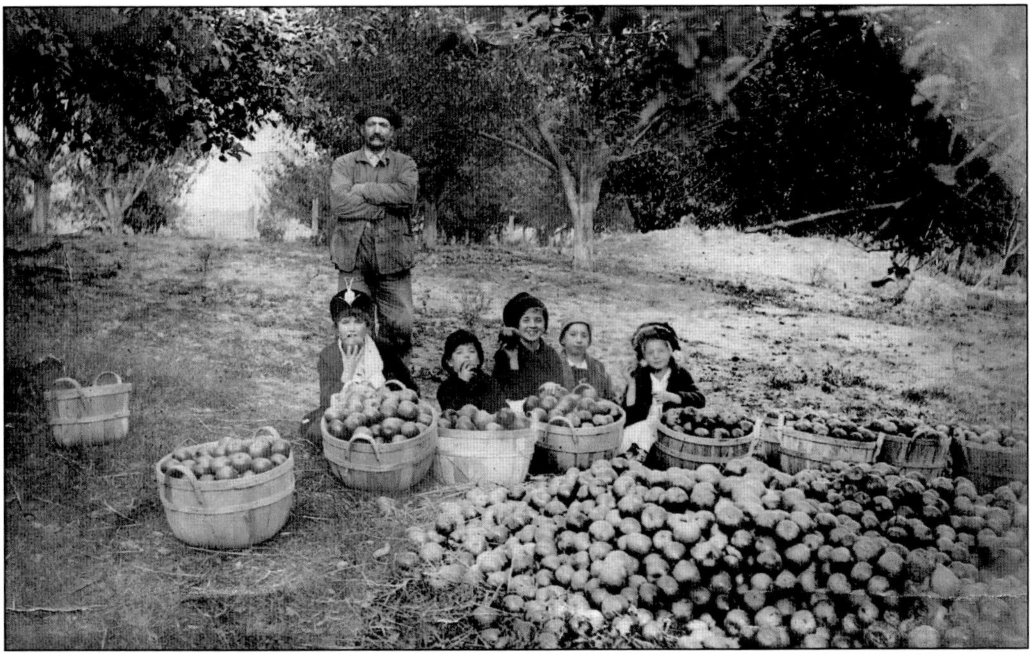

Jacob Vogel is out picking apples with a group of children in his orchard on Eight Mile Road. It looks like they are putting the apples in the baskets.

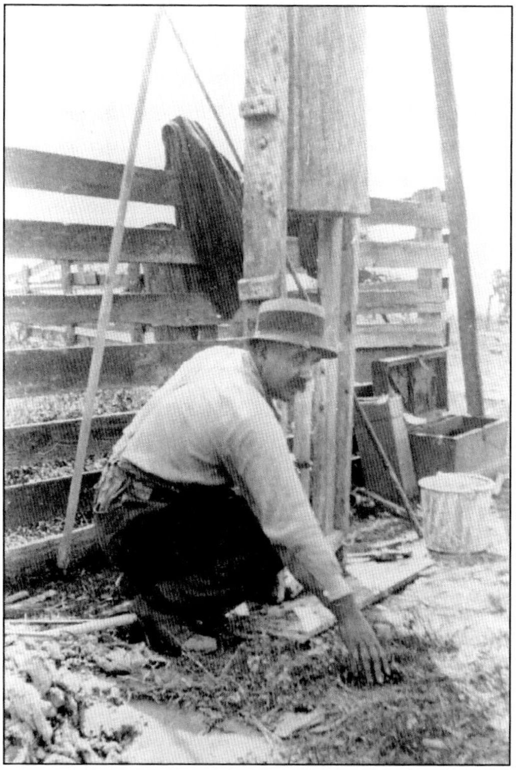

Theodore Cordes did not want to dig a well himself, so he found Charles Wahlfield in Dorr and brought him to Alpine Township. Wahlfield would go from farm to farm digging wells. People would feed him and put him up for the night.

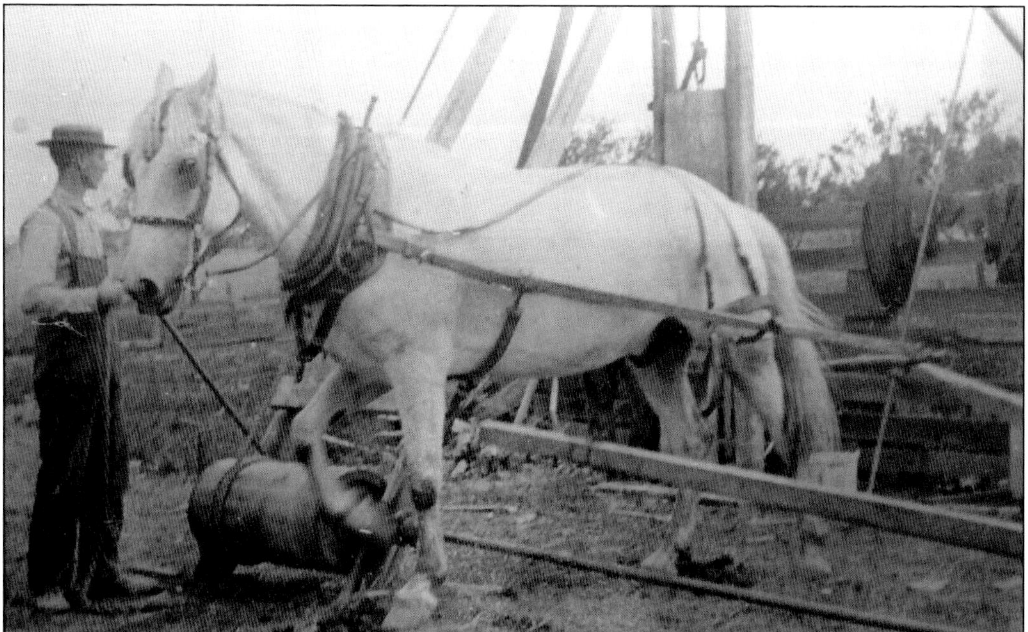

Charles's son Edward Wahlfield has a rope and pulley system going up and down with a 200-pound block to drive the pipe into the ground for a well. The power came from the horse going around in a circle, turning a small shaft that wound the pulley rope on a drum.

Six

CHURCHES

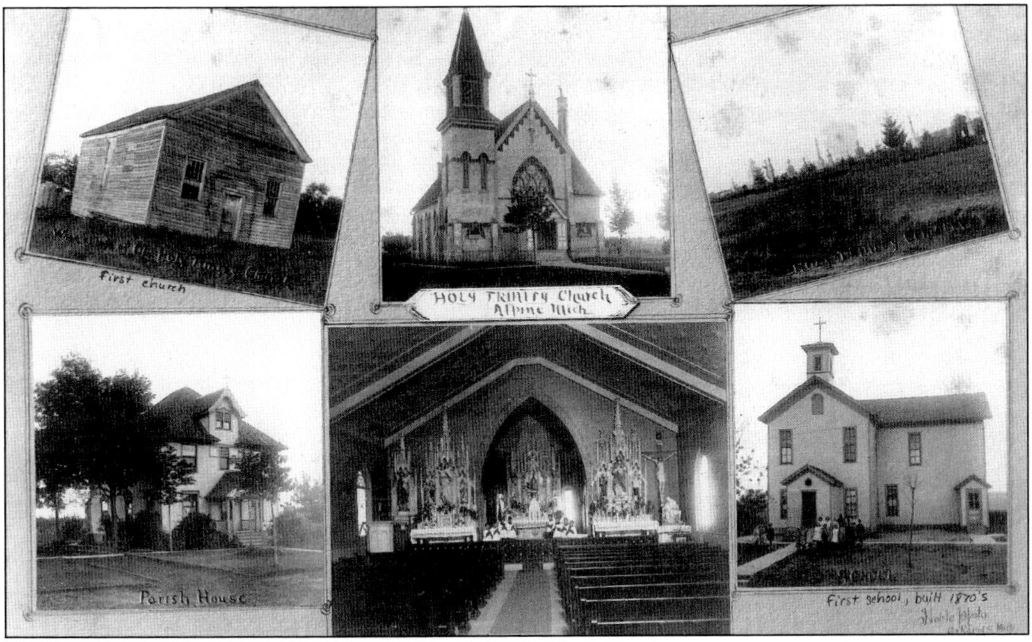

In 1848, the first church building for Holy Trinity Catholic parish was built on three acres donated by John Omlor on Baumhoff Avenue and Five Mile Road. On this postcard, all the buildings that went down in the April 11, 1965, tornado can be seen. The trees in the cemetery are small here. They grew to make this parish cemetery a very peaceful place to walk. All the trees are now gone.

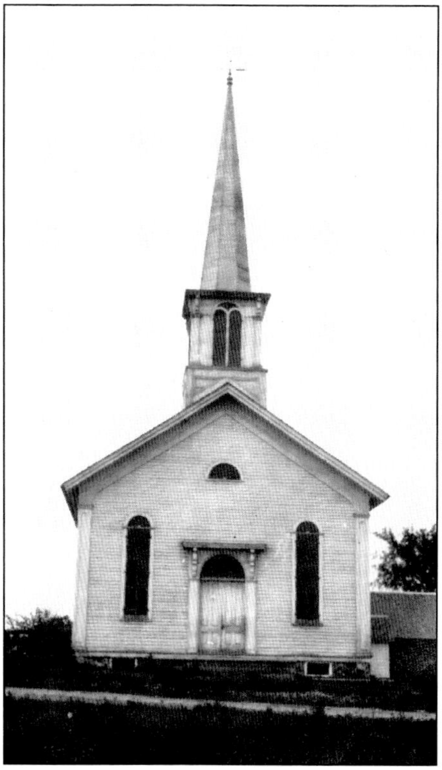

The registered name of the church on Ten Mile Road, west of Alpine Avenue, was the First Church of Alpine and Sparta at Ballards. This church still stands at the corner known as Ballards Corner. It was established in 1861.

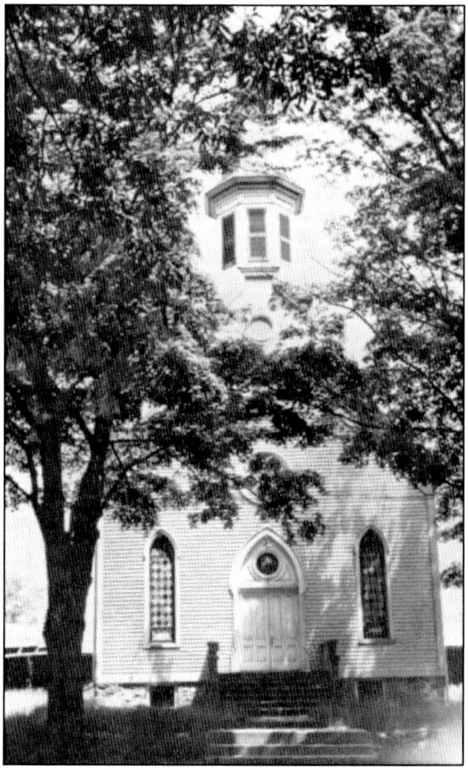

In 1868, the group that formed the Trinity Congregational faith community held meetings at Mill Pond School. James Bettes built this church, which was financed by Solomon Wright. It was dedicated on December 19, 1873. This first church building was destroyed in the 1965 Palm Sunday tornado.

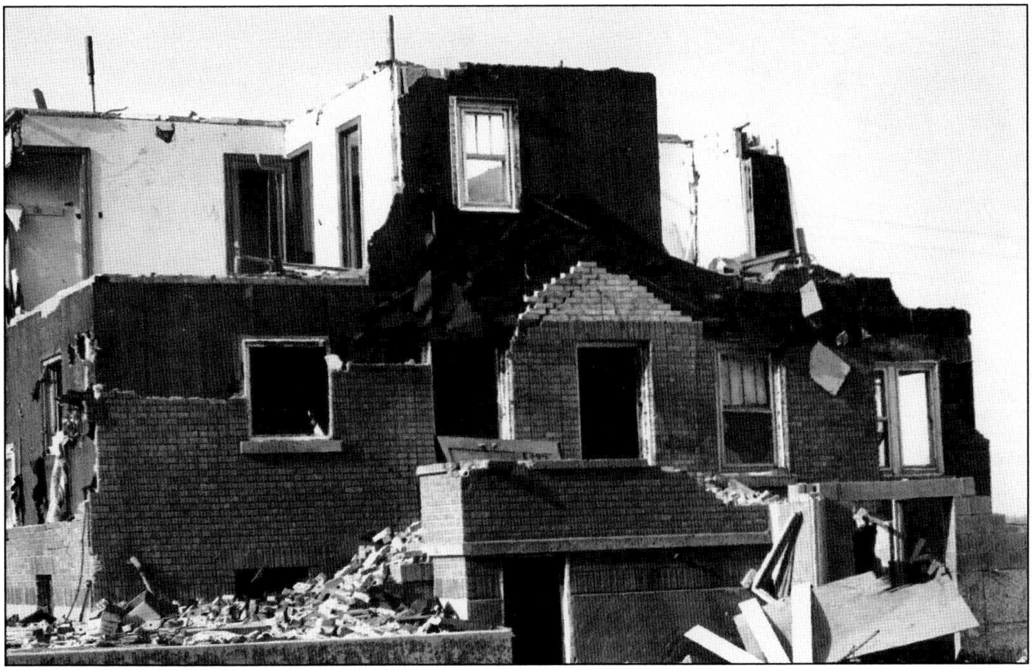

Alpine Township's greatest natural disaster was the Palm Sunday tornado that swept from southwest to northeast on Sunday, April 11, 1965. It severely damaged both Trinity Congregational Church on Four Mile Road and the Holy Trinity Church buildings. This is what was left of the priest's residence at the Holy Trinity parish grounds.

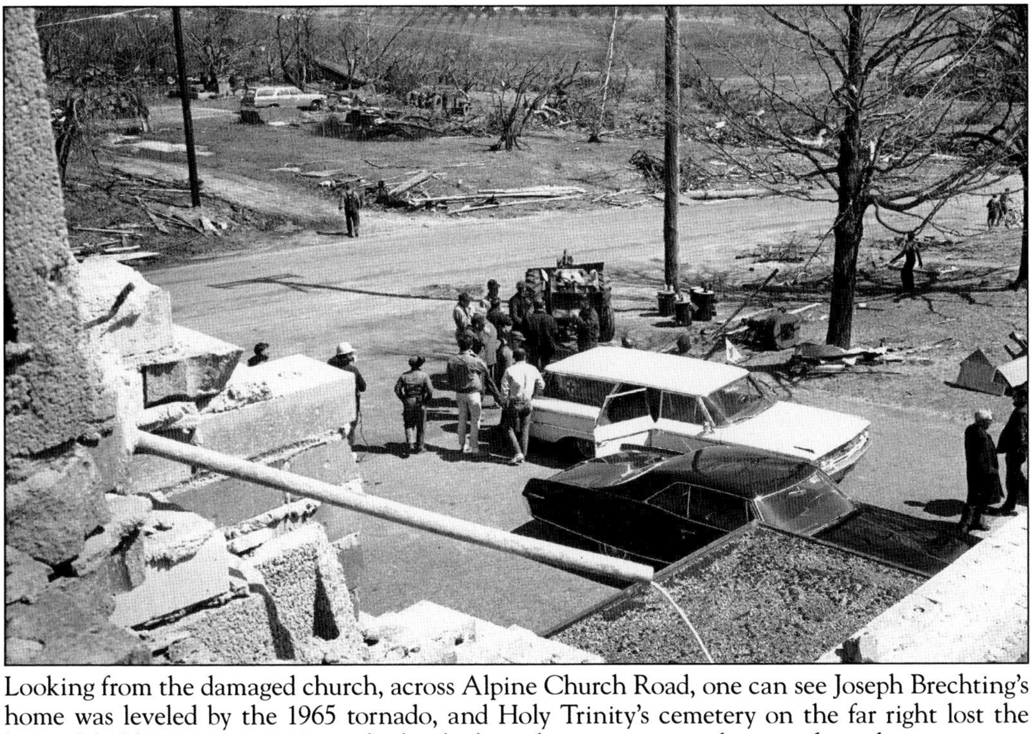

Looking from the damaged church, across Alpine Church Road, one can see Joseph Brechting's home was leveled by the 1965 tornado, and Holy Trinity's cemetery on the far right lost the beautiful old spruce trees. Horses had to be brought in to remove the trees from the cemetery.

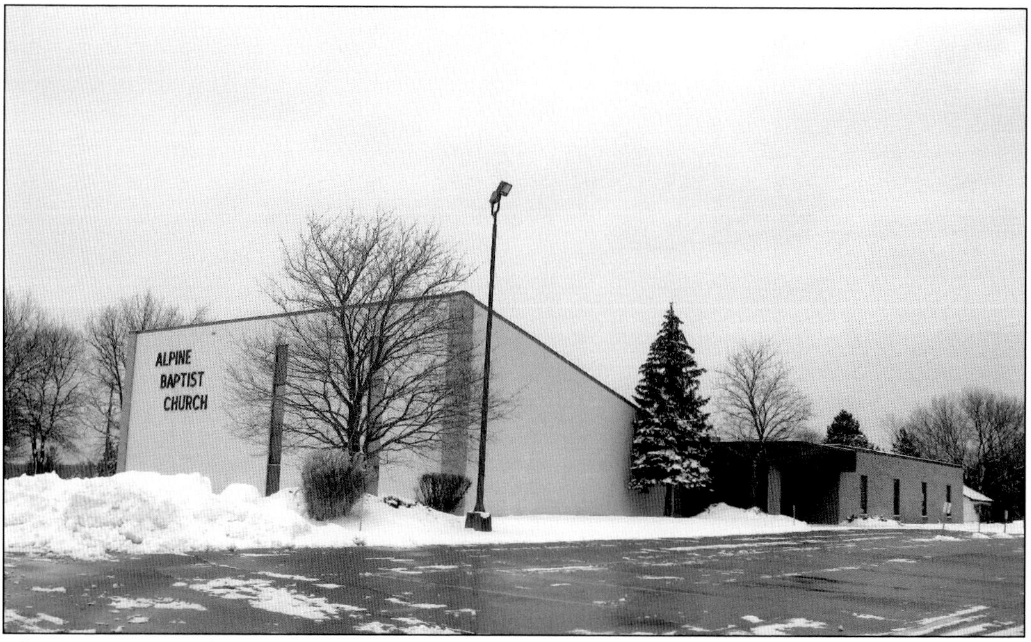

The First Baptist Church of Alpine and Walker was organized in 1856. The congregation's first church was located on what is now Four Mile Road. The congregation later moved to its present location on Seven Mile Road, east of Alpine Avenue.

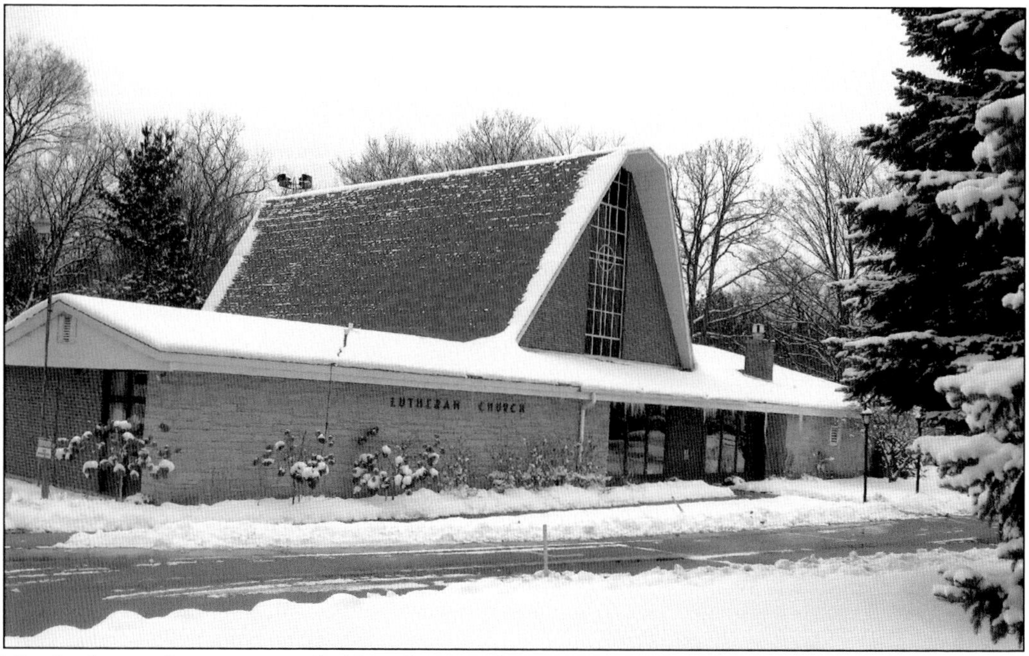

The Lutheran denomination held its first worship services on November 3, 1963, in the Stoney Creek School. It dedicated its Zion Lutheran Church building on Lamoreaux Drive on March 14, 1965. With the growth in the population of Alpine Township, the Maranatha Bible Church organized in July 1966. It was started as a mission in 1964 as the Calvary Undenominational Church on Stoney Creek Road.

Seven

SCHOOLS

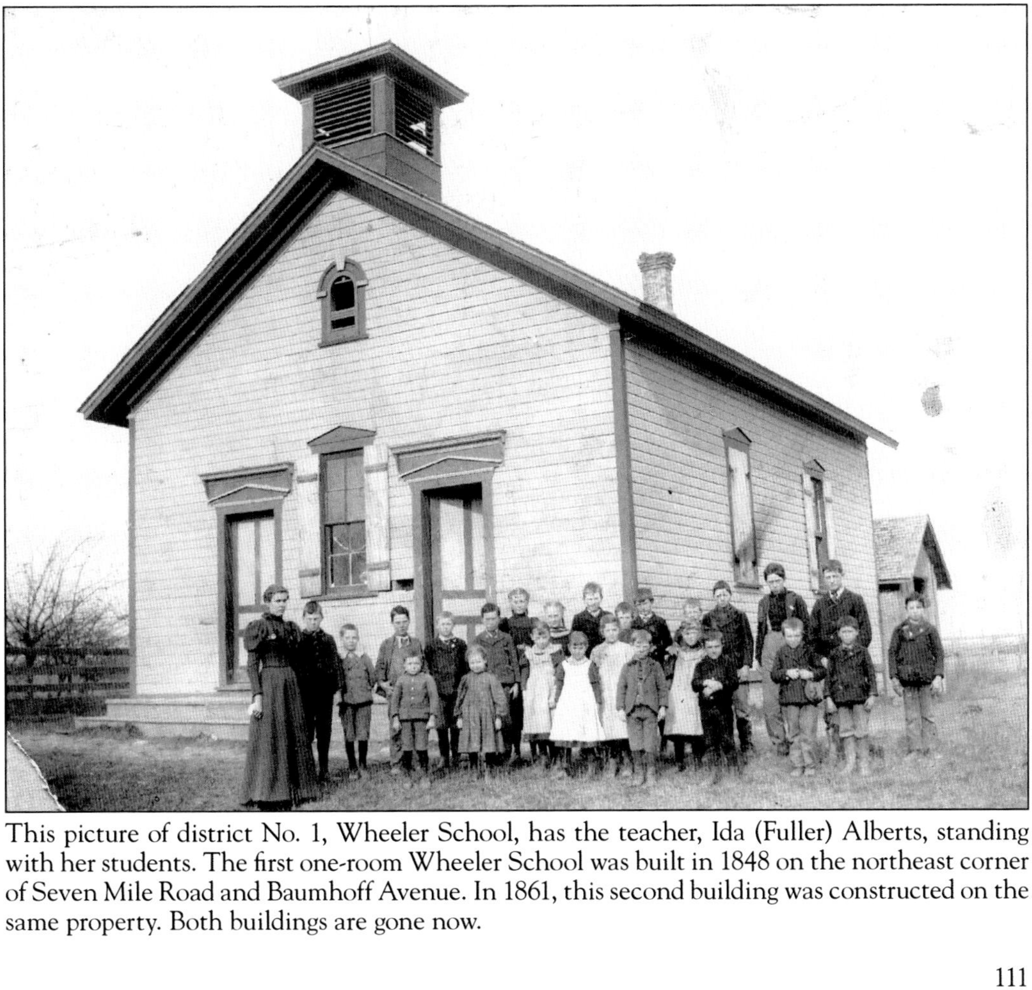

This picture of district No. 1, Wheeler School, has the teacher, Ida (Fuller) Alberts, standing with her students. The first one-room Wheeler School was built in 1848 on the northeast corner of Seven Mile Road and Baumhoff Avenue. In 1861, this second building was constructed on the same property. Both buildings are gone now.

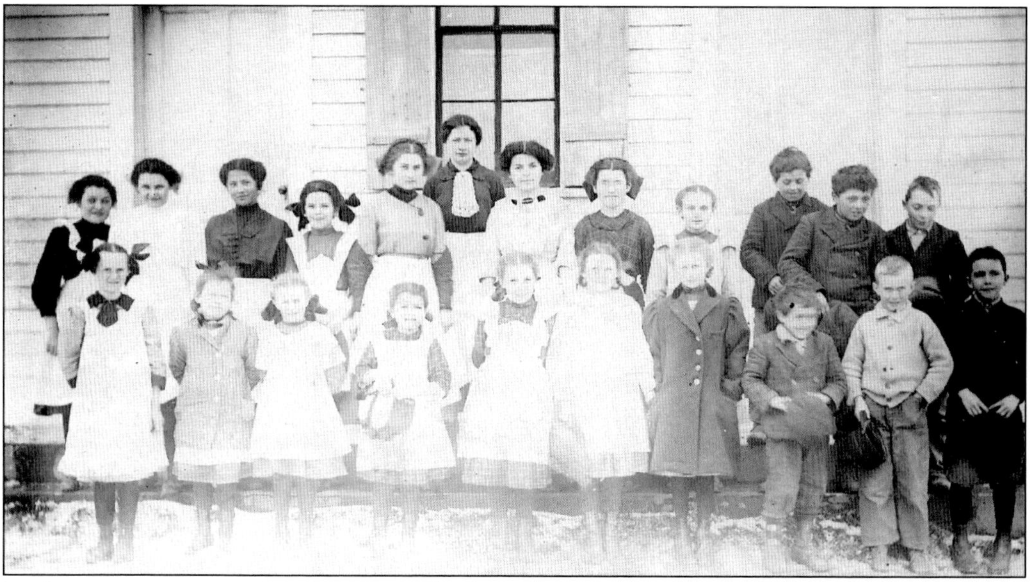

In this winter picture of students at Wheeler School, the girls are seen on the left and only six boys on the right. From left to right, the girls are (first row) Elizabeth Antor, Anna Antor, Martha Vogel, a Hillebrand girl, two unidentified girls, and another Hillebrand girl; (second row) Marie Alberts, Gertrude Alt, an unidentified girl, another Hillebrand, Theresa Antor, the teacher, two unidentified girls, and Mary Rothenthaler. The boys are thought to be Carl Steffens and Richard Alberts in front (third and second from the right) and Oscar Pitsch, Ed Pitsch, and Ed Steffens in back, from left to right.

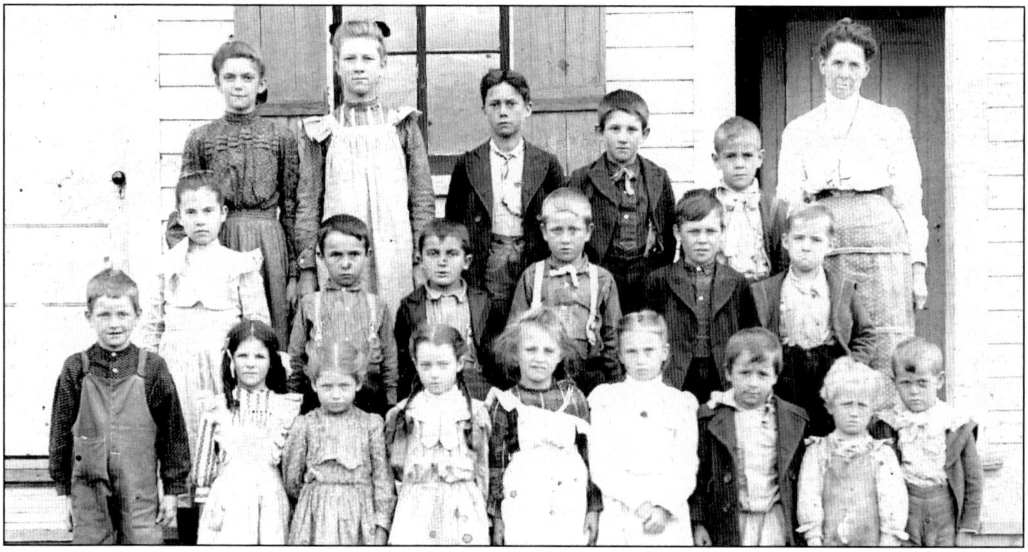

A third Wheeler School was build across the street on the northwest corner in 1881 and operated until 1948. It serves the township now as a community building where the Alpine Township Historical Commission office is located. In this picture, from left to right are (first row) Carl Steffens, Iva (Antor) Cordes, Florence (Fuller) Schoenborn, Princess (Fuller) Armock, Flora Cranmer, Clara May Eddy, Albert Cranmer, and two unidentified; (second row) Viola Thome, Bert Thome, Richard Alberts, O. Downer, Frank Antor, and unidentified; (third row) Julia (Steffens) Dressel, Alta (Downer) Cranmer, Earl Ruthardt, L. Downer, and two unidentified.

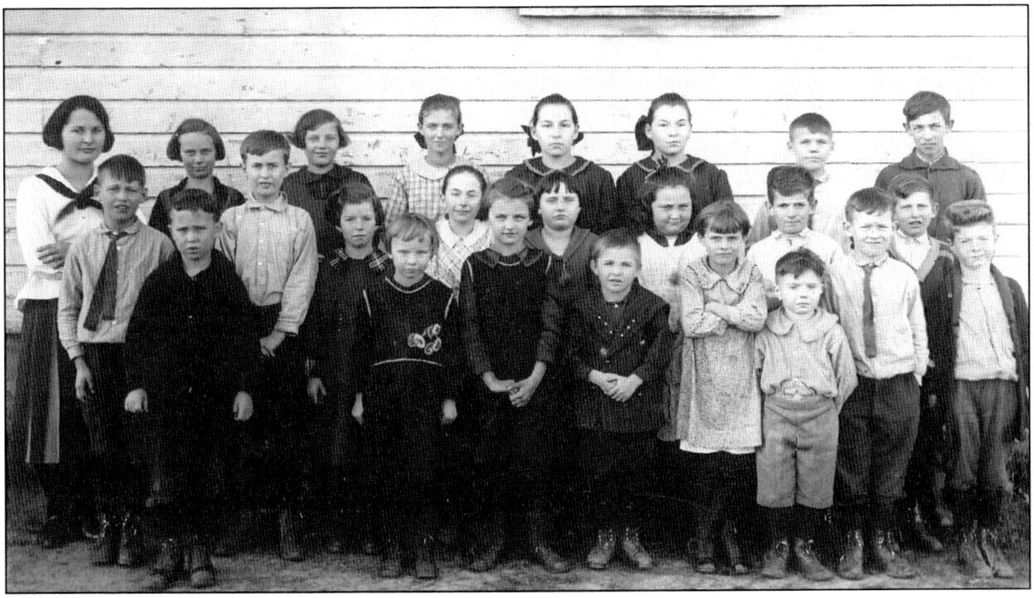

In 1923, Alice (Davenport) Klenk stands with her students. From left to right are (first row) Joe Wheeler, Hazel, Louise, and Lloyd Rusche, Emma Rothenthaler, Gerald Pitsch, Arthur Alt, and Kenneth Cranmer; (second row) Joseph Alt, Francis Alberts, Helen Cranmer, Agnes Steffens, Louise Pitsch, Alvina Pitsch, and Ed and John Rothenthaler; (third row) Alice Klenk, Genevieve Wheeler, Aleta Pitsch, Anna Rothenthaler, Evelyn and Ethlyn Alberts, Carl Alt, and Joe Rothenthaler.

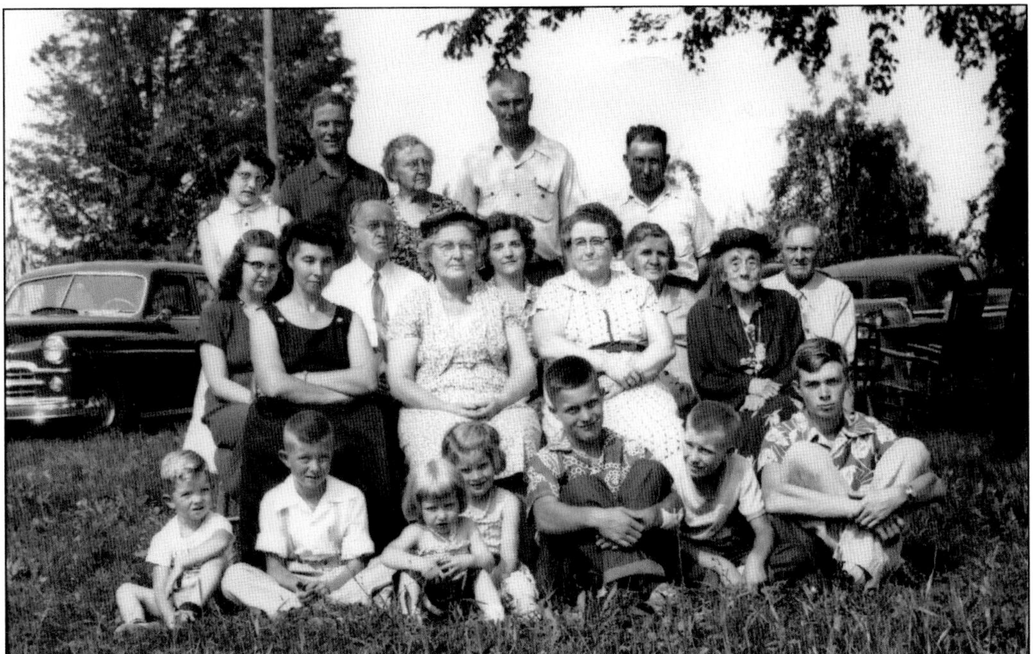

This is the Wheeler School picnic in 1953 with the Alberts and Cranmer families. The last annual picnic was held in 1955.

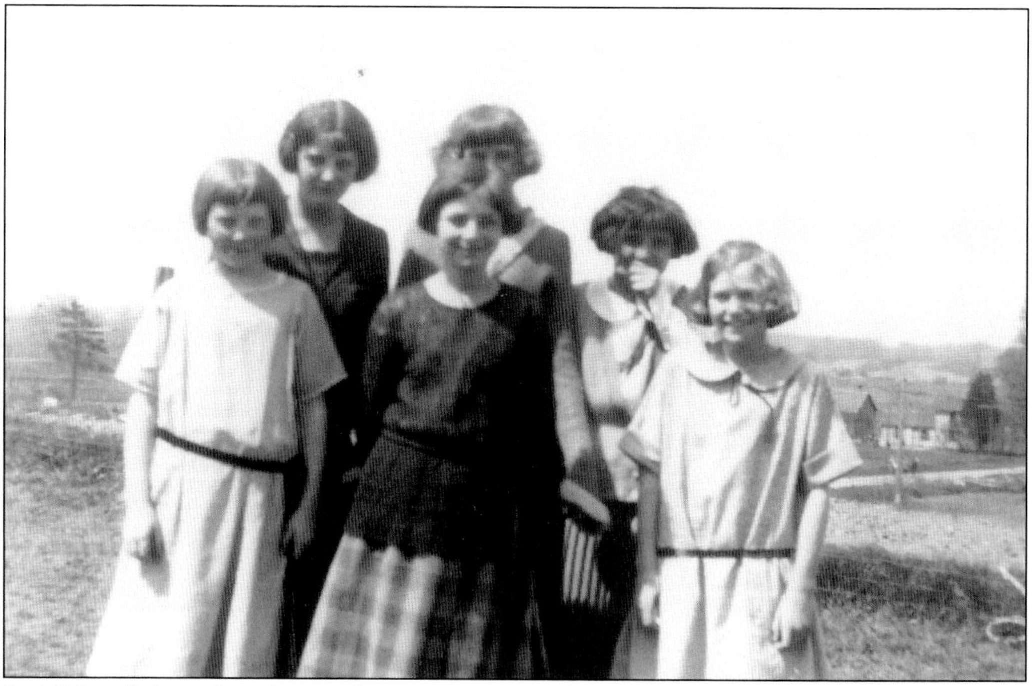

In 1924, eighth-grade girls pose for a picture. From left to right are (first row) Florence Platte, Myrtle Ross, and Elsie Ingersoll; (second row) Lora Pyard, Ella Fish, and Bertha Ostrowski.

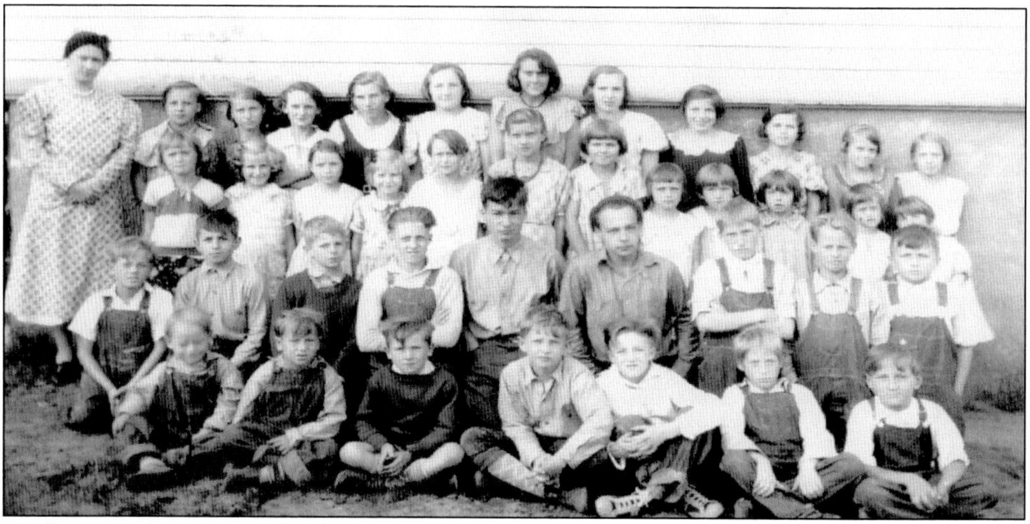

Students at the Koon School in 1934–1935 are, from left to right, (first row) the Whiting twins, Art Blair, unidentified, Bill Connell, Francis Lusk, and John Sawicki; (second row) Chuck Cheslek, Carl Vogel, two unidentified, Fritz Heinbeck, Donald Hudson, Harold Lusk, Richard Cheslek, and Raymond Lonnee; (third row) Regina Sawicki, Arlene Glass, Rosemary Lusk, Esther Skurka, Margaret Whiting, Stella Skurka, Annabelle Porter, Evelyn (Lonnee) May, unidentified, Catherine Hudson, Barb Cheslek, and June Lusk; (fourth row) teacher Mary Cavanaugh, Mildred McQueen, Martha Lusk, Margaret Whiting, Shirley Lusk, Evelyn West, Nina Whiting, Norraine (Heinbeck) Fix, Ann Marie Connell, Norrie Lonnee Christiansen, Helen (Cheslek) Pike, and Virginia Porter.

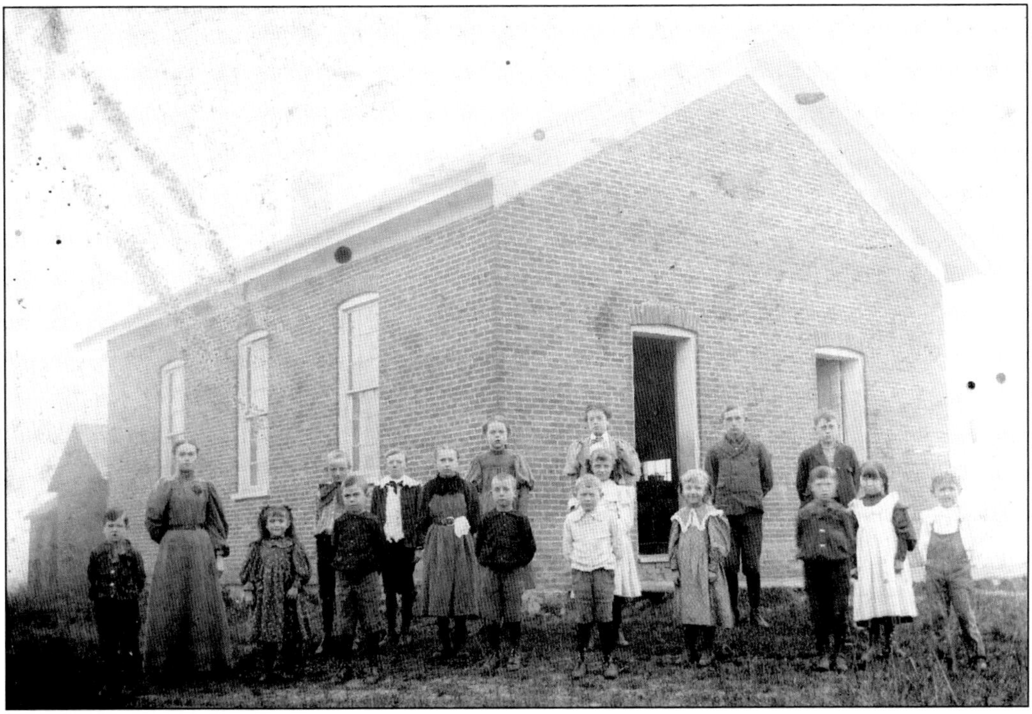

District No. 3, Red Brick School, fractional with Wright Township, was on the southeast corner of Stage Avenue at Six Mile Road. Erected in 1868, it was first called Wilson School.

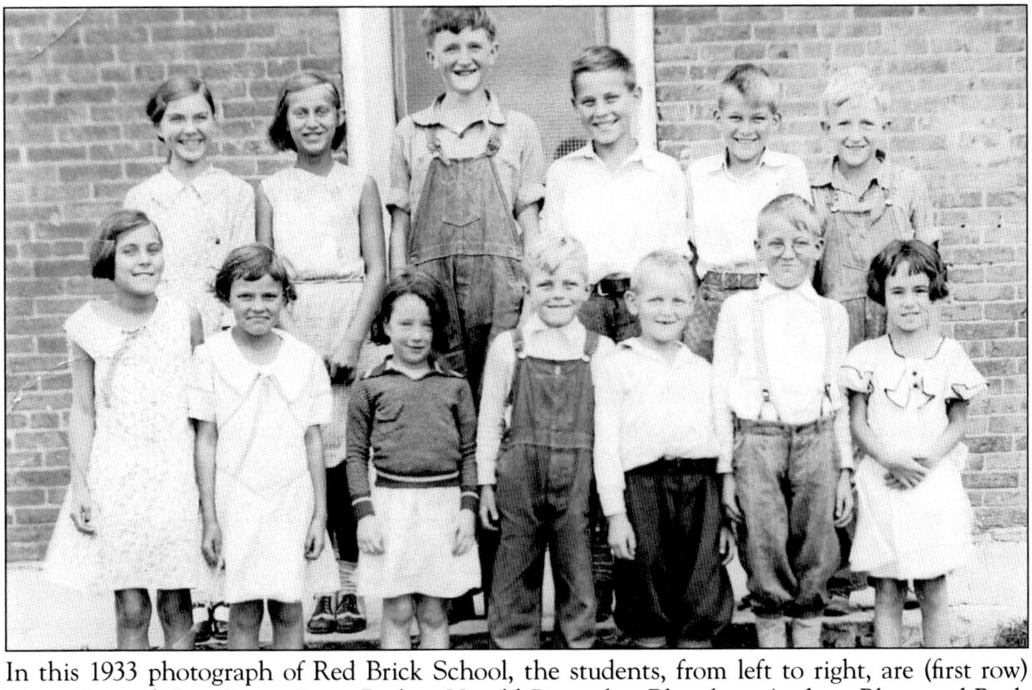

In this 1933 photograph of Red Brick School, the students, from left to right, are (first row) Marie Piccard, Iris Girou, Patty Barker, Harold Piccard, a Blow boy, Andrew Blow, and Ruth (Host) Darling; (second row) Lillian Plyman, Orpha Barker, Bill Van Dyke, Bus VanDyke, Art Terpstra, and John Blow.

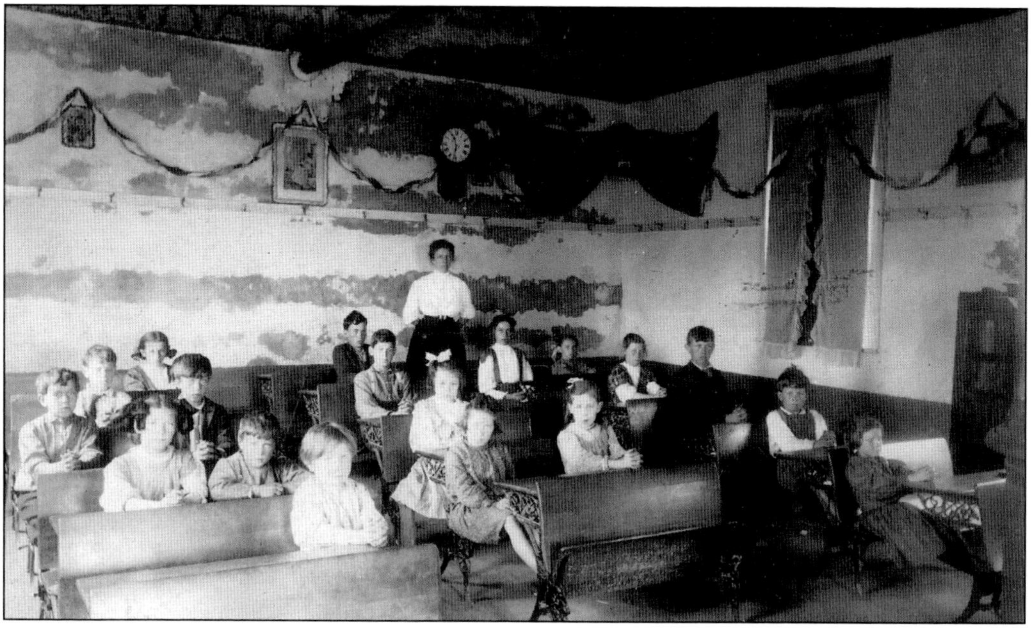

This is a photograph taken inside Red Brick School when Delsie Wells was the teacher.

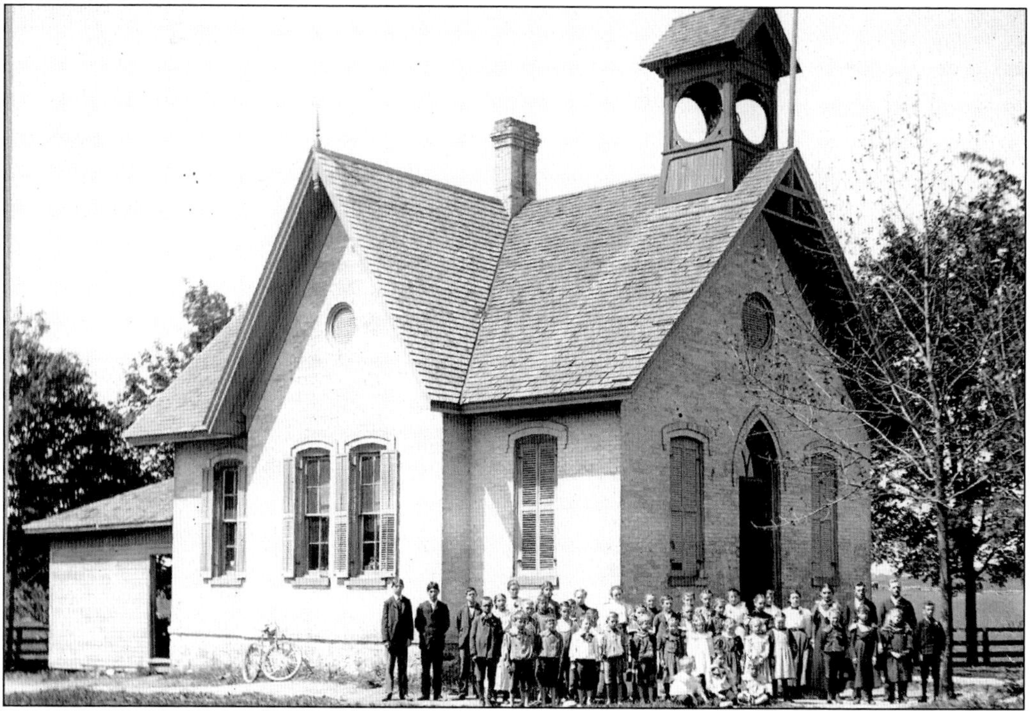

District No. 4, Ballard School, was on the south side of Ten Mile Road, just west of Sparta Avenue. It was called Rouse School in its earliest years. It was fractional with Sparta. One morning, when Vergie Guiles was teaching, a truck driver saw fire near the chimney of the school and stopped to help get the children out of the building. None of the 25 students were hurt. Guiles was so organized as a teacher that she was able to help all the students take their belongings with them when they went out the door.

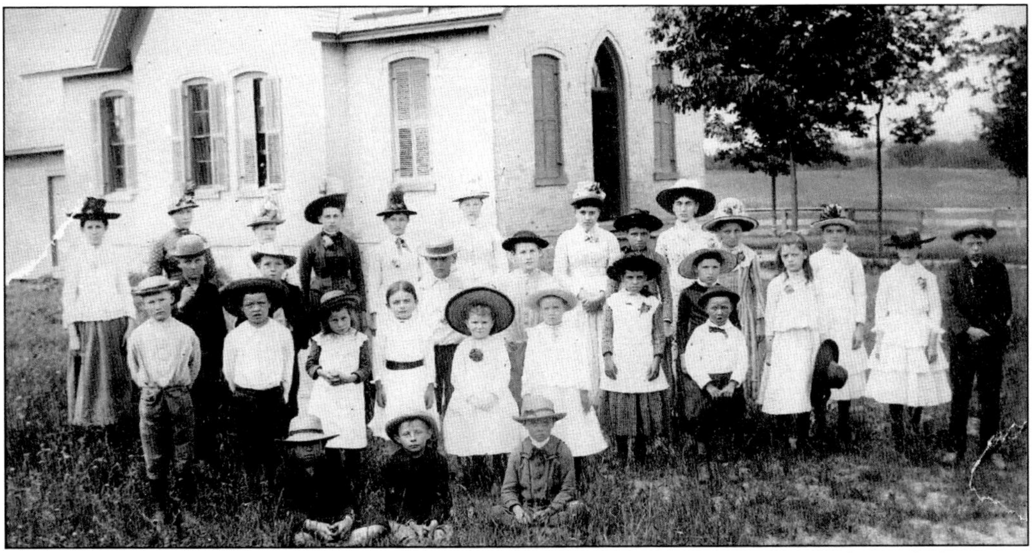

Among those seen here at Ballard School are Frederick Schindler, Mindon Culver, Clyde Paine, Jay Anderson, Nettie Culver, Clara Schindler, Lulie Hawley, Emma Miller, Ray McWilliams, Will Cummings, Forest Montgomery, Lowell Smith, A. C. Anderson, another Emma Miller, Grace Field, Ethel Bailey, Bertha Field, Wilhelmina and Lois Anderson, Ella Hawley, Bertha Johnston, Jane Anderson, Lena Hawley, Maud Miller, May Cummings, Edith Culver, Louise Schindler, Grace Place, and Oreley Brown.

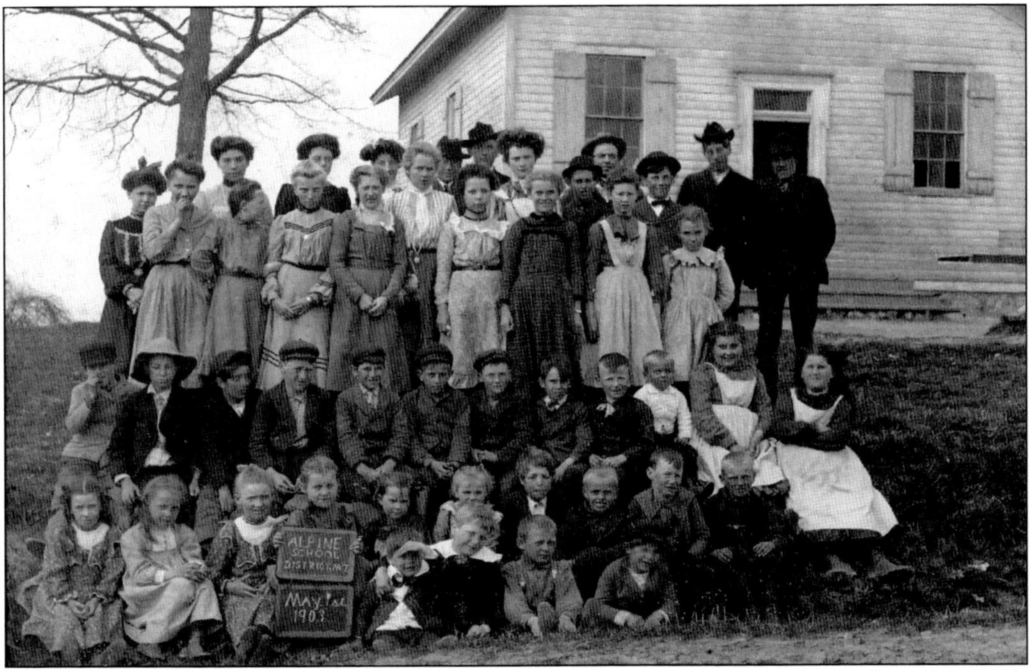

District No. 7, Colton School, fractional with Plainfield Township, was located on the north side of Seven Mile Road, east of Vinton Avenue. It was erected in 1869. In 1903, this picture was taken on May Day. Katie Dutmer is third from the left in the first row of students standing. Peter Dutmer is the sixth from the right in the third row of seated children. Maude DeWitt is second from the left in the last row.

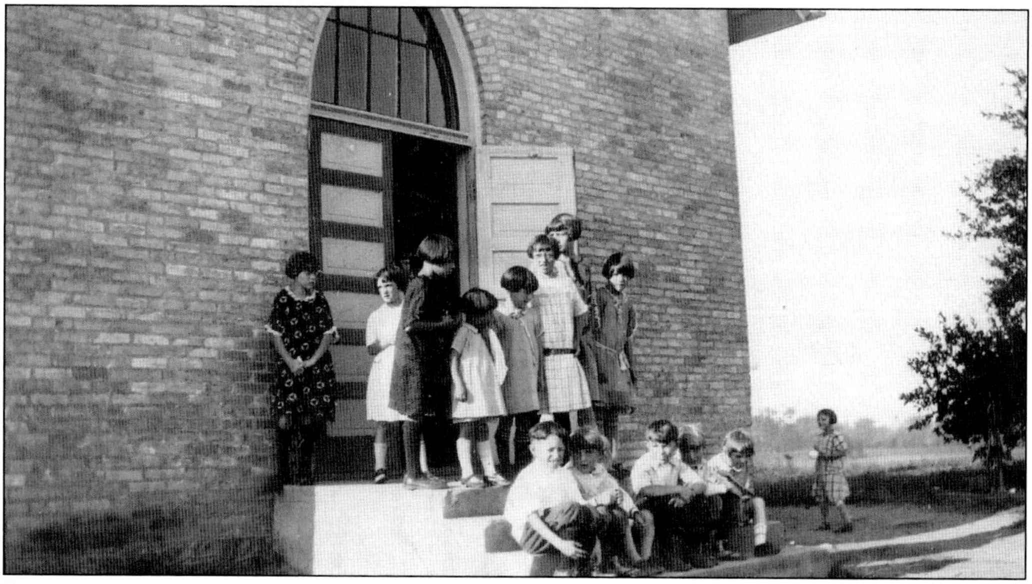

District No. 8, Pearsall School, was on the south side of Six Mile Road at Peach Ridge Avenue. It had been erected in 1851 and rebuilt later as White Brick School. The school building, shown here, burned down.

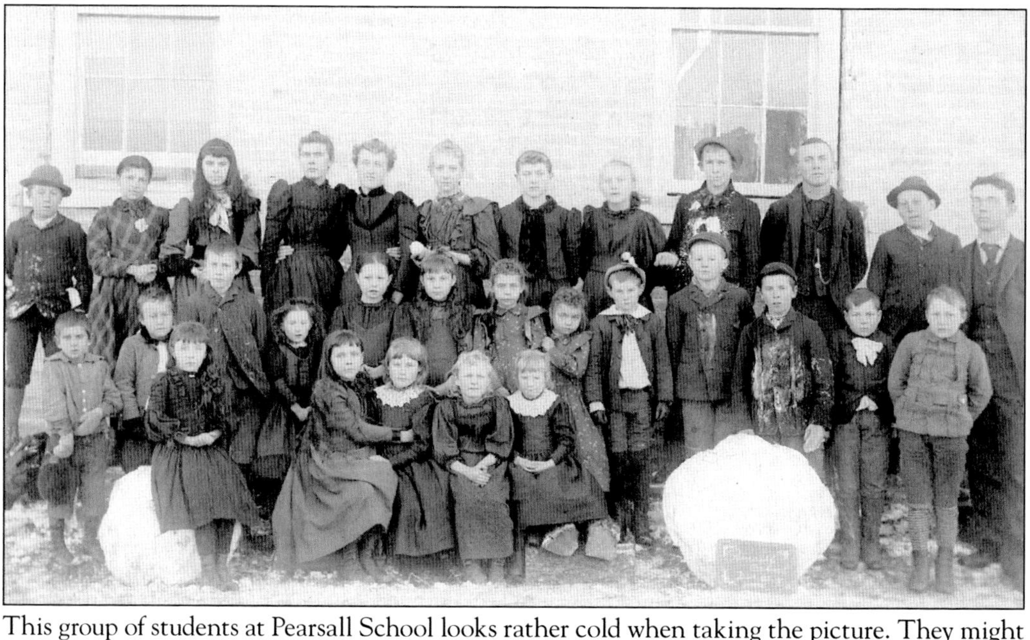

This group of students at Pearsall School looks rather cold when taking the picture. They might have enjoyed rolling up those snowballs for the picture.

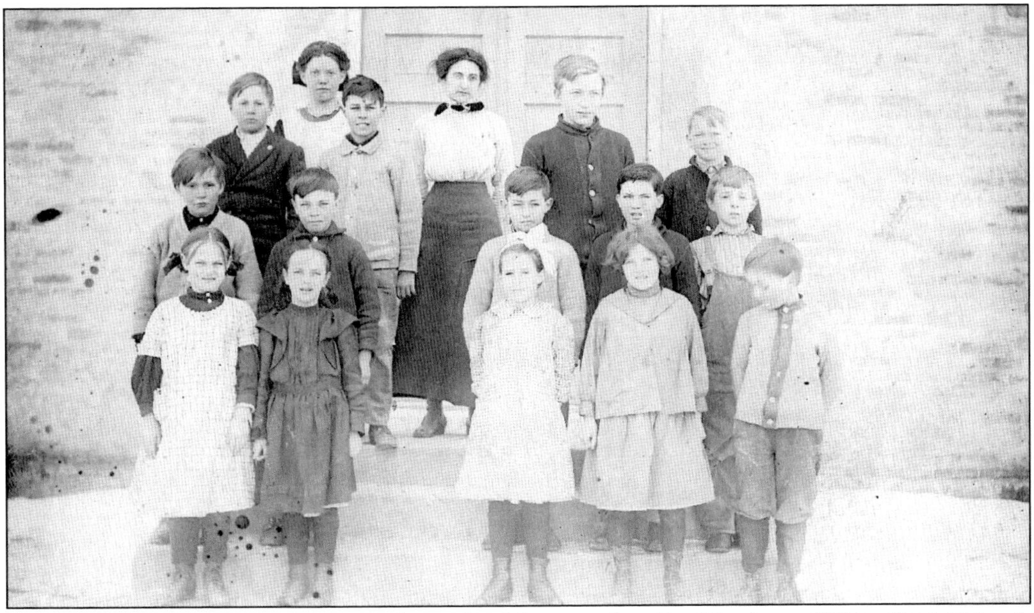

The students here are standing on either side of their teacher, Iva Hawley, at White Brick School, later known as Pearsall School.

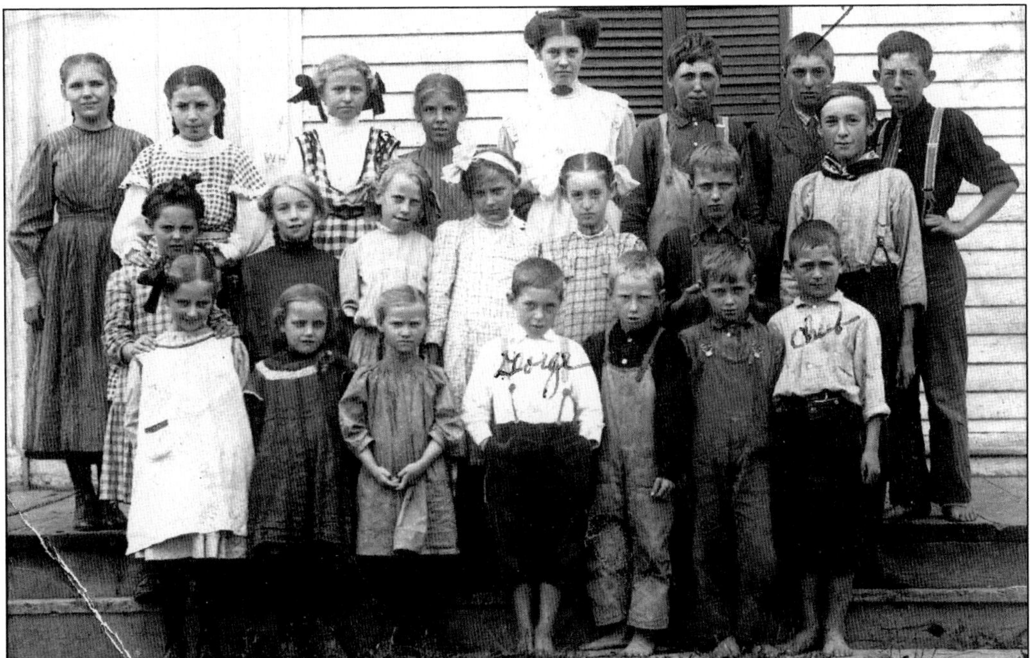

When someone knew the names of these children at a township school, the person wrote right on the photograph. What a wonderful group of children. It must have been warm enough to go without shoes for the children in the front.

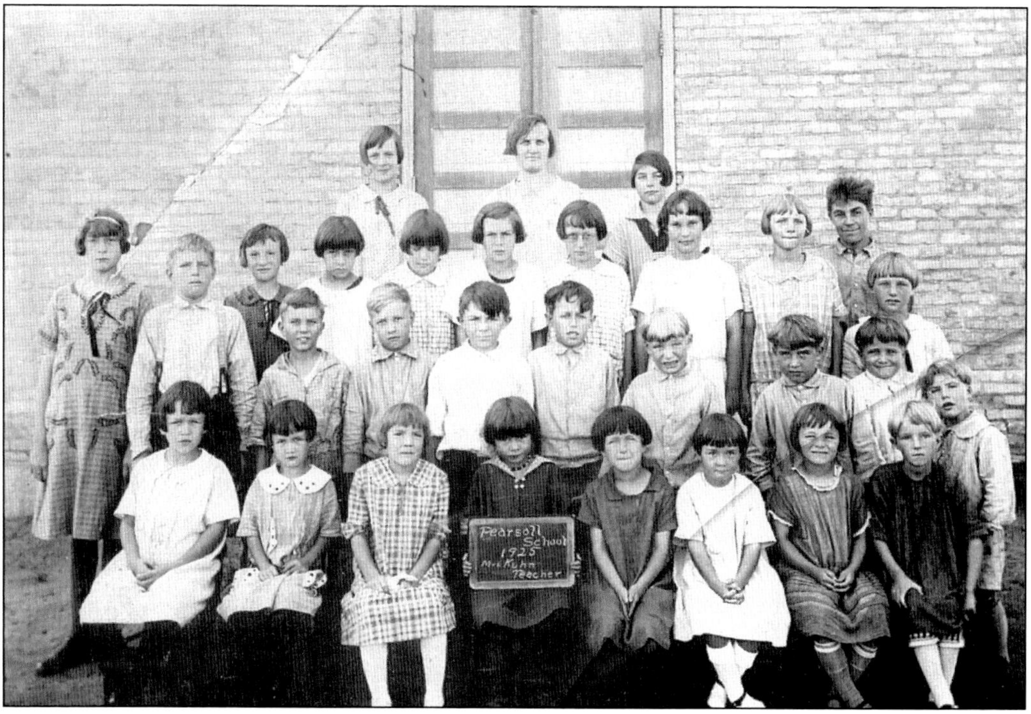

These are Pearsall School students in 1925.

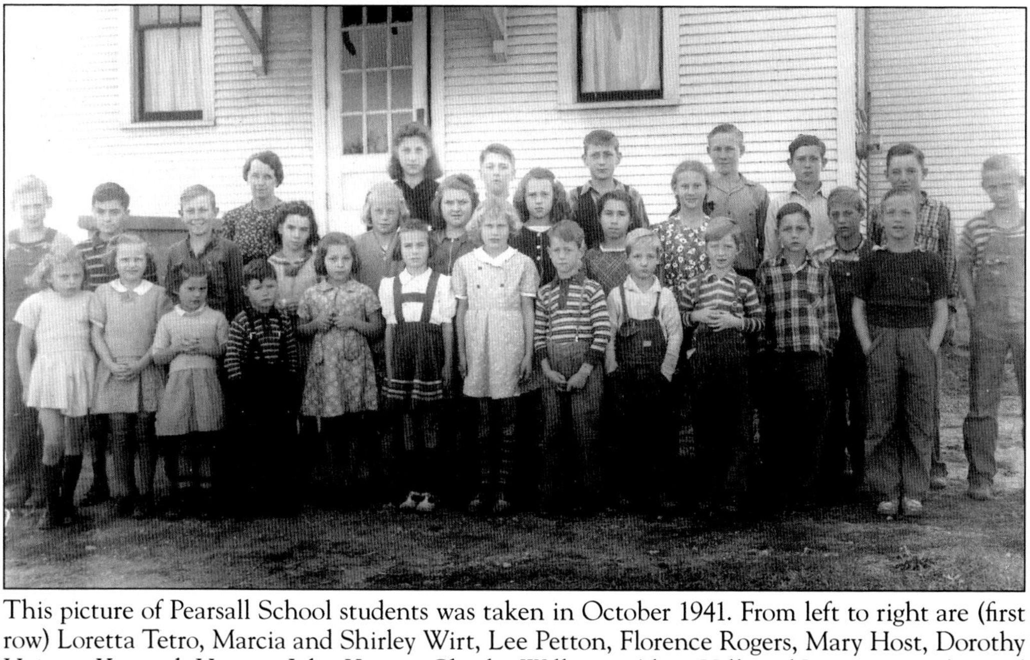

This picture of Pearsall School students was taken in October 1941. From left to right are (first row) Loretta Tetro, Marcia and Shirley Wirt, Lee Petton, Florence Rogers, Mary Host, Dorothy Haisma, Kenneth Haisma, John Kamps, Charles Williams, Alvin Hill, and Junior Heitz; (second row) George Kamps, Glenn and Edward Rogers, Kathleen Byrne, Doris Akers, Dolores Preston, Marion Haisma, Charlotte Host, Janet Akers, Nelson Kamps, and Marinus Kamps; (third row) teacher Marie Byrne, Grace Kamps, Charles Chase, Cornelius Kamps, Wilbur Rogers, Donald Haisma, and Rowland Hill.

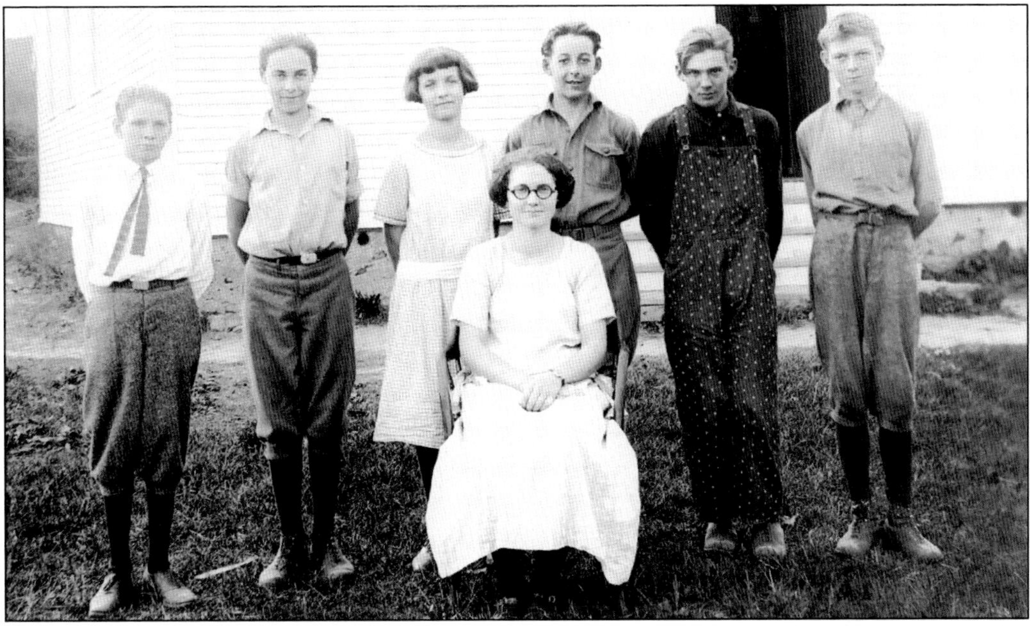

District No. 10, Boyd School, was on the northeast corner of Eight Mile Road and Fruit Ridge Avenue. It was erected in 1856 and was fractional with Wright Township. This year, at Boyd School, Aleta Vogel, who would later marry Jack Brown, was the teacher. This must be the graduating class, as Boyd School was always a one-room school, with all grades, until it was no longer used as a school. It was consolidated with the Kenowa Hills School system.

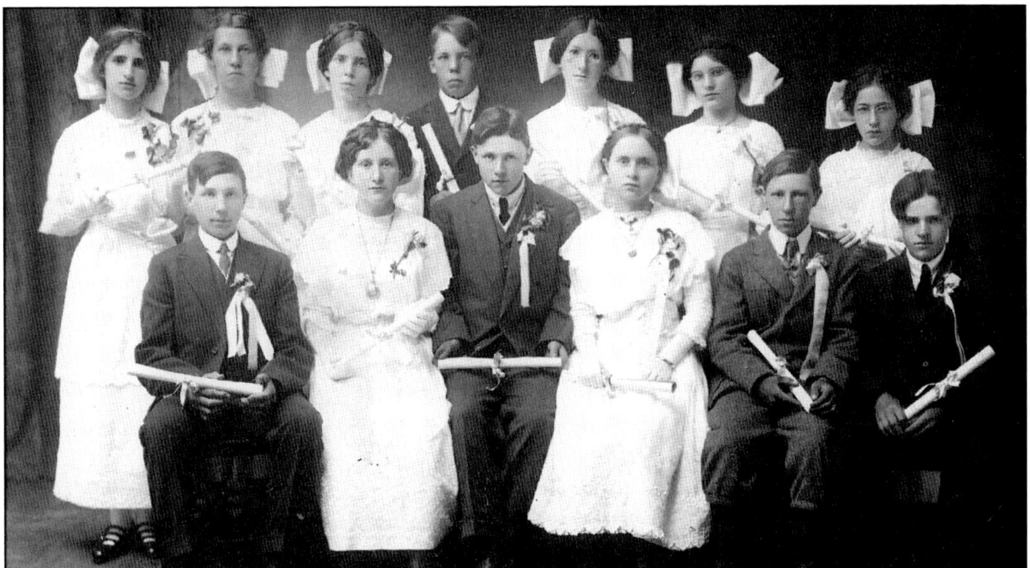

District No. 11, Cordes School, was on the west side of Cordes Avenue, near Alpine Church Road. It was erected in 1855 on the Eberhard Cordes property. Holy Trinity School was also in district No. 11 on Alpine Church Road. From left to right, the graduates of the eighth grade from district No. 11 are (first row) Ed or Bob Host, Josephine Wagner, Joe Scheidel, Ann Weber, Alfred or Bob Scheidel, and Ed Williams; (second row) Josephine Cordes, Grace Kremer, Freda Wahlfield, Clem Henze, Louise Schweitzer, Cora Meyers, and Louise Williams.

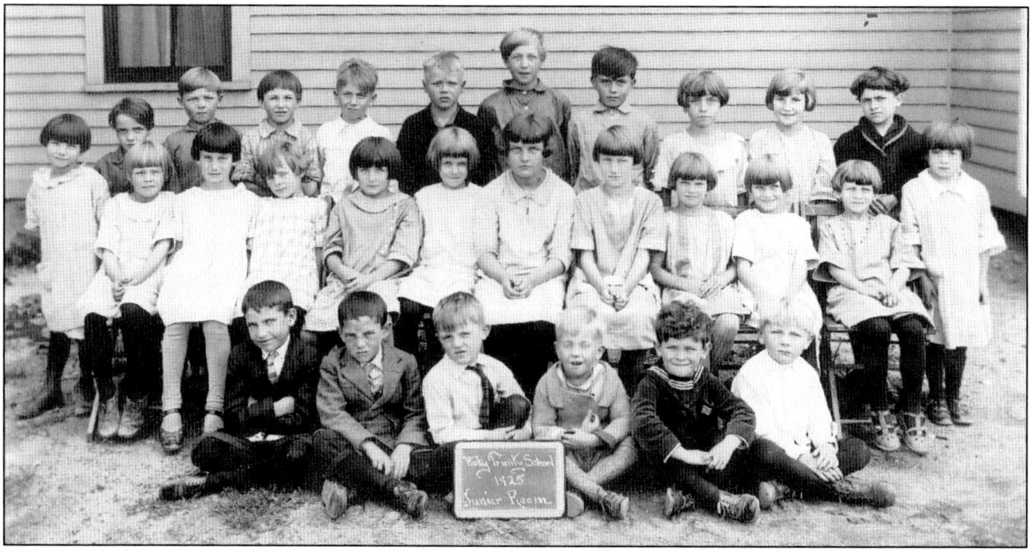

These are the 1925 students at Holy Trinity Catholic School's junior room. From left to right are (first row) Charles and Michael Zagummey, Edward Schweitzer, Claude Host, Edward Raisch, and Reynold Zerfas; (second row) Viola Pitsch, Anna Henze, Helen Brechting, Rita Brown, Louise Brechting, Lorraine Henze, Cora Young, Marian Brechting, Rita Schindler, Eileen Pitsch, Viola Zimmer, and Bernadette Brechting; (third row) Edward Fish, Frederick Zerfas, Lawrence Schafer, Norman Host, Carl Hendershot, Bernard Schafer, William Brechting, Marcella Cordes, Anna Wagner, and Frances Zagummey.

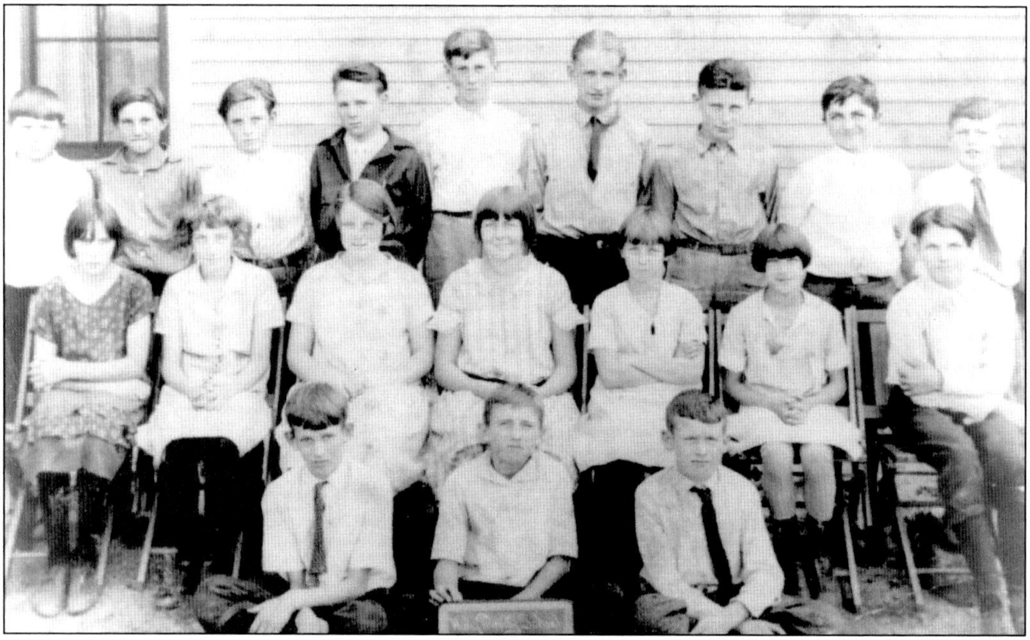

In 1925, this was the senior room at Holy Trinity. From left to right are (first row) Edward Brechting, Wilfred Cordes, and Arthur Alt; (second row) Dorothy Fish, Lillian Yost, Mary Smith, Irma Smith, Lavina Host, and Madelyn and George Schindler; (third row) Fred Homrich, Walter Schafer, James Smith, Joe Connell, Dick Brechting, Earl Zimmer, George Roberts, Frank Zagummey, and Joseph Alt.

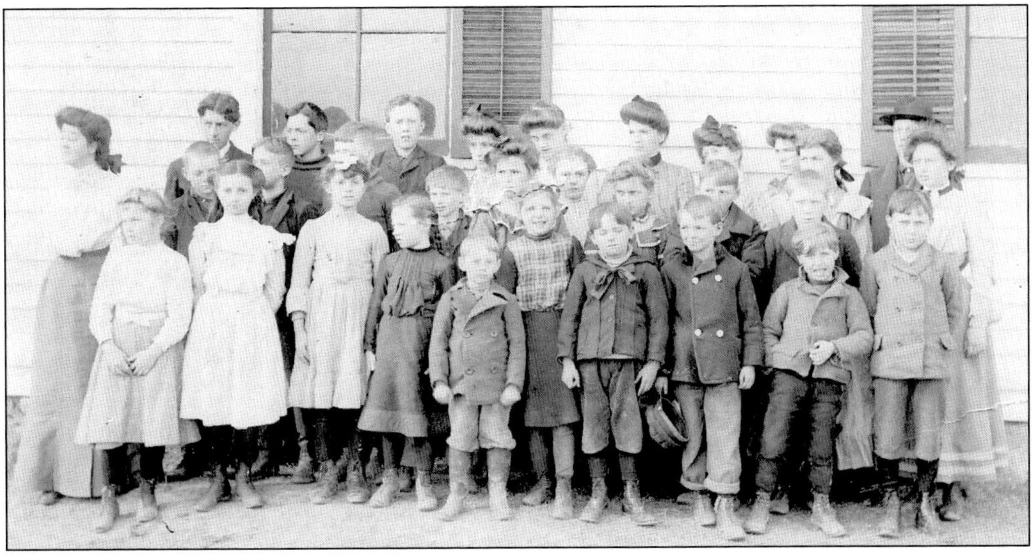

District No. 14, the Englishville School, was on the west side of Vinton Avenue, just south of Ten Mile Road. It was erected in 1852 on Richard English's property and was fractional with Sparta. Something must have happened to the left, as most of these students are looking that way and not at the photographer. A few students were very focused on what the photographer was doing.

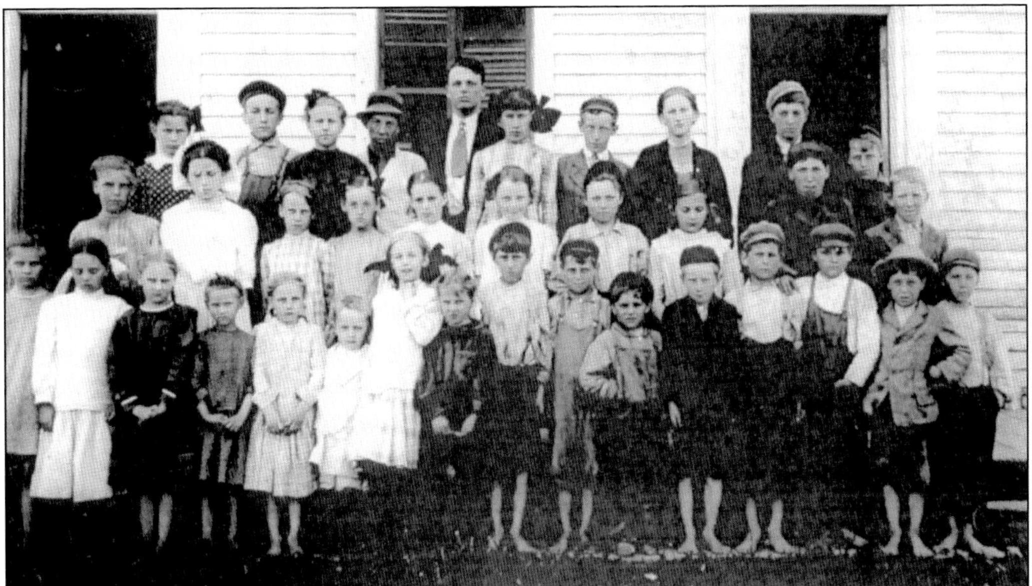

In 1910, Truman Jackson was teaching at the Englishville School. From left to right are (first row) Lena Myers, Clarisia Andrus, Alma Bullard, Mary Myers, Laura Hussey, John Kittler, Sylvia Watson, Fronie and George Webber, Bud Hussey, Zieke Centille, Martin Kittler, Harold Erhart, Andrew Centille, George Erhart, and Joe Webber; (second row) Fay Schultz, Ila McCready, Gertie Kittler, Bernice Smith, Lillian Hussey, Orsavilla Vinton, Tom Myers, Margaret Heinbeck, Walter Schultz, and Herman Kittler; (third row) Wysetta Church, John and Mary Webber, Cecil Smith, teacher Truman Jackson, Eva Kittler, Dillian Watson, Frances Church, Ellsworth Erhart, and Wilbur Hussey.

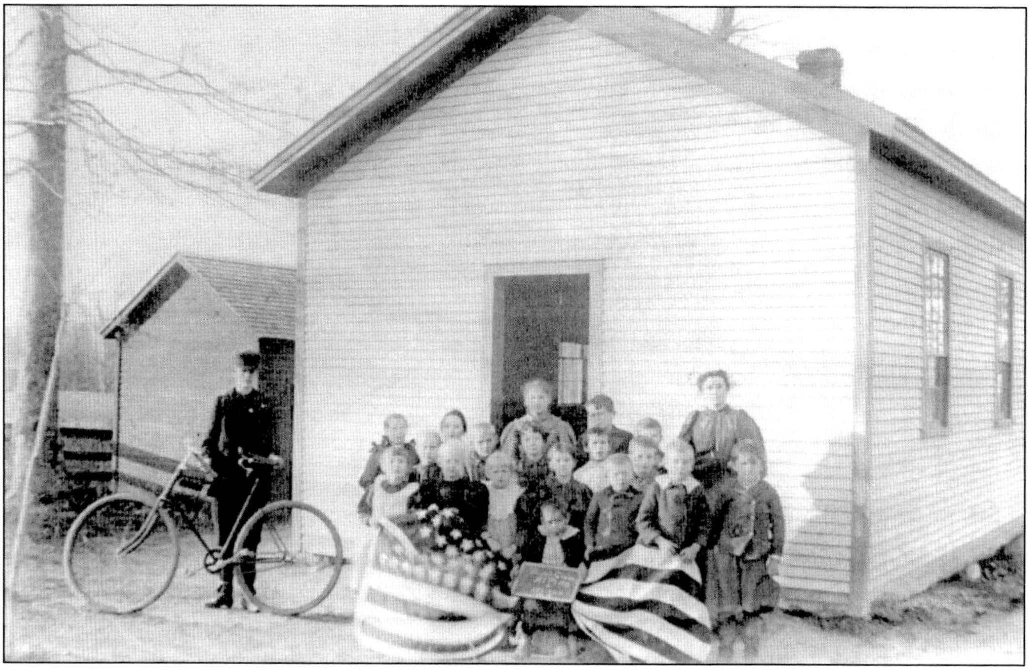

District No. 15, Beech Grove School, fractional with Walker, was on the northwest corner of Four Mile Road and Fruit Ridge Avenue. It was called Monroe School in the early years. In the first row, second from the left, is Helen (Bremer) Schantz.

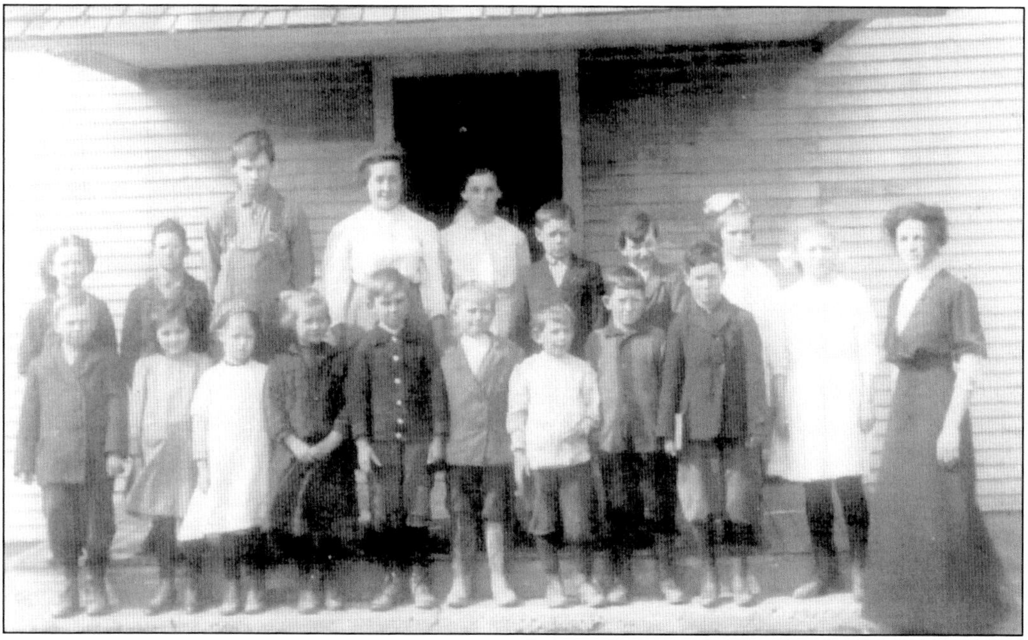

Margaret Allen is the teacher at Beech Grove School this year. From left to right are (first row) Ed Schindler Sr., Ethel Hart, Marion and Helen Hofacker, Harold Westrate, James Westrate, Chuck Roth, and Ward and George Walcott; (second row) Arlene Cummings, Harold Walcott, Hilton Hanson, Muriel Greiner, Eleanor Putnam, Lloyd Haradine, Bill Roth, Esther Putnam, and Winifred Westrate.

Eight

MILITARY AND EVENTS

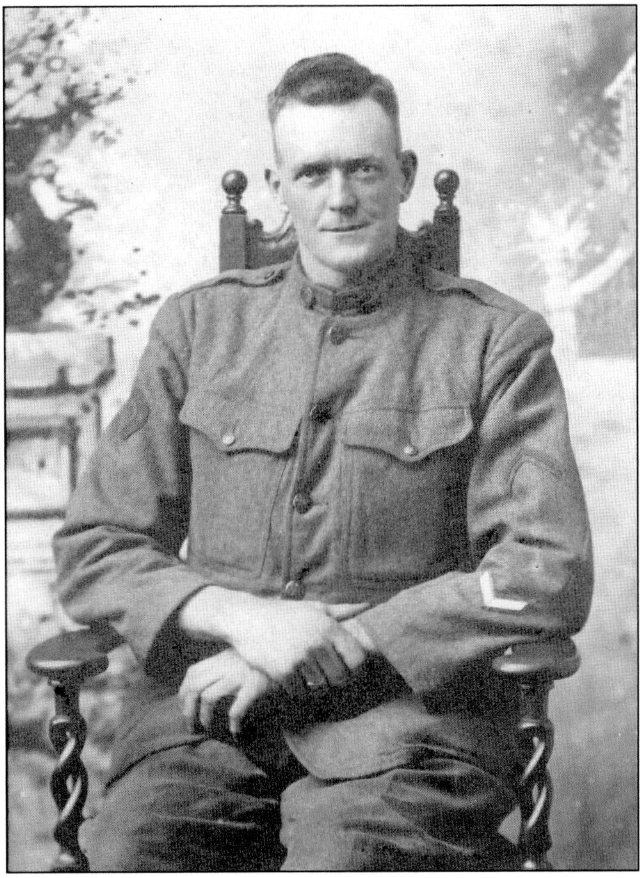

George Joseph Steffens served in the army during World War I. He was inducted on July 24, 1918, and had his basic training at Camp Custer. Steffens served until January 30, 1919.

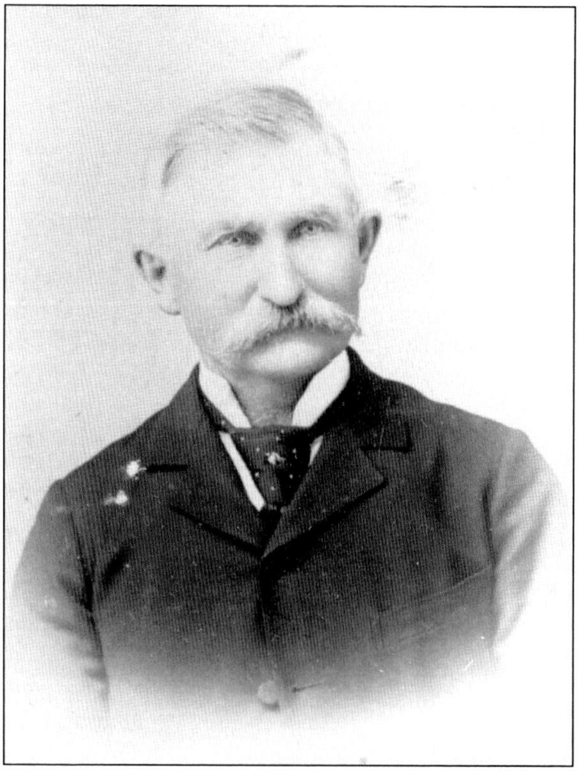

John Frederick Klenk enrolled on May 13, 1861, with the 3rd Regiment Michigan Infantry, Company C. He fought in the Battle of Bull Run. He was discharged on June 25, 1863, with a disability.

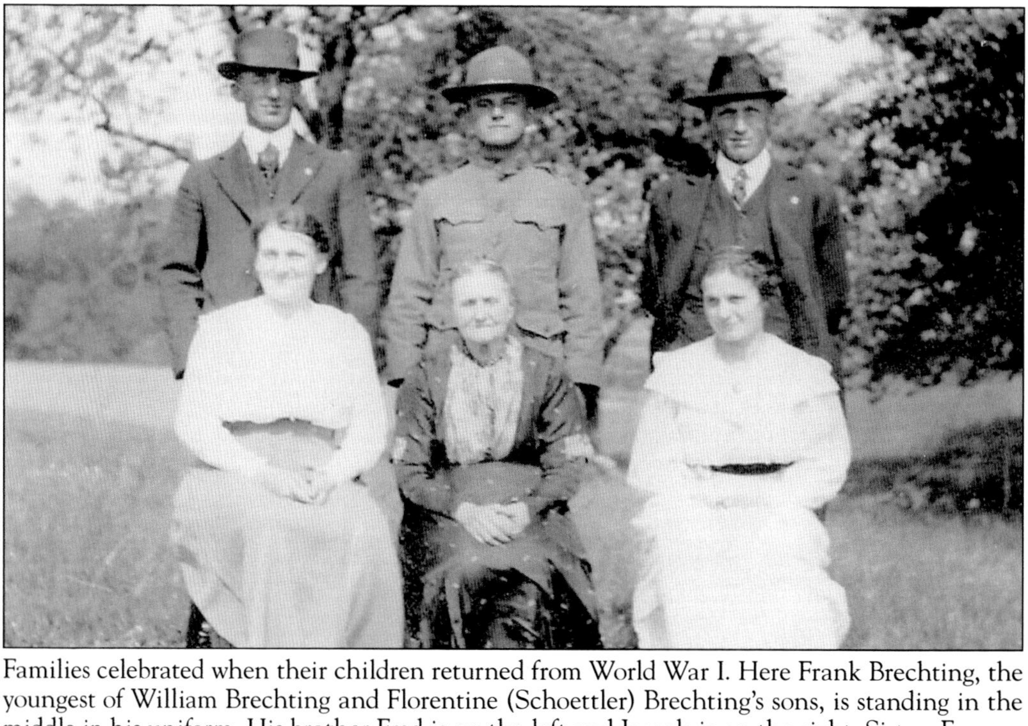

Families celebrated when their children returned from World War I. Here Frank Brechting, the youngest of William Brechting and Florentine (Schoettler) Brechting's sons, is standing in the middle in his uniform. His brother Fred is on the left and Joseph is on the right. Sisters Frances Ebers (left) and Mary Schweitzer are seated on either side of their mother, Florentine.

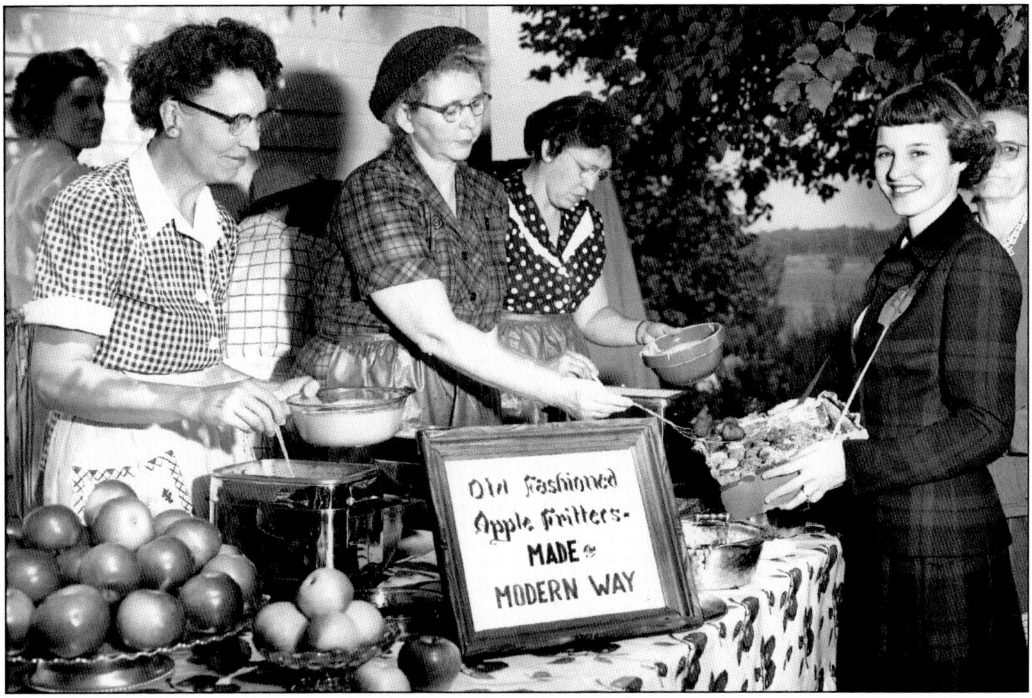

In 1950, the Peach Ridge Fruit Growers Association decided to host an annual picnic the next year, with a focus on the promotion of apples. It would be called the Apple Smorgasbord. Area women knew that apples could be used to enhance every dish at a meal, so every dish at the smorgasbord was made with apples. At this 1953 Apple Smorgasbord, the Michigan Apple Queen, Carol Fahling, is offering apple fritters made by, from left to right, Janet Kline, Gladys Davenport, and Alma Gillett. This year, the festivities were held at the George and William Kober farm.

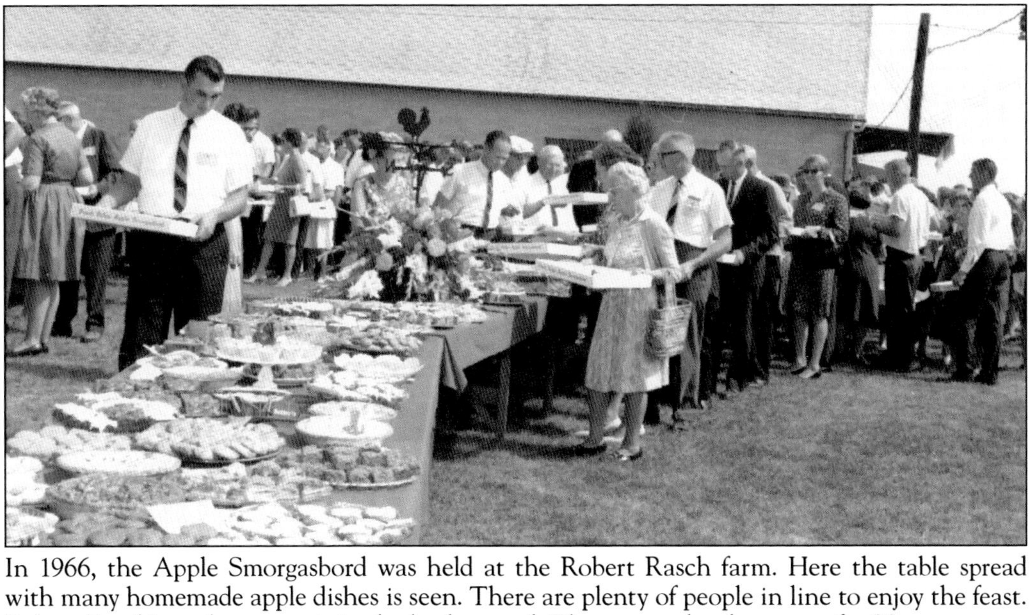

In 1966, the Apple Smorgasbord was held at the Robert Rasch farm. Here the table spread with many homemade apple dishes is seen. There are plenty of people in line to enjoy the feast. Robert Rasch's apple storage is in the background. The smorgasbord went on for 20 years.